D1251444

LAID TO REST IN
CALIFORNIA

A GUIDE TO THE CEMETERIES
AND GRAVE SITES
OF THE RICH AND FAMOUS

Patricia Brooks
and Jonathan Brooks

INSIDERS' GUIDE®

GUILFORD, CONNECTICUT
AN IMPRINT OF THE GLOBE PEQUOT PRESS

The prices, rates, and hours listed in this guidebook were confirmed at press time. We recommend, however, that you call establishments to obtain current information before traveling.

INSIDERS' GUIDE®

Text design: Casey Shain
Photo credits: p. 9, photos.com; pp. 147-48, Ronald Reagan Library; p. 295, Molly Mitchell; and p. 311, Luther Burbank Home & Gardens, Santa Rosa, California. All other photos by the authors.

Library of Congress Cataloging-in-Publication Data
  Brooks, Patricia, 1926-
   Laid to rest in California : a guide to the cemeteries and grave sites of the rich and famous / Patricia Brooks and Jonathan Brooks. —1st ed.
     p. cm.
   ISBN-13: 978-0-7627-4101-4
   ISBN-10: 0-7627-4101-5
   1. Celebrities—California—Biography. 2. Celebrities—Tombs—California—Guidebooks. 3. Cemeteries—California—Guidebooks. 4. California—Biography. I. Brooks, Jonathan, 1957-
II. Title.
   CT225.B76 2006
   929'.509794—dc22

                                                                                              2006019847

Manufactured in the United States of America
First Edition/First Printing

CONTENTS

To family members here and, hopefully, up there

ACKNOWLEDGMENTS

An unsung choir of office workers, too many to cite by name, at cemeteries throughout the state helped us locate various gravesites on or under their turf. We wish we could thank them individually for their generous assistance and information. The staffs at several cemeteries stand out in our memories for especially friendly welcomes and helpfulness. They are Angelus-Rosedale in Los Angeles, Pierce Brothers Valhalla Memorial Park in North Hollywood, Holy Cross in Culver City, San Gabriel Cemetery in San Gabriel, Desert Memorial Park in Cathedral City, Cypress Lawn in Colma, and Santa Barbara Cemetery in Santa Barbara. Millie at Woodlawn in Santa Monica deserves special mention for her patience and helpfulness.

A special bow of thanks goes to Mary Norris, our editor at Globe Pequot Press, unflagging in her support and enthusiasm for our project. We appreciate the work and patience of Amy Paradysz, who guided our manuscript through its labyrinthine paths to completion, and Casey Shain, master designer–artist, and the Globe art department for their presentation of many of our photographs.

Woody Allen once said, " . . . death is one of the few things that can be done just as easily lying down." The same can't be said for *writing about death,* but we wouldn't have missed a minute of it.

INTRODUCTION

We assume because you are reading this book that you share our interest in star gazing, the kind where you look down instead of skyward.

Star gazing at cemeteries is a favorite California sport, especially in southern California where so many of the constellations lie. One of the nicest things about a visit to celebrities' final abodes is that you'll always catch them at home. Death means never having to say you're out of town on business.

So many of the burial grounds in California are called memorial parks. The park idea in California seems to have been borrowed from the first Forest Lawn. But the concept of a graveyard that is scenic, natural, and wooded goes back even further, to the early nineteenth-century East Coast burial grounds, like Mount Auburn in Cambridge, Massachusetts, and the Woodlawn in the Bronx and the Green-Wood in Brooklyn, New York. They in turn pinched the idea from Cimetière du Père Lachaise in Paris. The oaks and maples of East Coast cemeteries give way in California to palms and cypress trees. Pines seem to be ubiquitous all over the country.

Parklike cemeteries are often attractions in themselves—magnets for joggers, birders, nature lovers, even writers seeking solitude for their compositions. In our modern, noise-accented environment, silence can be a much-cherished commodity, something cemeteries have, shall we say gravely, in spades.

Our intention in this guidebook is not to convince the skeptical of the pleasures of cemetery visits. If you have to ask what it is that makes graveyards appealing, this book may not be for you. Rather, it is an opinionated guidebook for the converted or at least the open-minded. You needn't be a taphophile to find this book helpful, but it doesn't hurt.

California is fertile soil for the rich, famous, and infamous. For more than 165 years the state has been a lure for those seeking wealth, fame, opportunity, and immortality. Explorers, naturalists, adventurers, fortune seekers, serious scholars, scalawags—all have been tempted to head west to California. From the first gold rush to the gold rush known as Hollywood, people from other parts of the country and the world have followed the dream of a golden-yellow brick road to happiness and success. Many have found one or the other, occasionally both. We have included almost 1,000 of them.

There wasn't the ghost of a chance of doing biographic sketches of *all* the underground residents we visited, but we have done skeletal sketches, which we call obits, as in obituaries, of some 250 of the most notable or notorious people you might be most interested in visiting. As for the others, by mentioning them in their final walk-off roles, we hope that when you visit a star, you'll look up some of the satellites as well. For instance, on a visit, say, to Inglewood Park Cemetery to pay final respects to Ella Fitzgerald, you will have the pleasant discovery of dozens of other lesser-known names there as well, such as fellow musicians Chet Baker and "Big Mama" Thornton, keeping her company unto eternity. Such surprises can give your visit a spirited finale.

To make this guidebook as helpful as possible, under each cemetery listing is a sidebar titled "Lunch Break." This includes suggestions of places to eat before or after your cemetery visit, in the event you have traveled many miles and are unfamiliar with the area. Another sidebar after certain obituaries is called "House Call," signifying that the individual's home is nearby and open to visitors. (In some cases a related museum, office, or other building of relevant interest is featured instead.) The address, phone number, and a few details about the place will help you in planning your trip. A third sidebar, which we call "Film Vault," is a reminder, in the case of an actor, actress, or director, of one of his/her films that we think especially memorable.

There are more than fifty cemeteries in Los Angeles County alone, some without any A- or even B-list luminaries. We have included twenty in the county for inclusion in this book, almost all of them with a casting call of big names. Overall, we have included almost fifty burial grounds throughout the state. We have organized each chapter alphabetically, first by towns within an area, then by cemeteries within a given town.

Of course, not all of California's subterranean stars are of the movie variety. California burial grounds reflect the western migration of our country's population and provide the final roll call for leaders in many other professions: authors, presidents (two), governors, senators, scientists, business tycoons, pioneers— earth shakers in a variety of fields.

A surprising number of people, many of whom we associate with another part of the United States, have met their judgment calls in this sunnier climate.

Who would have expected Indiana-born author Theodore Dreiser or New York–bred playwright Clifford Odets to stop their final presses in Forest Lawn in Glendale? Or that Truman Capote, born in New Orleans but a star of New York's glitterati, would end up, at least in part, in Pierce Brothers Westwood Village Memorial Park, Los Angeles? American mobility notwithstanding, graveyard visits are haunted by surprises.

A book about California burial sites can never be encyclopedic (though we believe this one to be the most comprehensive of any extant). People keep dying to get in, and we can never keep up with them all. As we were finishing this volume, newcomers kept checking in (or out). Richard Pryor, Shelley Winters, Don Knotts, Darren McGavin, Aaron Spelling, and Dana Reeve barely made the grave shift. By the time of our final deadline, we were thinking of that old movie *Death Takes a Holiday,* adding a frantic PLEASE! Please, no more new arrivals until after our book is published.

A few words about cemetery etiquette. While it is true that dead men tell no tales, that doesn't mean they aren't listening. More to the point: Cemetery visits aren't confined to star trekkers; funerals may be in progress or bereaved relatives may be visiting nearby sites, so keep your voices low. And by all means, tread carefully: Never touch or pick flowers or shrubbery anywhere on the grounds. Park as close to the side of the road as possible; avoid hogging access roads. If you treat them with respect, cemetery office personnel and grounds-keepers can be extremely helpful in unearthing graves. Oh, one other bit of unsolicited advice: Wear practical walking shoes for your grave hopping. Cemetery lawns, even the best-groomed ones, are often uneven, with surprising tilts, drops, and changes in turf. Don't be spooked by all this—be comfortable.

If your spirit is willing, your grave adventures can be incredibly rewarding, no bones about it. And if you've seen one cemetery, chances are you'll want to see them all, or at least another, then another, and another. The hunt for buried treasures can be addictive. How well we know! As Mort Sahl once said, "You haven't lived until you've died in California."

LOS ANGELES

Sprawling Los Angeles is a vast playground of the stars—
the deceased ones, that is. Although most are accessible, distances
are so great it takes awhile to navigate the traffic to the many
celebrity cemeteries even within the city limits. For those of us
devoted to the underworld, it's worth it.

ANGELUS-ROSEDALE CEMETERY

1831 WEST WASHINGTON BOULEVARD; (323) 734-3155; FAX (323) 734-3159

What we like about this vintage cemetery, which first opened its gates in 1884, is that it *feels* old. This is evident in much of the statuary and the intriguing private mausoleums that grace the cemetery's sixty-five acres, some shaped like pyramids, others like Greek temples. The entrance drive is flanked by rows of sentrylike palm trees, and the grounds are stippled with pines and palms. The surrounding brick walls have cutouts in the shape of crosses. This was the first cemetery in the area open to people of all races and religions.

The brick building that houses the office is on the right. Perhaps because Angelus-Rosedale is not a high priority for graveyard groupies, the office staffers often have time to chat about the permanent residents and the many sculptures on the grounds. One staffer urged us to look for the unusual gray granite sculpture of the woman in mourning that marks the Kercheval family grave site. At its base are the words "Until the day break, and the shadows flee away."

Among a number of Los Angeles mayors, military officers, Civil War generals, Congressional Medal of Honor awardees, and politicians, **William Thornton Glassell** (1831–1879; section M, lot 11, southeast corner) is a standout. A great-uncle of General George S. Patton, this Virginia native commanded the first Confederate submarine and later founded the city of Orange, California.

Angelus-Rosedale is the final address of **Frank Chance** (1877–1924; section N, lot 109, grave 2 NE), Hall of Fame first baseman and player-manager of the Chicago Cubs in the years in which they played in four World Series (yes, way, way back then). He was part of the dynamic infield double-play combo of "Tinker to Evers to Chance," a phrase still remembered today by baseball fans.

Another athlete taking time out here is **Henry "Hurricane Hank" Armstrong** (1912–1988; section 12, lot 53, grave 4 NW), the only professional boxer to hold three world titles at one time (featherweight, welterweight, and lightweight) and who is considered one of boxing's all-time greats.

You must remember this: **Dooley Wilson** (1886–1953; section D, lot 6, grave 5 NE), pianist-composer-actor, is here. He will live forever, or as long as the movie *Casablanca* is shown. In his role as the pianist Sam, he played it again, singing "As Time Goes By."

Also here are composer and lyricist **Andy Razaf** (1895–1973; section O, lot 116, facing the chapel, on the right, second row), best known for his jazz collaborations with Eubie Blake, and **Tim Moore** (1888–1958; section O, lot 120, grave 1 NW), who was Kingfish in the television version of the popular radio show *Amos and Andy*.

Bebop and jazz musician **Eric A. Dolphy Jr.** (1928–1964; section 10, lot 140, grave 1 NE) was a brilliant innovator known for his improvisational style; he played with Charles Mingus, John Coltrane, and others. There is also a cenotaph here honoring jazz great **Art Tatum** (1909–1956). His spirit may be willing, but his remains were removed and re-buried in the Great Mausoleum at Forest Lawn Memorial Park, Glendale.

In spite of her wishes, **Hattie McDaniel** (1895–1952; section D, lot 24) is here with a relatively new (1999) monument, just across the road from the office. The veteran character actress, whose performance as Mammy in *Gone With the Wind* won her a Best Supporting Actress Oscar in 1940, requested burial in Hollywood Forever Park. But in 1952 African Americans could not be buried in a "whites only" cemetery, even in southern California. She now has a monument here *and* in her first choice as well (Hollywood Forever Park; see page 59).

Other movie people at Rosedale include **Everett H. Sloane** (1909–1965; mausoleum, front wall north, niche 122), a skilled member of Orson Welles's radio repertory company, Mercury Theater. His premier film roles were in Welles's *Citizen Kane* and *The Lady from Shanghai*.

Marshall Neilan (1891–1958; section K, lot 35, grave 3 SW) was a big-name actor-director of the silent-film era, earning a whopping (for the 1920s) $150,000 per picture; chronic alcoholism did him in.

Forgotten today but distinguished in their time were **George Goodfellow** (1855–1910; mausoleum), felicitously named surgeon who was the first doctor to

operate on abdominal gunshot wounds with success, and **Phineas Banning** (1830–1885; section J, lot 40, grave 2 SE), a financier who owned Catalina Island and was influential in the development of Los Angeles harbor. **David Burbank** (1821–1895; section J, lot 222, grave 3 NW) was an entrepreneurial dentist and rancher who sold his 4,000-acre sheep ranch to a development company in 1886. The company named the spread Burbank in his honor.

Among life's less fortunate is **Pauline "Baby Sunshine" Flood** (1915–1917; section 7, lot 1, grave 2N-2W), a baby movie "actress" who appeared in nine films. Her brief career ended when she crawled in front of a moving truck.

LUNCH BREAK

A variety of real Greek dishes in gigantic servings can be found at **Papa Cristo's** (2771 West Pico Boulevard, Koreatown; 323-737-2970; www.papacristo.com). At night there's belly dancing and a contagious gaiety.

Louise Peete (1883–1947; section G, lot 19A, space 65), smooth-talking southern femme fatale, made a career of seducing rich men and killing them by driving them to suicide. She finally was caught and imprisoned, but when freed, killed again—this time a woman who had felt sorry for her and helped in her release. So much for pity: Peete got the gas chamber.

★*Grounds open 8:00 A.M.–5:00 P.M. daily. Office hours: 8:00 A.M.–5:00 P.M. Monday–Saturday. Map; restrooms. Annual one-and-a-half-hour tour second weekend of October.*

ANNA MAY WONG *1905–1961*

When Los Angeles-born Wong Liu Tsong, the daughter of a Chinese laundryman, began acting at age fourteen as a Hollywood extra, one of the first things she did was change her name. As Anna May Wong she had everything—beauty, intelligence, and ability—everything except the chance to play leading roles opposite Caucasian men and to earn the big bucks with which Hollywood studios rewarded their stars. For *Shanghai Express* (1932), one of her best-known films, she earned $6,000; the movie's star, Marlene Dietrich, received $78,000 or more.

It wasn't just about the money. Despite her looks and obvious sex appeal, Wong was turned down for romantic leads opposite white actors. She coveted the female lead in the film version of Pearl Buck's novel *The Good Earth,* set in China, but lost it to Luise Rainer, who had to be made up to look Chinese, as was Paul Muni, the male lead. Ironically, the antimiscegenation restrictions of the Hays office, which tightly controlled movie morality codes, wouldn't permit Muni to have a real Chinese woman as his movie wife. Go figure.

Though Wong never had a breakthrough Hollywood leading role, she eked out a long career, starring in English, German, and French silent films and touring in stage productions throughout Europe and the United States. Her career ended in 1960 with parts in *Portrait in Black* (with Lana Turner and Anthony Quinn) and *The Savage Innocents* (again with Quinn and Peter O'Toole). All in all, she made more than fifty movies, both silents and talkies.

She never married, but supposedly had an affair with director Marshall Neilan (also at rest here), among others. She died at age fifty-six from complications of heart disease and cirrhosis. Her unmarked grave is in section 5, lot 136, grave 3 NE, near a giant old olive tree.

CATHEDRAL OF OUR LADY OF THE ANGELS

555 WEST TEMPLE STREET;
(213) 680-5200; WWW.OLACATHEDRAL.ORG

Awesome is the word for the exterior of this new (2002) cathedral, designed by Spanish architect Rafael Moneo. The elegant, austere interior is vast space, softened and humanized by a series of twenty-seven tapestries by John Nava, depicting saints and religious scenes.

In the lower level of the cathedral, the mausoleum holds some 1,300 crypts and 5,000 cremation niches. The mausoleum can be reached by stairs or an elevator on the left rear side of the cathedral (when facing the altar). It is one of the few cathedrals in the United States where laypeople may be buried. Its long austere hall, made of Spanish limestone, is warmed by soft lighting from alabaster wall sconces.

> ## LUNCH BREAK
>
> For a lovely lunch, outdoors on the shaded patio in good weather, **Cafe Pinot** (700 West Fifth Street; 213-239-6500) is a true delight, with its California-French-style food and its handy location next to the Main Library.

There are six chapels, plus twenty-six stained-glass windows and nine lunettes from the old St. Vibriana cathedral, now restored to bright, vivid colors.

Relics of **St. Vibriana**, a third-century martyr whose remains were discovered in the Roman catacombs in the nineteenth century and brought to the old St. Vibriana cathedral, were transferred here. As the patroness of the archdiocese of Los Angeles, she has her own chapel, where her remains are now kept in a glass sarcophagus.

In the Bishops' crypt are several bishops and archbishops, as well as **Cardinal James McIntyre** (1886–1979), the first cardinal appointed to the western United States. He was originally interred at Calvary Cemetery. One of the few laypeople here so far is actress **June Marlowe** (1903–1984), who played Miss Crabtree in the "Our Gang" comedies. She was moved from San Fernando Mission Cemetery. ★ *Cathedral and mausoleum open 6:30 A.M.–7:00 P.M. Monday–Friday, 9:00 A.M.–6:00 P.M. Saturday, 7:00 A.M.–6:00 P.M. Sunday.*

GREGORY PECK 1916–2003

When you consider that Eldred Gregory Peck made more than fifty movies in almost sixty years, it is surprising to learn that he never intended to be an actor. In college, at the University of California, Berkeley, he majored in English, with the idea of going into medicine later. It was sheer chance that he was recruited, because of his 6-foot-

Gregory Peck

April 5, 1916   June 12, 2003

3-inch height, to play in a campus production of *Moby Dick.* Five more plays in college, and he was hooked.

After graduation Peck went to New York to study with Sanford Meisner at the Neighborhood Playhouse. His first years were spartan. He sometimes slept in Central Park for lack of money and worked at the 1939 World's Fair and as a tour guide for NBC. His first acting break came in 1942 as the lead in the short-lived Broadway play *Morning Star.* Later the same year he appeared in *The Willow and I.*

While learning freer movement and dance from Martha Graham, he injured his back so severely that he was exempted from military service. Years later the publicity machine at 20th Century Fox blamed his injury on rowing at college (he *was* on the crew at Berkeley). He later said it took him years to get the truth out. "In Hollywood," he said, "they didn't think a dance class was macho enough."

From Broadway, it wasn't long before Hollywood noticed the tall, handsome actor with the distinctive voice. In 1944 he made his first film, *Days of Glory,* followed by five big pictures that made him a bankable box office star: *The Keys of the Kingdom, The Valley of Decision, Spellbound, The Yearling,* and *Duel in the Sun.* When offered *Gentleman's Agreement* in 1947, Peck's agent tried to talk him out of it because of the sensitive subject matter (at the time), anti-Semitism. Peck insisted on making the picture. That same year he signed a letter criticizing the activities of the House Un-American Activities Committee (HUAC) for its blacklisting.

This was the first of many instances when Peck went against the common wisdom and did the right, not the opportune, thing. Years later he publicly opposed the Vietnam War, even while supporting one of his sons who was there fighting. Through the years Peck was involved in many humanitarian, liberal, and Democratic causes.

Friends tried to persuade him to run against Ronald Reagan for governor, but he declined, saying he had no ambition for politics.

FILM VAULT

The 1962 version of *Cape Fear* is still chillingly scary. Robert Mitchum as the creepy killer joins Peck in a fine cast that includes Polly Bergen, Martin Balsam, and Telly Savalas.

Peck once insisted, after receiving the Jean Hersholt Humanitarian Award in 1968, "I am not a do-gooder . . . I simply take part in activities I believe in." There were plenty of those, including the American Cancer Society and the National Endowment for the Arts. With actor friends Jose Ferrer and Dorothy McGuire, he founded the La Jolla Playhouse in 1949, which has become a landmark theater. He was also a founding patron of the University College, Dublin, School of Film.

In his long career Peck made a remarkable number of important, significant films and was nominated for a Best Actor Oscar five times, four of them during his first five years in Hollywood. He finally struck gold in 1962 with his role as the honorable lawyer Atticus Finch in *To Kill a Mockingbird*. While he often played heroic figures, Peck could also act against type, such as a Nazi in *The Boys from Brazil* (1978).

Peck's first marriage produced three sons. After an amicable divorce, he married Veronique Passani, with whom he had a boy and girl and a marriage of forty-eight years that ended with his peaceful death.

You don't need a map to find Gregory Peck's crypt. He was one of the first to take up residence here, in the third alcove on the left as you enter. His large beige marble wall crypt has his name and dates. Period. At the end of his alcove is a luminous stained-glass window.

PIERCE BROTHERS CHAPEL OF THE PINES CREMATORY

1605 SOUTH CATALINA STREET; (323) 731-5734

A visit to this, Los Angeles's oldest crematorium (1903), is easily combined with a trip to Angelus-Rosedale, located just around the corner on West Washington. The chapel is an attractive circular building with neoclassical columns and detailing, though somewhat rundown now. There are few high-wattage superstars here, but

this is the final address of scores of actors, directors, and other film personnel whose hard work and steady efforts were the underpinnings of many a successful Hollywood movie. Finding them is not easy. It depends on the helpfulness (or lack thereof) of the office staffers on any given day.

Here you'll find **Edmund Gwenn** (1875–1959; ashes in vaultage), impish character actor best known as Santa Claus in the classic *Miracle on 34th Street* (1947), and **Margaret Dumont** (1889–1965), whose Amazonian presence was an important plot element in *A Night at the Opera, Duck Soup,* and five other Marx Brothers films, in which she played the foil and/or assertive would-be love interest of Groucho.

British-born **Nigel Bruce** (1885–1958; vault 35167) is at peace here. A character actor, Bruce is best remembered as Dr. Watson, Basil Rathbone's trusted sidekick in the fourteen Sherlock Holmes films made between 1939 and 1946. **Jean Hagen** (1923–1977), less famous than her onetime husband Franchot Tone, played in scores of movies, among them *Singin' in the Rain* (as Lina Lamont, silent star), *The Asphalt Jungle, Adam's Rib,* and *The Big Knife.*

At one time everybody's favorite character actor was **Thomas Mitchell** (1892–1962; ashes in vaultage), whose drunken doctor in *Stagecoach* (1939) won him an Oscar for Best Supporting Actor and who played stellar roles in *Gone With* the Wind, It's a Wonderful Life, and other hits. Character actor **H. B. Warner** (1875–1958) is no household name today, but from the silent movies through the 1950s he was a stalwart in hundreds of films. Special triumphs were *A Tale of Two Cities, You Can't Take It With You,* and *It's a Wonderful Life.*

One bona fide star on the premises is British-born **Herbert Marshall** (1890–1966), who was a mainstay of many films of the 1930s and 1940s. Frequently cast as a sympathetic, world-weary lead or weak second lead, he occasionally played a villain (as in *Foreign Correspondent,* 1940). Some of his big hits were *Trouble in Paradise* (1932), *The Letter* (1940), *The Little Foxes* (1941), *The Razor's Edge* (1946), and *Duel in the Sun* (1946).

LUNCH BREAK

For something cheap, spicy, and different, try **BCD Tofu House** (1201 South Los Angeles Street; 213-746-2525). It's no-frills Korean food, one of a small chain, with three other handy locations in Koreatown.

Not everyone at Pierce Brothers Chapel is movie connected. Explorer **George Palmer "G. P." Putnam** (1887–1950) was better known as Amelia Earhart's husband than as the publisher and author he was, yet he directed the flights that made her famous.

And not everyone who came here stayed. In the case of several onetime residents, it was "here yesterday, gone today." Walter Huston (1884–1950), the first of three generations of a multitalented film family, was cremated here, but his ashes were lost for twenty years. Mysteriously, his son John found them at a New York funeral home and buried them at a family ranch in California. When Walter's second wife died in 1973, the much-traveled ashes were dug up and buried next to her in a Fresno cemetery. That seems to be the last judgment. ★ *There are no grounds to speak of. Office hours: 8:00 A.M. – 4:30 P.M. weekdays.*

PIERCE BROTHERS WESTWOOD VILLAGE MEMORIAL PARK

1218 GLENDON AVENUE; (310) 474-1579

Talk about big things in small packages! This tiny, hard-to-find burial ground—just off Wilshire Boulevard and surrounded by high-rise buildings in Westwood—is easily overlooked, yet it's hidden in plain sight. If you enter the alleyway to the AVCO Theater parking lot, the cemetery is to the right. A single road leads around the main area, section D, which resembles a grassy village green punctuated by pepper trees and pines, with many graves and markers in the grass. You may park at the side of

the drive and easily explore the green and several semi-enclosed sanctuaries with wall crypts that are on the east side of the green.

Once found, Westwood Village is a mother lode of celebrity sightings, with probably more famous bods per square foot than any other cemetery extant—about 200 at our last count. A-list actors, directors, producers, composers, musicians, a Persian poet—all are at rest here, just a few steps from the busyness of their former lives. Situated on a plot of land a mere 100 by 150 yards, Westwood is also the easiest of any burial ground to explore in a limited time. In short, it's the one to have when you're having only one.

Clustered among the inhabitants are actress **Eve Arden** (1909–1990; section D, lot 81), best known for wisecracking roles in many movies, an art form she perfected in the early television series *Our Miss Brooks;* **Jim Backus** (1913–1989; section D, west end of the green), movie and television actor (he was the millionaire on *Gilligan's Island*) who gave voice to the cartoon character Mr. Magoo; and **Robert Stack** (1919–2003; Room of Prayer, to the right of Marilyn Monroe), longtime movie leading man best known as the straight-arrow G-man in the television series *The Untouchables*.

Other actors of prominence here are **Richard Basehart** (1914–1984; central ash garden), who played in *Moby Dick* and *Cry Wolf*, among many other films; **Lloyd Nolan** (1902–1985; center of green, 75 feet south of Sanctuary of Tranquility), whose many films included *A Tree Grows in Brooklyn* (1945) and *Hannah and Her Sisters* (1985), his last; **Cornel Wilde** (1915–1989; section D, behind a tree), the actor who played Chopin in *A Song to Remember* (1945) and later a director; **Richard Conte** (1910–1975; section D, lot 62), who made many films, from *Call Northside 777* (1947) to *The Godfather* (1972); and **Lew Ayres** (1908–1996; section D, west end of lawn), whose greatest role was in *All Quiet on the Western Front* (1930) and who was Ginger Rogers's second husband.

John Cassavetes (1929–1989; in front and to the right of Armand Hammer's mausoleum) wore two Hollywood hats. As an actor he played in *Rosemary's Baby* (1968) and was nominated for an Academy Award for a supporting role in *The Dirty Dozen* (1967). As a director he made *A Woman Under the Influence* (1974) and several other independent films. Ingenue **Donna Reed** (1921–1986; section D, lot 110) starred in many films, but her best known are *It's a Wonderful Life* (1946) and *From Here to Eternity* (1953).

After hours, Westwood might be jamming underground with all the musicians and bandleaders here: **Buddy Rich** (1917–1987; Sanctuary of Tranquility, right side), brilliant jazz drummer; **Stan Kenton** (1911–1979; ashes scattered in Garden of

Roses), jazz bandleader; and **Les Brown** (1912–2001; Garden of Serenity, wall niche), whose Band of Renown was popular in the 1940s.

    Mel Torme (1925–1999; section B, lot 114, first road left, near the curb just beyond the entrance), popular vocalist of the 1940s and 1950s, known as the "Velvet Fog," is singing right along, as are **Carl Wilson** (1946–1998; section D, center), lead singer and co-founder of the Beach Boys, and **Roy Orbison** (1936– 1988; section D, lot 97, center lawn section, between two trees), popular rockabilly singer and songwriter. **Sammy Cahn** (1913–1993; section D, next to Orbison in center lawn) wrote many award-winning songs, including "High Hopes" and "Love and Marriage." In a more classical mode, cellist **Gregor Piatigorsky** (1903–1976; section D, lot 154) is also at rest herein.

    "Miss" **Peggy Lee** (1920–2002; Garden of Serenity, inside, on the left), as this popular jazz singer was *always* introduced on stage, made famous such songs as

"That's Why the Lady Is a Tramp," "I've Got It Bad and That Ain't Good," "Why Don't You Do Right?" and her signature "Is That All There Is?" She recorded more than 650 songs—blues, jazz, swing, Latin, even rock—and composed some, too. Her grave marker, like her many introductions, reads "Miss Peggy Lee" and "Music is my life's breath." Her grave site is as beautiful as she was, with a polished granite bench in front of three fountains in an oblong pool.

Westwood is home to other notables besides actors and musicians. Husband-and-wife historians **Will Durant** (1885–1981) and **Ariel Durant** (1898–1981) are in section D (small urn plaque near a tree bench). Their fifty-year research project, *The Story of Civilization,* a monumental popular series of volumes on the history of mankind, is still read today.

It seems fitting that both **Eva Gabor** (1919–1995; in front of Hammer mausoleum) and **Eddie Albert** (1906–2005; section D, lot 61) are in the same final acreage, as they shared billing as spouses on television's popular sitcom *Green Acres.* Eva was probably the most talented of the gorgeous Gabor sisters, appearing in *Gigi* and other films. Albert's five decades of acting—both on Broadway and in over eighty films—gave him lengthy credits, from *Brother Rat* (both stage and screen versions) to *The Longest Yard* (1974), with time-out in the U.S. Navy in World War II, for which service he received a Bronze Star. Among his other films were *The Teahouse of the August Moon, The Sun Also Rises, The Heartbreak Kid,* and *Roman Holiday,* for which he received a Best Supporting Actor nomination. Albert was also a vocal spokesman for environmental and ecological causes. He passed to greener acres from pneumonia, a complication of his Alzheimer's disease. He is here, along with his real-life wife, actress **Margo Albert** (1917–1985), who was a niece of Latin bandleader Xavier Cugat.

Also at rest here is **James Wong Howe** (1899–1976; north wall; nine rows up, fourth from right, Sanctuary of Tranquility), an award-winning cinematographer whose name was on hundreds of movie credits for three decades, beginning in the 1930s. He won two Oscars, for *The Rose Tattoo* (1955) and *Hud* (1963). **Irving "Swifty" Lazar** (1907–1993; section D, main lawn), high-profile actors' and writers' agent, represented A-list clients, among them Humphrey Bogart, Lauren Bacall, Gregory Peck, Noel Coward, Ernest Hemingway, and Tennessee Williams. Lazar was as visible a presence on the Hollywood scene as any of his famous clients, annually hosting a popular Oscar party.

On the premises as well is **Nader Naderpour** (1929–2000; section D, south end of the lawn), a Persian poet better known in his native Iran than in the United States.

Surprise residents are **G. David Schine** (1929–1996; section D, right side of the green, first row) and his wife, former Miss Universe **Hillevi Rombin Schine** (1933– 1996), who died together in a plane crash. Schine, the onetime colleague of the notorious Roy Cohn and U.S. senator Joe McCarthy, later became a respectable producer, putting his Washington playboy days firmly behind him.

Fanny Brice (1891–1951), comedienne of vaudeville, stage, and radio, was reinterred here from Home of Peace Memorial Park and resides in quiet dignity up four steps, through a locked gate, behind the rose garden beauty of the Garden of Serenity and the path where Walter Matthau rests. The headstone of **Eric Douglas** (1958–2004), Kirk's troubled actor son, lies next to Matthau's on the right.

Westwood shelters several victims of horrendous crimes, notably two budding actresses. **Dominique Dunne** (1959–1982; section D, lot 189), daughter of author Dominick Dunne, appeared in *Poltergeist* and was killed by a boyfriend, and *Playboy* model and "Playmate of the Year" **Dorothy Stratton** (1960–1980; section D, lot 170), was murdered by her estranged husband, Peter Snider.

Bob Crane (1928–1978; center of lawn), reinterred here from Oakwood Memorial Park in Chatsworth, was Colonel Hogan, the lead in *Hogan's Heroes,* which thrived on television from 1966 to 1971. What could be more unexpected than a comedy about a World War II Nazi prisoner-of-war camp becoming a TV hit? Try the real-life predilections of Crane himself. After he was savagely murdered in a Scottsdale, Arizona, motel room, Crane's secret life as a swinger and photographer of sexcapades came to light. Not a pretty story.

Ernest Lehman (1915–2005; section D, unmarked, next to Ray Conniff), one-time Broadway publicist and writer of short stories and novellas before moving to

Hollywood, made it big as a screenwriter. His first effort, *Executive Suite* (1954), was followed by *Sabrina, The King and I, Somebody Up There Likes Me, The Sweet Smell of Success* (adapted from his own novella), and *North by Northwest* (an original screenplay and one of Alfred Hitchcock's most popular films). The 1960s and 1970s brought more Lehman successes: *West Side Story, The Sound of Music* (widely credited with saving MGM from bankruptcy), *Who's Afraid of Virginia Woolf?* (an adaptation), *Hello Dolly!,* and *Black Sunday.* Lehman had four Oscar nominations and received an honorary Oscar in 2001.

LUNCH BREAK

Delicious contemporary California food is just a hop-skip away at **Napa Valley Grille** (1100 Glendon Avenue; 310-824-3322). An open kitchen, fine wine selection, charming vineyard mural, and relaxing decor make this a great choice, especially nice for Sunday brunch. For something cheaper, faster, and still nourishing, try **Noodle Planet** (1118 Westwood Boulevard; 310-208-0777).

A newcomer is Don Knotts (1924–2006; north side of drive in first row, facing Armand Hammer mausoleum), the actor/comedian who played Deputy Barney Fife on the *Andy Griffith Show.* ★*Grounds and office open 8:00 A.M.–5:00 P.M. daily. Map; restrooms.*

TRUMAN CAPOTE *1924–1984*

It is difficult to think of Truman Capote—wispy and fey, with a little boy voice and 5-foot-3-inch height—as a ladies' man, but for many years after his first success as a novelist he was the darling—witty, gossipy, and clever—and confidante of prominent New York society belles. His first book, *Other Voices, Other Rooms,* published in 1948, quickly became a best seller and pushed its twenty-three-year-old author into the limelight, a place he never willingly left.

The Grass Harp followed, establishing him as a southern novelist, which he only partly was. Though born in New Orleans, he lived most of his life—from age eight—in New York City, with time out for school in Ossining, New York, and Greenwich, Connecticut. For a while, he was The Next Big Thing, as success followed success. He won two O. Henry awards for short stories; wrote a Broadway musical, *House of Flowers;* and did a screenplay rewrite for *Beat the Devil.*

Capote then changed direction, producing some superb nonfiction: *New Yorker* magazine articles and *In Cold Blood,* a book about brutal murders in Kansas—a pacesetter in the field of fact-written-as-compellingly-as-fiction. With *Breakfast at Tiffany's* he was back with his light touch, and he returned to the South in two charming memoirs of childhood, *A Christmas Memory* and *The Thanksgiving Visitor.*

Television talk shows, readings, and social extravaganzas like his exclusive, much publicized "Black and White Ball" in Manhattan followed. Then things began to unravel, with a pattern of alcoholism, drugs, and nervous breakdowns. What finally did him in professionally and personally was the publication of the first chapter of *Answered Prayers,* a never-completed roman à clef memoir in which he bitchily carved up the society women who had been his best friends. Talk about self-destructive!

Even Capote's death provided fodder for gossip and quarrels. He succumbed, of liver disease complicated by drug use and phlebitis, while in Hollywood on a visit to his friend Joanne Carson, former wife of television host Johnny Carson. His long-time lover-companion, Jack Dunphy, and other friends from East Hampton, New York, wanted to take his remains home, stating that Truman loathed Los Angeles and would not want to spend his afterlife there. The Solomon-ian denouement was that half the ashes went back to New York; the rest Joanne Carson put into a wall crypt at Westwood Village. The marble-walled crypt is on the outside wall of the Corridor of Tenderness, near the park entrance.

JAMES COBURN *1928–2002*

Often described as the actor with the "piano key smile" (before Jack Nicholson came on the scene), James Coburn was considered as "cool" as they came. He first caught attention with his performance as the laconic knife-throwing vigilante in the popular 1960 western *The Magnificent Seven,* no small feat considering with whom he had to compete for screen time (Steve McQueen, Yul Brynner, Charles Bronson, Robert Vaughn, et al.).

Coburn drove home his screen "cool" as an Aussie POW in the ensemble cast of *The Great Escape* (1963), one of the few characters who actually *did* escape. He continued doing supporting roles in popular movies until the spy-film parody *Our Man Flint* (1966) and its sequel *In Like Flint* (1967) gave him star status. Despite the popularity of those films, he never really caught on with audiences as a leading man, though a movie he starred in and produced in 1967, *The President's Analyst,* has become a deservedly true cult film. Another notable performance of that era was his starring role in 1973's *The Last of Sheila,* a twist-filled whodunit. Coburn was functionally crippled for over a decade due to rheumatoid arthritis, which he attempted to cure with countless unorthodox treatments. He was finally able to perform on-screen again in the 1990s, earning a deserved Best Supporting Actor Oscar in 1999 for his role as Nick Nolte's father in the scathing *Affliction.*

James Coburn was fatally felled by a heart attack. He rests now inside the Garden of Serenity (right side) beside three rough-hewn fountains in a pool, opposite Peggy Lee. Coburn's side of the polished bench he shares with his wife, **Paula Josephine Coburn** (1955–2004), reads "James Harrison III–'I go bravely on . . .' James Coburn." Her side of the bench says "Love is the answer."

RODNEY DANGERFIELD *1921–2004*

What epitaph would one expect to find on Rodney Dangerfield's gravestone? Something about a lack of respect? Well, forget about it. Even in death, Rodney didn't get the respect his stage persona craved.

Born Jacob Cohen on Long Island, New York, the son of a vaudevillian, he tried his hand at stand-up comedy under the name Jack Roy. Years of off-and-on struggles followed, then came a big break on *The Ed Sullivan Show* under the name Rodney Dangerfield. He later appeared repeatedly on *The Tonight Show,* always wearing his signature costume of a plain black suit with white shirt and bright red tie, the knot of which he tugged at nervously as he delivered his self-deprecating one-liners. (Samples: "My wife likes to talk during sex–last night she called me from

Detroit," "I saw a guy jogging nude—I asked why? He said 'cause you came home early!" "I told my bartender to surprise me—he showed me a naked picture of my wife!")

What really cemented Dangerfield's popularity was his role as the crass Ron Czervik in the cult film *Caddyshack* (1980), which introduced him to a delighted young audience. He followed his stardom by opening a comedy club in New York called Dangerfield's, which launched the career of many a young comic. He continued doing stand-up and was featured in a series of popular television ads for Miller Lite beer. Among his later films were *Easy Money* (1983), *Back to School* (1985), as the self-styled animated dog in *Rover Dangerfield* (1991), and *Meet Wally Sparks* (1997). A notable (out of character) film appearance was as a sadistic, molesting father to Juliette Lewis in Oliver Stone's controversial *Natural Born Killers* (1994).

Dangerfield died of complications during heart valve surgery. On entering the hospital, when asked by reporters how long he'd be there, he said, typically, "If all goes well, about a week. If not, about an hour and a half."

His white shirt and red tie are now part of the Smithsonian Institution's permanent collection, but his headstone can be found in the Chapel Garden Estate, with the epitaph "There goes the neighborhood."

ARMAND HAMMER *1898–1990*

Considering that he lived much of his life in the shadows, it is surprising that the only private mausoleum—the most visible presence at Westwood Village—belongs to Armand Hammer. The stately edifice is on the left as you enter the cemetery grounds. It contains his father Julius, mother Rose, and brother Victor, an avid art collector and expert.

Born in New York City of Russian Jewish parentage, Armand earned a medical degree from Columbia University. Even so, he became a businessman-entrepreneur and spent much of his adult life commuting between the Soviet Union and the United States, trading Russian furs and minerals for American wheat, tractors, and other machinery. He later sold Russian art and artifacts in the Western world.

Even during his lifetime, Hammer's connections to the USSR

HOUSE CALL

The nearby **UCLA Hammer Museum** (10899 Wilshire Boulevard; 310-443-7000; www.hammer.ucla.edu), now part of the university though not on the campus, is a short stroll from the cemetery. It contains Hammer's legacy of fine art, with emphasis on French impressionists, graphic art, and old masters. Special exhibitions of avant-garde artists are held regularly. The museum also has a well-selected gift and art book shop.

always seemed mysteriously vague and questionable, considering that his commutes were during the hostile decades of the cold war. With the cold war over, it has been documented since Hammer's death—by Soviet, FBI, and Britain's MI-5 files—that his businesses were mere fronts for espionage, serving as conduits for paying Soviet spies in the United States.

Hammer's last venture and most solid success was his investment in Occidental Petroleum, a small California firm that he managed and manipulated—partly through lobbying and bribery—to turn into the eighth-largest oil company in the United States. He did this via backdoor deals with Libya's infamous dictator, Colonel Muammar Gadhafi.

BURT LANCASTER *1913–1994*

The son of a mailman, Burt Lancaster (born Burton Stephen Lancaster in New York City) lived the dream life of countless ten-year-old boys. He joined the circus as an acrobat, and during World War II he served in the U.S. Army in North Africa and Italy.

After the war Burt turned to acting, and tumbling from Broadway to Hollywood landed his first film role opposite Ava Gardner in *The Killers* (1946), based on Ernest Hemingway's short story. Critics and audiences flipped over Lancaster's debut, he quickly bounded into nine more films released in the next three years, and his movie career was flying. All these breaks without an hour spent on acting lessons! Though he was thirty-two years old when he made his first film, he soon made up for lost time, clocking more than eighty movies in his long career.

While his roles in his early pictures were mostly as a handsome tough guy, he got the chance to demonstrate his acrobatic background in *The Flame and the Arrow* (1950) and *The Crimson Pirate*

FILM VAULT

Ranking high in Lancaster's successes and just as high as a movie in its own right is *Sweet Smell of Success* (1957), a tough, cynical look at New York nightlife that holds up remarkably well. His acid-tongued newspaper columnist J. J. Hunsecker (said to be loosely based on Walter Winchell) and Tony Curtis as a wannabe are brilliant, and so are the jazz score, Alexander Mackendrick's direction, the script, and the camera work of James Wong Howe.

(1952), teaming with his close friend from his circus days, Nick Cravat. There were also leading parts in such varied genres as tough Western (*Vengeance Valley,* 1951), sports bio (*Jim Thorpe, All American,* 1951), and army drama (*From Here to Eternity,* 1953, for which he was nominated for an Oscar). He even played the ruler of a south sea island (*His Majesty O'Keefe,* 1954).

As Lancaster's acting résumé grew, so did his versatility, and he alternated between pure entertainment fare and impressive dramatic projects, many of which he also produced. Several of his films were important ones that challenged him, such as *All My Sons; Come Back, Little Sheba; The Unforgiven; Judgment at Nuremberg; Birdman of Alcatraz;* and *Seven Days in May.* Oscar came calling in 1960, when he received the Best Actor statuette for his performance as the charismatic charlatan Elmer Gantry.

Lancaster often took less than his usual acting fee to produce a project he believed in, or to appear in the film of a director he respected and wanted to work with, such as *The Leopard,* directed by Luchino Visconti. He was honored with a fourth Academy Award nomination for *Atlantic City* (1980); his final role was in the popular *Field of Dreams* (1989). Soon after that film's release, Lancaster suffered a severe stroke, but that didn't prevent him from marrying for the third time the next year (at age seventy-eight). His two earlier marriages produced five children.

Burt Lancaster somersaulted from the earthly circus into the next world at age eighty, following a heart attack. On the lawn, at the far right, Lancaster's small square bronze grave marker is eight spaces in from the curb, directly across from the Sanctuary of Love.

JACK LEMMON *1925–2001*

It seems fitting that Jack Lemmon, who made ten movies with Walter Matthau, should be buried near his off-screen buddy, on the south end of the park in the Chapel Garden Estate, by the office. To his left is Carroll O'Connor; to his right, fittingly, is Billy Wilder, for whom he made some great movies—*Some Like It Hot, The Apartment, The Fortune Cookie*—and one not-so-great, *Buddy Buddy*.

FILM VAULT

Some Like It Hot (1959) may not be the best movie farce of all time, but we can't think of a better one. The premise of two musicians on the lam from the Mob is enhanced by performances by Lemmon, Tony Curtis, and Marilyn Monroe, who never hit a wrong note. Then there's that super script by Billy Wilder and I. A. L. Diamond and Wilder's laser-fast directing.

Lemmon was born to privilege in Boston, attended the right prep schools, and graduated from Harvard. He began his theatrical career as a piano player in a New York bar, but before long was in several television soap operas and showed his budding comic skills in *Room Service* on Broadway.

A move to Hollywood led to his debut in the forgettable *It Should Happen to You.* Prime-time comedy roles followed—in *Mr. Roberts* (for which he won a Best Supporting Actor Oscar), *The Apartment, Phfffft!, Irma la Douce,* and *The Out-of-Towners.*

He soon proved he was not just another pretty face/empty space, by moving with ease to serious dramatic parts—in *Days of Wine and Roses, Save the Tiger* (another Oscar, this time for Best Actor), *Missing,* and *Glengarry Glen Ross.* For all his wide-ranging performances, he is probably best remembered for the manic *Some Like It Hot.* Some of his many films may have been lemons—but Jack never was.

OSCAR LEVANT *1906–1972*

From the 1930s to 1950s, Oscar Levant was as famous to radio and movie audiences as talk-show guests are in this era. The difference is that he had real wit.

Born in Pittsburgh, Pennsylvania, to a Russian Orthodox Jewish family, Levant was a piano prodigy. From the late 1920s over the next twenty years, he composed scores for twenty movies as well as classical compositions for orchestras. He also composed, conducted, and/or acted in four Broadway shows. Many considered him a genius for his piano and composing ability, along with his obvious high intelligence.

As a pianist and dour, sarcastic companion he appeared in six movies, among them *Rhapsody in Blue* (1945), *The Barkleys of Broadway* (1949), and *An American in Paris* (1951). He also wrote three books of memoirs—*A Smattering of Ignorance* (1940), *Memoirs of an Amnesiac* (1965), and *The Unimportance of Being Oscar* (1968)—all of which were well received.

He was a frequent guest on *The Jack Paar Show* and from 1958 to 1960 had his own show on Los Angeles's KTOP-TV, which became controversial because he made too many snide wisecracks about real people. As a raconteur and black humorist, Levant couldn't be matched. If he were alive today, he would be a constant on cable television.

Levant's shtick was his hypochondria and neurosis. He once said, "I only make jokes when I am feeling insecure" and "Once I make up my mind, I'm full of indecision." Other much-quoted lines were "There's a fine line between genius and insanity. I have erased this line," "Underneath this flabby exterior is an enormous lack of character," and "I've given up reading books. I find it takes my mind off myself."

When Frank Sinatra Jr. was kidnapped, Levant commented, "It must have been done by music critics," and he once said, "I knew Doris Day before she was a virgin." He commented to Harpo Marx about his girlfriend, "She's a lovely person. She deserves a good husband. Marry her before she finds one."

He loved poking fun at himself as well, as in "Roses are red, violets are blue, I'm schizophrenic and so am I," "What the world needs is more geniuses with humility; there are so few of us left," and "I am no more humble than my talents require."

He liked to say, "I don't drink; I don't like it; it makes me feel good" and "I envy people who drink—at least they know what to blame everything on."

Levant became addicted to prescription drugs in later life. His second wife, June Gale, frequently had him committed to mental hospitals. But she remained married to him for almost thirty-three years, until his fatal heart attack. On the creamy marble walls of the Sanctuary of Love is Levant's niche, last row, bottom on the right side.

DEAN MARTIN 1917–1995

When Dean Martin (born Dino Crocetti), crooner and straight man for antic comedian Jerry Lewis, broke up the couple's enormously popular ten-year partnership in 1956—after they had made sixteen films together—the conventional wisdom was that Lewis would easily go it alone because he was the funny man, the goofy slapstick artist who "made" the team. Martin's career, critics predicted, would wither and fade. Were they ever wrong! Lewis's career sputtered, but Martin—largely because of his close ties to Frank Sinatra's Rat Pack—thrived as a quasi-serious actor and a recording artist.

His movies—*The Young Lions, Some Came Running,* and a number of lighter ones, like *Oceans 11* with the Rat Pack—enhanced his reputation as an actor as well as a songster. Several of his records—"That's Amore," "Return to Me", "Volare," and "Everybody Loves Somebody"—sold more than one million copies. His *Dean Martin Show* survived nine years on television, during which time his cabaret and nightclub appearances with Sinatra consolidated his image as a genial, laid-back, slightly boozy pal, always with a drink in hand. The drinking, a prop at first, morphed into the real thing near the end.

Frequent handwritten messages attached to his wall crypt in the Sanctuary of Love (third row on the left, three up from the bottom) attest to the fact that Martin had scores of adoring fans and to them he is still missed. His niche marker reads, fittingly, "Everybody loves somebody sometime."

WALTER MATTHAU 1920–2000

A fairly recent arrival at Westwood Village, Walter Matthau had a long career, beginning after World War II. A New York City native, he appeared on Broadway in such plays as *Will Success Spoil Rock Hunter?* and *A Shot in the Dark.*

His first movie role was in 1955 in *The Kentuckian* in which he played a villain, a type he would reprise in a number of films, including *Charade* in 1963. He made some sixty movies playing, believably, both serious and comic roles. Though not

conventionally handsome, he did well in romantic comedies, such as *Cactus Flower* (1969), *A New Leaf* (1971), and *House Calls* (1978).

Superstardom came relatively late for Matthau. He was forty-five when he was cast in 1965 as Oscar Madison, the sloppy character in the Broadway play *The Odd Couple,* opposite Art Carney as neat Felix. In 1968 the play became a movie, with Matthau in the same role but Jack Lemmon as Felix. The chemistry between the two actors was palpable and the beginning of a longtime movie partnership and off-screen friendship. In 1969 Matthau won a Best Supporting Actor Oscar for his role as the shyster lawyer in *The Fortune Cookie,* which also starred Lemmon. In all, the two made ten films together.

In his later career Matthau often specialized in playing cantankerous elders, as in *Grumpy Old Men* in 1993 and *Grumpier Old Men* in 1995, both with Lemmon. By this time their performances were so broad, they seemed to be mailed in.

Lemmon and Matthau now reside forever in nearby plots of land. Matthau and his second wife, actress **Carol Marcus Matthau** (1924–2003), whose first husband was the author William Saroyan, share a headstone against the outer wall of the Garden of Serenity, several stones down from old pal Lemmon. The Matthau grave site has a flecked granite bench, with these words on the side: "We only part to meet again. We will with thee go forever."

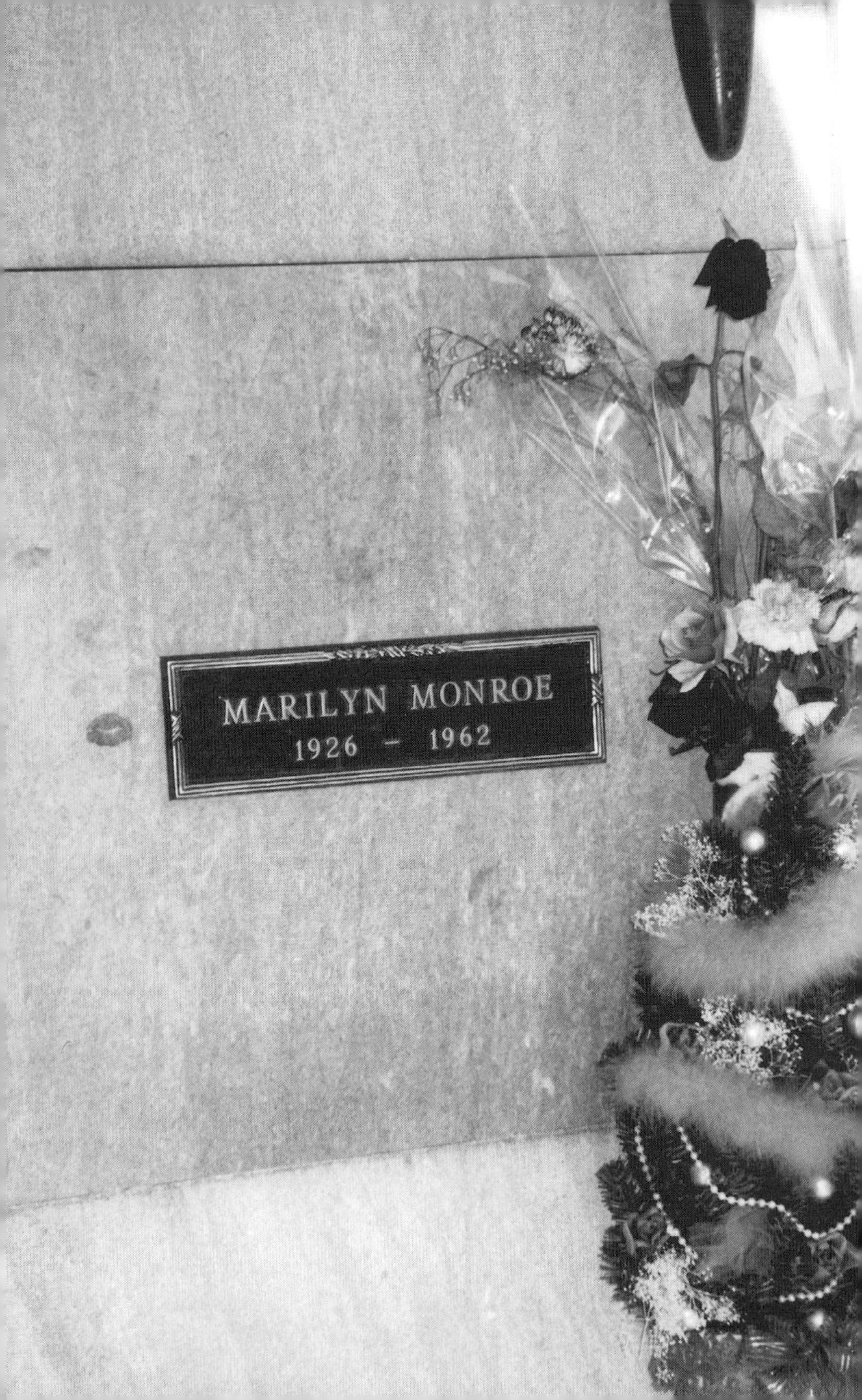
MARILYN MONROE
1926 - 1962

MARILYN MONROE *1926–1962*

MM's is the grave most tourists seek. We have observed Japanese tour groups marching in tandem to her crypt in the Corridor of Memories (the second tier up from the floor, in the beige marble wall near the entrance at the north end of the park), then march right out, without a glance at the other intriguing residents. A flower vase attached to the crypt usually sports a fresh bouquet. For many years, before he moved to Florida, Joe DiMaggio, Marilyn's third husband, left a bouquet on the anniversary of her death. A memorial service held here on her August 5 anniversary still attracts hundreds.

The marble around her bronze marker is often stained with lipstick kisses, proving, we suppose, that her fans are of both sexes. A marble bench dedicated to Marilyn is positioned opposite her crypt. Even in death this blond siren—who began life as Norma Jean Mortensen (or Baker, depending on which source you believe)—continues to lure admirers. Hugh Hefner, publisher of *Playboy* magazine, has reserved the crypt to her left.

From her early impact films, *The Asphalt Jungle* and *All About Eve,* to *The Seven Year Itch, Bus Stop,* and *The Misfits,* she filled the screen with her presence—her voluptuous figure, wiggle, innocent smile, and breathy little-girl voice. She proved she could do comedy in *Some Like It Hot* and *How to Marry a Millionaire,* but she desired to be taken seriously as a dramatic actress and even studied at the Actors Studio in New York.

She had big yearnings, which three marriages, numerous affairs, psychiatry, and the adulation of fans couldn't satisfy. Her short life was star-crossed by drugs, insecurities, insomnia, habitual and clinically wayward tardiness (she'd be hours late, both in life and on movie sets,

HOUSE CALL

Marilyn's last home, where she died, is at 12305 Fifth Helena Drive in Brentwood. An unpretentious abode on a cul-de-sac off Carmelina Avenue, it is the last house on the left—privately owned, but a magnet for passionate fans to drive by.

which drove directors and her fellow actors crazy), and bouts with mental illness. Her final curtain, a mysterious suicide—after she'd been fired from her last movie, then reinstated—has been the stuff of films, plays, biographies, and endless gossip. Was it really suicide, or murder, or a fake attempt for attention that went awry? We'll never know. Never mind that if she were alive today, she would be eighty years old. To generations of movie fans, she is still the *only* Marilyn, an authentic legend.

CARROLL O'CONNOR *1924–2001*

While Carroll O'Connor will always be Archie Bunker to fans of television's *All in the Family,* this Irish Catholic New Yorker had a large body of movie and television work before he was tapped by producer Norman Lear to play Archie. Ironically, O'Connor grew up in Queens, the setting of *All in the Family,* but his Queens was Forest Hills and his real family was more educated and middle class than Archie's. His father was a lawyer, his mother a schoolteacher, and his two brothers became doctors. O'Connor even did a stint as an English teacher, something the philistine Archie would have scorned.

O'Connor joined the U.S. Merchant Marine during World War II, then attended college at the University of Montana (where he earned an MA) and in Ireland (where he married in 1951) before deciding to become an actor. His film and television work was extensive. Before becoming Archie forever, he played in *Lonely Are the Brave* (1962), *Cleopatra* (1963), *In Harm's Way* (1965), *Hawaii* (1966), *Point Blank* (1967), *The Devil's Brigade* (1968), and *Kelly's Heroes* (1970), among others. He also appeared in a number of television dramas, like *Gunsmoke, I Spy, The Fugitive,* and *The Wild, Wild West.*

When Lear sought him out, O'Connor was living in Italy. He agreed to play Archie thinking the show was so outrageous, it wouldn't last long. Within a year it became the highest-rated sitcom on television, and it thrived for the next six sea-

sons. O'Connor's round Irish face seemed perfectly suited to Archie Bunker, though Archie's nationality is never mentioned.

One more irony of Archie-versus-Carroll: Whereas the premise of the role was Archie's bigotry and right-wing point of view, O'Connor was an outspoken liberal and supporter of many progressive causes. What made Archie so believable was that O'Connor played him straight, with the nuances of real life, not as a one-dimensional cartoon.

O'Connor's next big television hit was as Sheriff Bill Gillespie in the small-screen version of *In the Heat of the Night,* which ran for seven years (1988–1995). In addition to acting in the show, he wrote and directed a number of episodes and was executive producer. Throughout the 1970s and 1980s he acted in many made-for-TV dramas, including a remake of the movie *The Last Hurrah,* starring as Frank Skeffington. In 1990 O'Connor was inducted into the Television Hall of Fame.

Carroll O'Connor is now at peace in Chapel Garden Estate, to the right of the headstone of Jack Lemmon.

GEORGE C. SCOTT *1927–1999*

This marvelous actor often played angry, brooding men, and people who worked with him said that was sometimes the way he was in real life. Once, when he was rehearsing a film, an actress mentioned to the director that she was afraid of Scott. His response was, "Everybody is."

Maybe there were reasons. Virginia-born, George C. Scott lost his mother when he was eight years old and was raised by his father, a corporate executive. After a stint in the U.S. Marine Corps, young Scott studied journalism at the University of Missouri, but soon left for Broadway and an acting career.

Though he was hardly a pretty boy, he landed good roles on stage in *The Andersonville Trial* and even played Shakespeare's *Richard III*. One of his first movies was *Anatomy of a Murder* (1959), and a string of hits followed: *The Hustler, Dr. Strangelove or: How I Learned to Stop Worrying and Love the Bomb, The Yellow Rolls-Royce, Petulia, Patton, The Hospital*. All in all, he made over forty movies.

FILM VAULT

Despite his more famous roles, we have a soft spot for *Petulia* (1968), a quirky, offbeat film Scott made with Julie Christie (at her best and most beautiful), with a star-rich cast and the light touch of Richard Lester as director.

As in *Patton,* Scott often played intense, complex men. Nominated four times for an Academy Award, Scott refused the Oscar for *Patton,* saying others were just as deserving and the entire awards concept was a sham. He could play comedy and leading men as well, as in *Petulia* (1968) and *The Hospital* (1971), a sardonic black comedy. In the perennially popular television version of *A Christmas Carol,* Scott's Scrooge was a masterpiece.

His personal life was often as turbulent as his movie roles. He married and divorced actress Colleen Dewhurst twice, then married the much younger Trish Vandevere. They were separated at the time of his death. Tales of abusive conduct with his wives and other women dogged his reputation, but no one can deny his exceptional talent.

Scott's large headstone is just in front of the Garden of Serenity (a little irony there), left of Walter Matthau, along the south side of the park, next to the drive.

BILLY WILDER 1906–2002

A law student turned journalist turned scriptwriter turned escapee from the Nazis—it all sounds like a Billy Wilder movie, but actually it's the précis of his own early life. Samuel Wilder, as he was born (in Sucha, Austria), was nicknamed "Billy" by his mother, who had spent several years in the United States and was fascinated by Buffalo Bill Cody. Billy was educated to be a lawyer, but found scriptwriting for silent movies in Berlin more fun—that is, until Hitler came to power.

That's when Wilder left, knowing fewer than a hundred words of English on his arrival in Hollywood. With the help of Peter Lorre and other European friends, he got a job as a scriptwriter, collaborating with Charles Brackett. They worked together for twelve years and co-wrote eleven movies, including *Midnight* and *Ninotchka* (both 1939), *Hold Back the Dawn* and *Ball of Fire* (both 1941), and *Lost Weekend* (1945).

More than twenty-five films followed, either written or co-written (with I. A. L. Diamond and others), directed, and/or produced by Wilder.

> ### FILM VAULT
>
> Most of Wilder's oeuvre holds up surprisingly well, but **Sunset Boulevard** (1950) remains one of our all-time favorite movies, one we can see over and over again. It was also Wilder's favorite of all his films. The story's great, so is the clever script, and so are the performances by Gloria Swanson, William Holden, and Erich von Stroheim. And how about that opening scene?

Among these were *Double Indemnity* (which Wilder co-wrote with Raymond Chandler), *A Foreign Affair, Sunset Boulevard, Stalag 17, Sabrina, The Seven Year Itch, Love in the Afternoon, Witness for the Prosecution, Some Like It Hot, The Apartment,* and *The Fortune Cookie.* At one time he had fourteen straight hit movies.

Wilder was obviously a quick study. Not only did he learn English fast (though he always spoke it with an Austrian accent), but his grasp of American life, culture, and idiom was also lightning fast. One look at his most successful films, and it's hard to believe a non-native-born person could have written them. Quick, racy, hilarious dialogue was a Wilder specialty. If you had to encapsulate his genius with one word, it might be "audacious." There wasn't any subject he was afraid to tackle.

Though thoroughly American in subject matter, his films were infused with European sophistication and cynicism—a combination that gives them special flair. Even though he mastered serious drama, romance, film noir, and melodrama, his greatest talent was for comedy. In sixty years of moviemaking he accrued twenty-one Oscar nominations and took home six of the statuettes, two for *The Lost Weekend* and two for *The Apartment*.

Tastes changed in the late 1960s and 1970s, and Wilder's successes were fewer. Still, he is now recognized as one of the few Renaissance men of movies, talented at writing, directing, and producing. If he had to choose, he would probably have called himself a writer first. President Clinton awarded him the National Medal of Honor, one of many honors he received in a lifetime of filmmaking. He died of pneumonia at ninety-five.

In the Chapel Garden Estate section, Billy Wilder's large headstone is to the right of Jack Lemmon, who starred in five Wilder films. Under Wilder's name, the polished granite stone has this sentence: "I'm a writer, but then nobody's perfect." As usual, Wilder has the last word, even from the grave.

NATALIE WOOD *1938–1981*

With her luminous brown eyes and petite beauty, Natalie Wood—born Natasha Gurdin in San Francisco to Russian immigrant parents—dominated the screen. Whether it was in childhood roles in *Miracle on 34th Street* and *The Ghost and Mrs. Muir,* or as a teenager in *Rebel Without a Cause* and *The Searchers,* or later as a young woman in *Splendor in the Grass, Gypsy,* and *West Side Story,* she proved herself to be a believable actress.

Wood began acting at age five and died at forty-three, having spent most of her life making movies. Her mysterious death had aspects of a movie tragedy. She drowned on a dark night, a short distance from her and her husband's (actor Robert Wagner, whom she had divorced and remarried) yacht, where she, he, and guest Christopher Walken had gathered earlier.

That Natalie Wood is still remembered is evident by the potted geraniums, gardenias, and fresh flowers at her grave, a simple bronze marker engraved with a Russian cross and rose. It lies five stones in from the curb in section D, lot 60, near an old tree.

DARRYL F. ZANUCK *1902–1979*

Among Tinseltown insiders, Darryl F. Zanuck is known as one of the most successful goyim in moviemaking history. A Protestant in an industry whose leaders were mostly Jewish immigrants, he was arguably the most dominant of all, with a golden touch in the movies he produced.

His is a remarkable story. Born into a lower-middle-class family in Wahoo, Nebraska, he grew up in two dysfunctional families. His parents divorced when he was thirteen and both bailed on him, leaving him in his grandparents' care. Later, he rejoined his mother in Los Angeles and lived with her and her second husband, an abusive alcoholic who beat his wife and threw Darryl across the room. Young Darryl couldn't get away fast enough. He joined the army, fought in Belgium in World War I, then came home to manual jobs as a steelworker, factory foreman, and professional boxer. All the while he nursed the dream of being a writer, and eventually sold a script to Hollywood producer Irving Thalberg.

Though poorly educated, Zanuck had a knack for storytelling and inventing plots seemingly made for movies. He also showed fine editing skills. He worked for Mack Sennett, Charlie Chaplin, and Carl Laemmle, then joined Warner Brothers in 1924, writing scripts for the Rin Tin Tin dog series. In three years he leapfrogged to executive producer. Under his aegis at Warner Brother, *The Jazz Singer* was made in 1927 and he produced *Little Caesar* (1930) and *The Public Enemy* (1931), stirring up a public appetite for gangster films.

In 1933 Zanuck co-founded 20th Century Pictures and two years later joined it with the Fox Film Corporation, creating the behemoth that became 20th Century Fox. *The Grapes of Wrath, 42nd Street, How Green Was My Valley, Laura, Gentleman's Agreement, The Razor's Edge,* and *Viva Zapata!* were all produced on Zanuck's watch.

What made Zanuck stand out from his fellow moguls and studio heads were his skills at collaboration with superb directors—John Ford, Joseph Mankiewicz, and Elia Kazan among them. He believed in them and in the movies with his imprimatur. In short, he made the movies he wanted to make, dozens of them, including *A Letter to Three Wives, No Way Out, Five Fingers,* and *All About Eve,* which garnered six Oscars, including one for Best Picture.

In 1956 Zanuck left 20th Century Fox, but returned in 1961 to oversee production of *The Longest Day* (1962) and *The Sound of Music* (1965). Both were such big hits, they made the company solvent again in an era that was changing from big studios to smaller independent film companies. He was the last of the mighty moguls to retire (in 1971), with a track record of 165 films.

In prime company as always, Zanuck's grave is in the grass, center section D, lot 173, lawn center, six rows in from the drive, to the left of a large olive tree. A long, oversize bronze marker (bearing the 20th Century Fox logo), it delineates in nineteen lines of raised type many of the highlights of his lengthy career. His wife, **Virginia Fox Zanuck** (1906–1982), shares the same locale; her gravestone is below his, with sixteen lines delineating *her* accomplishments. One of her greatest may have been keeping her marriage alive, despite Zanuck's numerous flings with stars and starlets.

FRANK ZAPPA *1940–1993*

It's odd that Frank Zappa, whose persona and entire career seem to have been designed to attract attention, would be buried in an unmarked grave. From the release of his first record album *Freak Out,* with his band the Mothers of Invention (the record company insisted that he add the "of Invention" part) in 1966, he was a force on the music scene that couldn't be ignored. That signature double album was difficult to classify, as were most of the following fifty-plus records released in his relatively short life.

Musically, Zappa incorporated jazz, blues, rock, doo-wop, and classical elements with song subjects ranging from sociopolitical commentary and satire to sexual and scatological themes. These combinations often had the effect of endearing him to rebellious youths and repulsing their parents, which was precisely what he aimed to do. Album titles reflect this: *We're Only in It for the Money, Burnt Weenie Sandwich, Uncle Meat, Hot Rats, One Size Fits All, You Can't Do That on Stage Anymore.* Zappa also produced many struggling "fringe bands," empathizing with their difficulty finding audiences for their talents.

He played drums in his Lancaster, California, high school band, and around that time discovered the discordant avant-garde music of composer Edgar Varese, which would become a huge influence on Zappa's own future avant-garde works. It's perhaps appropriate that his first musical instrument was the drums, because for his entire adult life he truly marched to his own beat, rejecting much of what American society deemed routine. This trait can be seen even in the naming of his four children: Moon Unit, Dweezil, Ahmet Rodan, and Diva.

It was perhaps Frank Zappa's penchant for mixing social and political satire with complex and groundbreaking music that kept him from ever catching on with the mainstream in the United States, though he had a loyal international following. Czechoslovakian president Vaclav Havel, a longtime fan, even offered Zappa the job of special ambassador to the West on trade, culture, and tourism. Then-president George H. W. Bush's secretary of state, James Baker, successfully pressured Havel to change his mind, resulting in the honor being downgraded to *unofficial* cultural ambassador.

By this time Frank was fighting the prostate cancer that would kill him at age fifty-two. His illness also forced him to cancel his plan to run for president of the United States. Always a believer in the power of the people to effect social change, Zappa had long established "get out the vote" registration booths at his concert venues.

Frank Zappa left Gail, his wife of twenty-five years and a staunch political activist, and their four children to carry on his legacy. Unearthing him at Westwood is an undercover job, but he is tucked into an unmarked grave in section D, lot 100, by a large tree, between actors Lew Ayres and Jim Backus on the west edge of the green.

HOLLYWOOD AND NORTH HOLLYWOOD

The land mass isn't enormous in this geographic sidecar to Los Angeles, but the concentration of departed talent is, with major burial grounds located within jogging distance of one another.

H O L L Y W O O D

FOREST LAWN CEMETERY

6300 FOREST LAWN DRIVE, HOLLYWOOD HILLS; (800) 204-3131; FAX (323) 769-7317

Smaller, though as pristine as the mother lode in Glendale just a few miles away, *this* Forest Lawn opened in 1948 on 400 or so acres. With so many movie actors in residence, it is probably fitting that Warner Brothers Studios is a neighbor across the road.

This Forest Lawn has the same rules as its parent: neither specific descriptions of graves provided at the office nor information on location of grave sites, and no help to visitors, except for a generic map listing various courts and sanctuaries. Here, as in Glendale, you must rely on the kindness of strangers—i.e., gardeners, groundskeepers, and maintenance workers—to find the locations of your favorite stars.

The grounds are immaculately tended, and the property sprawls over rolling hills and lawns, past blossoming shrubs, trees, elaborate courtyards, and a plethora of marble statuary of a classical, art nouveau, and contemporary nature. One thing here that we didn't see at Forest Lawn Glendale: a sign saying PLEASE LOCK YOUR

CAR AND REMOVE VALUABLES. The property seems too pastoral for such precautions to be necessary.

Wander the curving road up to the Courts of Remembrance, on the east side of the grounds, which yield a harvest of so many well-known names that listing them all would be like a casting call for a DeMille movie. If you use as a guidepost Bette Davis's impressive white sarcophagus on the left of the entrance to the Courts, enter and walk to the right. Turn right and you will find the black and green marker of **Charles Laughton** (1899– 1962; crypt 310), the celebrated English character actor who played comedy and drama with equal aplomb over a film career that spanned more than three decades. His role of roles was as Captain Bligh in *Mutiny on the Bounty* (1935), with the lead in *The Private Life of Henry VIII* (1933) a close second.

BROCCOLI

ALBERT R. BROCCOLI

DANA BROCCOLI

Diagonally across from Laughton at #2175 is **Clyde Beatty** (1902– 1965), a famous animal trainer whose wall crypt features a bronze plaque with a beautiful bas-relief of a reclining lion. At the left side of the Courts of Remembrance, a left turn reveals the marker of **Albert "Cubby" Broccoli** (1909–1996; crypt 65A), producer of the James Bond movie hits.

Beloved comedienne **Lucille Ball** (1911–1989), of *I Love Lucy* fame, has vacated her crypt in the Courts of Remembrance columbarium to be reinterred with her mother and other family members in Lakeview Cemetery in her childhood hometown, Jamestown, New York. No matter where her remains are now, everybody still loves Lucy. Multitalented **Steve Allen** (1921–2000; Columbarium of Brilliant Dawn) was an actor, director, writer (of over fifty books), pianist, composer, and lyricist, but was best known as creator and first host of *The Tonight Show.*

Elsewhere on the grounds, where Memorial Drive meets Crystal Lane, tucked in for eternal sleep is **Dorothy Lamour** (1914–1996; Enduring Faith, two graves in from the E curb), the glamorous movie star best known as the love interest in the Bob Hope–Bing Crosby "Road" movies. She popularized the South Seas sarong, which she wore in many films, so being "planted" near three large palm trees seems only natural. Her neighbor in Enduring Faith (lot 2083, across from Hillside) is **Marjorie Main** (1890–1975), Ma to Percy Kilbride's Pa in nine Ma and Pa Kettle hillbilly movies.

McLean Stevenson (1927–1996; Columbarium of Valor, niche G, 64660), forever remembered as the benign Lieutenant Colonel Henry Blake in television's long-running comedy series *M*A*S*H,* was also a cousin of Adlai Stevenson. Comedian **Godfrey Cambridge** (1933–1976) is on call in Murmuring Pines, block 5443.

Telly Aristotle Savalas (1921–1994), best known as the lollipop-sucking, hard-boiled cop in television's *Kojak,* rests from his TV labors in the Garden of Heritage, final alcove on the left (the only one with no statue in it), tucked into the northwest corner.

Tough guy in 1930s and 1940s films **George Raft** (1895–1980) now resides in the Sanctuary of Light, vault 2356, third from left, two spaces up from the bottom.

His neighbor is **Freddie Prinze** (1954–1977; vault 2355), who was the first Latino star of a television sitcom, and whose suicide ended a promising career.

In the Sheltering Hills section, plot 1999, five rows to the right of Gene Autry, is **Jack Webb** (1920–1982), star of television's police drama *Dragnet.* Another TV detective, actor **William Conrad** (1920–1994), is in Lincoln Terrace, plot 4448, on the other side of the Lincoln statue, halfway down the lawn, next to a small tree on the right. He starred in the *Cannon* television series.

Two reliable performers in the Morning Light section are **Edgar Buchanan** (1903–1979; grave 7780), the comic actor famous for his role of Uncle Joe in TV's *Petticoat Junction,* and **Dan Duryea** (1907–1968; grave 7883), who played treacherous heavies and turncoats in scores of movies. In the same section is **George Stevens** (1904–1975; grave 8034), director of dozens of excellent movies, dramas and

comedies alike, spanning some thirty years. His films include *Quality Street, Gunga Din, Woman of the Year, The Talk of the Town, The More the Merrier, Shane, The Diary of Anne Frank,* and *Giant* (for which he won an Oscar).

When the death knell sounded for **Rod Steiger** (1925–2002; Courts of Remembrance, Columbarium of Providence), this pull-all-stops actor who could do it all (leads, characters, accents, heavies, psychotics) left behind a fifty-year body of work that includes *On the Waterfront, No Way to Treat a Lady, The Pawnbroker* (Oscar nomination), and *In the Heat of the Night* (Best Actor Oscar). *Grounds open 8:00 A.M.–9:00 P.M. daily.* ★*Office hours: 8:00 A.M.–5:00 P.M. daily. Map; restrooms; flower shop; gift shop.*

GENE AUTRY *1907–1998*

Better known in recent decades as the owner of the California Angels baseball team (later named Anaheim Angels and now Los Angeles Angels of Anaheim) than as the singing cowboy star on which he built his fame and fortune, Autry was also a highly successful businessman.

Orvon Gene Autry, as he was born, near Tioga, Texas, was the grandson of a Methodist minister. His family moved to Ravia, Oklahoma, and in 1925, when he left high school, young Gene got a job as a telegrapher for the St. Louis–San Francisco Railway. His hobby was singing and playing the guitar at local dances. After meeting Will Rogers, who encouraged him, he took up performing full-time, first on local radio, billing himself as "Oklahoma's Yodeling Cowboy."

That was in 1928. Three years later he signed a recording contract with Columbia Records and worked in Chicago on the *National Barn Dance* radio program. In 1932 he had his first hit record, "That Silver-Haired Daddy of Mine," a duet with Jimmy Long, another railroad man. In 1934 Autry made his first movie, as part of a cowboy quartet in *In Old Santa Fe,* and then starred in a twelve-part serial called "The Phantom Empire."

From then on until 1940, he made forty-four movies for Republic Pictures, all B westerns. His persona was quickly established. His real name was his movie name, and he had his own horse, Champion, and sidekick, Smiley, plus the chance to sing in each film. His easy, pleasing voice and genial personality caught on with the public. By 1937 he was filmdom's top western star, a popularity that peaked during the early 1940s.

In addition to "That Silver-Haired Daddy of Mine," among the many songs that Autry popularized were "The Last Roundup," "Tumbling Tumbleweeds," "Mexicali Rose," "Take Me Back to My Boots and Saddle," and "Back in the Saddle Again."

Serving during World War II as a pilot with the Air Transport Command, he returned to find he had been overtaken in box office popularity by Roy Rogers. Yet Autry's career was not over. He had a weekly radio show from 1940 to 1956 on CBS

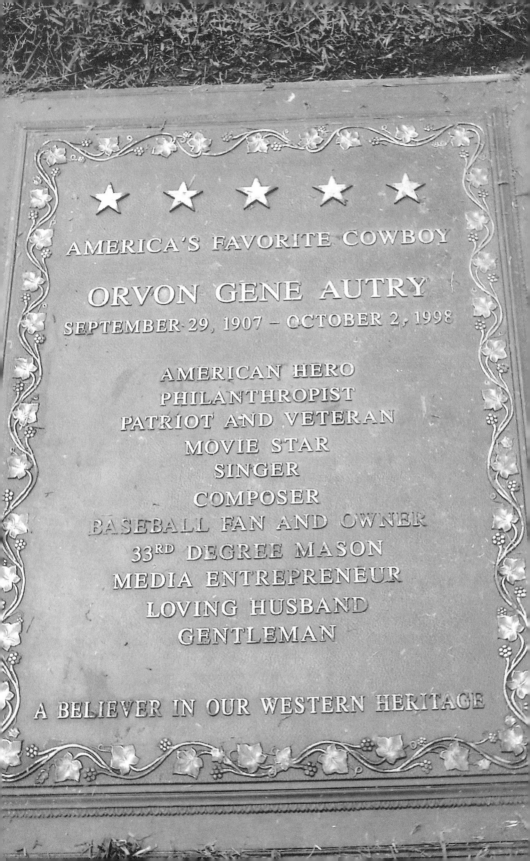

called *Gene Autry's Melody Ranch*. After the war, he formed his own film production company and made more westerns. In 1950 he produced his own television show for CBS. In all, he made over 600 records and some 100 movies.

In 1964 he left the ol' corral for a new career investing in real estate and radio and television franchises, and by 1982 he sold TV station KTLA for $245 million. For many years he was listed in *Forbes* magazine as one of the 400 richest Americans. His estimated net worth late in his life was $320 million. In 1960, hoping to secure broadcast rights for baseball's new expansion team, the Angels, he was persuaded to buy the team. By all reports, he was a genial owner.

HOUSE CALL

Autry National Center (4700 Western Heritage Way, Griffith Park; 323-667-2000), formerly the Gene Autry Western Heritage Museum, depicts the history of America's western movement, using movies, audiovisual materials, and many objects from Autry's large collection of western art and memorabilia.

Gene Autry's last roundup, his hard-to-miss grave, is near the main gate on the right in the Sheltering Hills section, six rows in and in front of a large white statue of a woman holding a child.

BETTE DAVIS *1908–1989*

Even in death, Ms. Davis commands center stage, as her imposing white marble sarcophagus (located against the left outer wall of the Courts of Remembrance) testifies. Below her name and those of her mother **Ruth Favor Davis** (1885–1961) and sister **Barbara Davis Berry** (1909–1979) are the words "She did it the hard way." That's no doubt true, for the spunky actress with the distinctive vocal style (much mimicked by comedians) fought hard and often with Jack Warner, head of Warner Brothers—battling for better roles, better scripts, better directors, and better pay—and she usually won. She was sometimes called "the fourth Warner Brother" for her toughness.

Her fights paid off in blockbuster roles that showcased her enormous talent, making her Hollywood's leading dramatic actress of the late 1930s and 1940s. These were some of her bull's-eyes: as a sluttish waitress in *Of Human Bondage* (for which she *should* have won a Best Actress Oscar); an actress in *Dangerous* (for which she did); a gangster's moll in *Kid Galahad;* a dying society girl in *Dark Victory;* a voracious matriarch in *The Little Foxes;* a romantic lead in *Now, Voyager;* and an English queen in *The Private Lives of Elizabeth and Essex.* Her tempestuous relationship with her co-star in that last film, Errol Flynn, may have kept her from playing Scarlett O'Hara.

DAVIS

RUTH FAVOR DAVIS | BARBARA DAVIS BERRY

BETTE DAVIS

Supposedly she and Flynn were offered as a package to MGM for *Gone With the Wind,* but both refused to play opposite each other again.

In fifty-eight years, Davis made almost ninety films, playing comedy, tragedy, and most emotions in between, winning eight Oscar nominations. One of her greatest performances came later in life—as Margo Channing, an aging actress in *All About Eve.* The film won six Oscars, but not one—though it should have—for Best Actress. She did it the hard way all right. In spite of unconventional good looks, she proved herself to be one of Hollywood's greatest actresses ever. Movies she made long after her prime—*What Ever Happened to Baby Jane* (1962) and *Hush . . . Hush, Sweet Charlotte* (1964)—were huge hits, but don't look to them for Davis at her best.

Her personal life wasn't as successful as her career. She was married four times; had one child with her third husband, William Sherry; and adopted two children with her fourth husband, actor Gary Merrill (her co-star in *All About Eve*). Her natural child, B. D. Hyman, wrote a savage tell-all book about Davis as a mother. Though the majority of people in the know said the book was mostly fiction, Davis admitted her career always came first, before marriage, children, friendships, anything. The greatest actress of her era wasn't perfect, but for moviegoers she was—and still is—plenty good enough.

LEO DUROCHER *1905–1991*

Baseball has had its share of colorful characters, but few have matched "Leo the Lip" Durocher. As a scrappy shortstop for the St. Louis Cardinals during the 1930s era of the obstreperous Gas House Gang, he mixed it up with the best of them—Dizzy and Daffy Dean, Pepper Martin, and Joe Medwick—as competitive off the field as on. He also played for three other teams and was considered a real hustler.

Durocher carried his combative style into managing, which he did for four clubs—the Brooklyn Dodgers, New York Giants, Chicago Cubs, and Houston Astros—until battles with Astros players and bosses led to his retirement in 1973. His glory days as a manager were with the Dodgers. But while in Brooklyn, he got into trouble with the influential Catholic Youth Organization for his affair with married actress Laraine Day. (They eventually wed each other, eloping to Mexico in 1947, divorcing in 1960.)

He earned his "Leo the Lip" nickname because of his frequent confrontations with umpires and feuds with players, owners, and the press. Yet his aggressive style helped turn the lackluster Dodgers into a winning team and later led the Giants to a World Series victory (in 1954), proving—to himself at least—that his mantra "Nice guys finish last" worked.

A nice guy he wasn't, at least publicly: He was fined and suspended often, and was fired and rehired several times by the Dodgers' owners. In 1947 he was suspended for one year from baseball, for allegedly hanging out with known gamblers. His association with shady characters—gamblers, bookmakers, and mobsters—haunted his later career and kept him from the Hall of Fame until 1994, three years after his death.

At one time he shared a house with George Raft, a close buddy.

Durocher's tough-guy image was burnished by his autobiography, *Nice Guys Finish Last*. It's an arguable theory, and "Leo the Lip" is right there to argue it. Look for him in the Hillside section, lot 3311, space 2—a spot from which no umpire can evict him.

JOSEPH FRANK "BUSTER" KEATON *1895–1966*

Buster Keaton, arguably the best of all silent-movie comedians, was often overshadowed by Charlie Chaplin. But time has given critics new appreciation of his multiple skills: his acrobatics (he did all his own incredible stunts), his nuanced deadpan, and his all-round creativeness. Anthony Lane, a *New Yorker* critic, once wrote that "he was just too good, in too many ways, too soon." Certainly Keaton peaked early.

From age three he was part of his parents' vaudeville act. His nickname came from a fall down a flight of stairs as a baby, which left him miraculously unharmed. Harry Houdini, a fellow performer, said, "That's some buster your baby took!" But Buster took far worse in childhood. Part of the act was for his father to throw little Buster all over the stage—an act that would be shut down today for child abuse.

In 1917, at age twenty-two, Keaton met Roscoe "Fatty" Arbuckle, a big (in all ways) silent star, who introduced him to films. They collaborated on two-reelers, with Keaton's roles getting bigger and bigger. Soon he was producing his own films at his own studio.

From 1920 to 1929 many of his best and most celebrated films were made by Keaton himself, among them *The General, The Navigator, Sherlock Jr.,* and *The Cameraman.* One of his innovations as a director was the use of a split-screen. In the 1930s Keaton's star faded, not because of talkies (he had a good voice), but through a series of poor luck, a bad deal with MGM that didn't recognize his range, his alcoholism, and two unfortunate marriages.

His first marriage, to Natalie Talmadge, one of Norma's sisters, ended with a divorce settlement in which she took everything and refused him the right to see their two sons (he was reconciled with them ten years later). His second marriage to a nurse during an alcoholic binge ended in three years, after which she won half of everything he owned. His third and final marriage to Eleanor Norris worked out better, surviving until his death. Although she was twenty-three years his junior, she helped him salvage his career.

By the 1940s he, um, bounced back, and the 1950s brought a new appraisal of his remarkable talents. There were television guest appearances, cameos in *Around the World in 80 Days* and *A Funny Thing Happened on the Way to the Forum,* and two short back-to-back TV series, *The Buster Keaton Show* (1950) and *Life With Buster Keaton* (1951).

Keaton was happiest when working, so when he contracted lung cancer, his wife and doctor kept the diagnosis from him. For a man of his temperament, it was probably better to think he had chronic bronchitis. It kept him busy and happy until near the end.

Buster Keaton's present perch is in Memory Lane, in front of the Court of Liberty steps. On the grass, to the right of the George Washington memorial, he is next to the stone wall. He may be immovably there, but his star still shines brightly around the universe.

ERNIE KOVACS *1919–1962*

Never as big a household name as Jackie Gleason or Jerry Seinfeld, Ernie Kovacs remains revered by a loyal group of fans, critics, and comedians who loved his icon-oclastic style, satire, and originality. After a mundane start as a struggling actor, this Trenton, New Jersey–born performer found his métier in television, a new medium in 1949 when he became the host of a Philadelphia-based cooking program.

Natural irreverence and a talent for visual gags led him quickly to network television and a series of short-lived shows, which left critics in stitches. Kovacs's deadpan style, quirky stunts, miming, and oddball characters—like the Nairobi Trio (musicians dressed in gorilla costumes), Percy Dovetonsils (Ernie as an effete poet who read nonsensical works), and Miklos Molnar (Ernie as a drunken Hungarian chef)—were unique at the time and a great inspiration to other comics.

What made his work even more a treat was that he wrote it himself. In the era of live television, his show had a funky spontaneity lacking today. Kovacs also proved he really *could* act, as his role as a policeman in the movie *Our Man in Havana* demonstrates. He died at the top of his form—as host of a series of television specials—from driving his car into a telephone pole, after a late night of partying and drinking. Admirers can only speculate on whether he would have climbed to even higher heights of creativity.

Across the road from Bette Davis's memorial, facing the Courts of Remembrance, is a large oval of lawn. Kovacs's gray granite grave marker is dead center and somewhat hard to spot. It is in fifteen stones from the curb and twenty-five rows down, next to his daughter **Mia Kovacs** (1959–1982), whose marker reads "Daddy's Girl, We all loved her too!" Ernie's stone states "'Nothing in moderation'— We all loved him." Another daughter is here as well—**Kippie Raleigh Kovacs** (1949–2004), whose epitaph reads "Ernie's beloved daughter, brave and beautiful, adored sister, mother and friend, we all loved her so!"

FRITZ LANG *1890–1976*

Like his contemporary Alfred Hitchcock, director Fritz Lang was an alumnus of the German expressionist school of film. Also like Hitchcock, Lang had a fondness for advancing the story through camera images rather than relying on scripted dialogue.

Few directors have had as lasting an impact on all who followed as Lang did with his Dr. Mabuse films (about a brilliant arch-criminal) and the visually striking *Metropolis* (1927). The latter is Lang's most famous movie, which is still required study in college film courses. He brought Peter Lorre to stardom by casting him as the child killer who nonetheless elicits sympathy in 1931's stellar film *M*, a veritable "how to" for future directors.

Born Friedrich Anton Christian Lang in Vienna, Austria, he studied engineering and art before serving in World War I and suffering multiple wounds. He broke into film by writing horror movies; becoming a director was an easy fit. He was famous in Europe, making films that still stand up today, usually focusing on twisted criminal elements in the underbelly of society. With the ascendancy of Hitler's Third Reich (which banned his last film), Lang fled Nazi Germany and relocated in Hollywood, where he had immediate impact with 1936's *Fury,* a powerful film about mob violence and revenge, starring a young Spencer Tracy.

Lang worked steadily through the 1940s and 1950s, and his work was continually well received. Among his unforgettable film noirs is 1944's *Ministry of Fear* with Ray Milland. Even when he turned to the western in *Rancho Notorious* (1952), Lang painted it from his own dark palette, though the film (co-starring Marlene Dietrich and Mel Ferrer) was shot and released in color. He returned to hard-boiled noir with *The Big Heat* (1953) and *While the City Sleeps* (1956). In all, Lang wrote and/or directed over fifty films. In time, though, he became disillusioned with the Hollywood studio system, and retired in 1963.

Fritz Lang's final credit is the Enduring Faith section, just to the right of plot 3818, second in from the curb.

STAN LAUREL *1890–1965*

Separate at last. It's something of a surprise on discovering the white marble marker stating "Stan Laurel–A Master of Comedy" that there is no Hardy in sight. Here is Laurel alone, ensconced in the fieldstone wall, up a few steps toward the mosaic of Liberty, behind the giant statue of George Washington in the Court of Liberty.

What made Laurel and Hardy special were the contrasts: tall, skinny, perpetually perplexed, English-accented Laurel and fat, bumptious, blowhard, know-it-all American Oliver Hardy (1892–1957). Laurel, born in Ulverston, in the lake country of England, had only a grammar school education and was in show business from the get-go; Hardy, Georgia-born, studied law briefly and trained as a singer at the Atlanta Conservatory of Music. Director Leo McCarey brought this disparate twosome together and directed all their shorts, many of which are comic masterpieces. Laurel had early training in pantomime, which shows clearly in his perfect timing. Their slapstick routines are flawless—and hilarious.

Of the more than twenty films (not counting cameo appearances) they made together, their best feature is considered to be *Sons of the Desert* (1933), with *The Flying Deuces* (1939) a close runner-up. But true fans (and they are legion) have their own favorite sequences as well as films.

The two buddies shared a proclivity for marriage: Laurel six times, Hardy three. Two years older than Hardy, Laurel outlived his partner of thirty years by eight years, but after Hardy's death, he stopped working.

The gravestone of Stan Laurel's last wife, Russian singer **Ida Kitaeva Raphael** (d. 1980), is in the ground, just below his wall memorial. If you're desperately seeking Ollie, he's at Pierce Brothers Valhalla Memorial Park in North Hollywood.

LIBERACE *1919–1987*

Don't expect Wladziu Valentino Liberace—Lee to friends—to hide discreetly in some hillside locale or obscure mausoleum crypt. This flamboyant showman continues to call attention to himself. You'll find him residing in a splendid white marble sarcophagus in the Courts of Remembrance, ornamented with Florentine designs and a piano with the candelabra on it that were his trademarks in life. Above the tomb stands a draped marble figure (his muse perhaps). With him are his mother ("our beloved mom") and older brother, George.

Trained as a classical pianist, Liberace debuted with the Chicago Symphony Orchestra in 1940, but he was drawn to popular music and created a persona that made him the star of supper clubs. Then came his own television program, for which he won two Emmy Awards, for best entertainment show and best male performer.

Critics called him the "Candelabra Casanova." Such barbs prompted him to quip, "I cried all the way to the bank," a remark later copied by others. Critics also questioned his sexual orientation; he even won a lawsuit against one of them who suggested he was homosexual. Growing up in a repressive era when gays kept to the closet, he constantly denied his homosexuality—while mincing, winking, and flaunting pink tuxedos and a llama fur coat covered in sequins and rhinestones. He basked in outrageous parodies of himself—one time flying across the stage in the guise of a winged purple bird. Even so, he made and spent millions and was dear to the fluttering hearts of fans, mostly older women, who must have been surprised when he died of AIDS.

HARRIET NELSON *1909–1994*
OZZIE NELSON *1906–1975*
ERIC "RICKY" NELSON *1940–1985*

Unlike other 1950s–1960s television series portraying "perfect" white middle-class families, *The Adventures of Ozzie and Harriet,* which made the transition from a popular 1940s radio show to television in 1952, actually starred the real-life Nelson family, rather than actors portraying a family. This lent an authenticity to early white-bread television fare. Not to say that the Nelsons weren't white-bread, but they were perceived as authentic. And television audiences following the show witnessed the Nelson children, David and Ricky (born Eric), grow up before the camera.

Ozzie was a successful bandleader (of Ozzie Nelson Band fame) beginning in the 1930s, marrying Harriet Hilliard, the band's vocalist, in 1935. Their younger son, Ricky, became a musical star on his own in the age of "teen idols," filling the gap when Elvis Presley was drafted into the army. Ricky proved to be more than a novelty, having several hits ("I'm Walkin'," "Travellin' Man," "Hello, Mary Lou," and "Garden Party," among others) in a successful musical career that lasted over two decades. He also appeared as an actor in more than one popular film, including co-starring with John Wayne in Howard Hawks's *Rio Bravo* (1961).

Talent obviously runs deep in the Nelson family. Ricky's accomplished offspring include the twins Gunnar and Matthew, who make up the hard-rock band Nelson, and daughter Tracy, an actress with many television credits.

Wife, husband, and son are making their final curtain calls in the Revelation section, up a steep hill from Evergreen Drive (at the Crystal Lane intersection), two rows up past a large tree, marker #3540. Ozzie and Harriet are buried next to each other, and Ricky is just above and to the right of his parents.

JOHN RITTER *1948–2003*

Sons of famous fathers don't always fare so well. John Ritter, youngest son of singing cowboy actor Tex Ritter, is an exception. It probably didn't hurt having Tex as a father, but John, with his boyish good looks, charm, and great comic timing, could surely have made it on his own.

A graduate of Hollywood High School, he was interested in architecture and psychology when he began studying at the University of Southern California, but he was urged to take an acting class and quickly became hooked. He switched his major, graduated with a BA in drama, and began looking for work. His only real experience at the time was accompanying his father on a troop tour in Germany in the late 1960s.

His first breakthrough job was as the young minister on the television series *The Waltons*. When the comedy sitcom *Three's Company* debuted, Ritter seemed like a new face, and a delightful one at that. Good writing and a charismatic cast kept the show on the air for years and earned Ritter an Emmy and Golden Globe. Later, he made several movies, including the farce *Noises Off* in 1992, *Sling Blade* in 1996, and *Bad Santa* in 2003.

Eight Simple Rules for Dating My Daughter, a sitcom in which Ritter played the father, not the date (time flies!), had good reviews its first two seasons. While rehearsing for a new season, he became ill, was rushed to the hospital (the same one where he was born), and died in surgery of aortic dissection, which seems to have been misdiagnosed at first. Especially with his talent, fifty-five was way too young to die.

Located in the Court of Liberty, lot 1622, Ritter's in-the-ground grave bears the words "Beloved husband, father, brother, son and friend" with a quote at the bottom: "And in the end, the love you take is equal to the love you make . . . Beatles."

HOLLYWOOD FOREVER PARK

6000 SANTA MONICA BOULEVARD;
(323) 469-1181 OR (877) 844-3837;
WWW.FOREVERNETWORK.COM

This venerable burying ground, formerly called Hollywood Memorial Park, was one of the first parklike cemeteries in the West when it was founded in 1899. One of the founders was Isaac Newton Van Nuys, who also founded Van Nuys, California. The cemetery is located across from Paramount Studios; from certain grave sites the gigantic HOLLYWOOD hillside sign is visible. In 1998, after years of benign neglect, the cemetery was bought by Tyler Cassity of St. Louis, Missouri, through a corporation called Hollywood Forever Inc., for the then-bargain price of $375,000. It was then renamed Hollywood Forever Park.

A medium-size burial ground of sixty acres in the heart of Hollywood, it is as crowded with celebrities as Oscar night—a virtual pantheon of movie gods and goddesses (more than 400 of them). For decades the famous and infamous were dying to get in. Pines, palms, cypresses, ancient oaks, and various weeping trees—along with marble mausoleums, monuments, and soaring statuary—are rampant. The new ownership has improved the grounds and established a flower/gift shop opposite the administration building's office at the left of the entrance. In the shop you can buy a map and check the tour schedule. The flat grounds are very walkable, and graves are well enough marked that the map isn't a necessity.

The park has also gone Hollywood, adding an attraction: An organization called Cinespia shows old movies Saturday evenings in warm weather (for a fee/donation), projecting them on the outer wall of the main Cathedral mausoleum, with state-of-the-art sound equipment. (How's that for a drive-in theater?)

There are blue-chip locals here as well as movie stars. Overseeing everyone in the park is the towering obelisk of **General Harrison Gray Otis** (1837–1917) and his wife, **Eliza Otis** (1833–1904). General Otis was a Civil War hero who made his name as editor and publisher of the *Los Angeles Times*. Other *Times* family members here are publisher **Harry Chandler** (1864–1944; section 12) and his wife, **Marion Otis Chandler** (1866–1952; same location). Harry Chandler built the *Los Angeles Times* into the most powerful newspaper on the West Coast.

Philanthropist **William A. Clark Jr.**'s (1877–1934) Greek Revival temple mausoleum occupies its very own island in a graceful lake, around which blue herons and white egrets swoop. The temple, which cost $500,000 when it was built in 1921, can be reached via a 40-foot granite bridge.

In the large marble Cathedral mausoleum, with beautiful Tiffany-style win-

dows, among many wall crypts of note you will find **Peter Finch** (1916–1977; corridor A, crypt 1224), the English actor who starred in *Sunday, Bloody Sunday* and who died just as he was reaching the top of his game. Posthumously, he received a Best Actor Oscar for *Network.*

Vintage actors at rest throughout the park include **Norma Talmadge** (1893–1957; front left in Abbey of the Psalms, Shrine of Eternal Love, Talmadge room, corridor G-7), silent star, comedienne, and paramour of Mack Sennett; **Ann Sheridan** (1915–1967; Chapel columbarium, second floor, east wall), sweetly sexy "Oomph Girl" in 1940s Hollywood movies; and **Joan Hackett** (1934–1983; Abbey of the Psalms, Sanctuary of Faith, corridor D-3, crypt 2314), personable supporting actress, whose crypt (and cryptic) message reads "Go away—I'm asleep."

Taking a permanent sabbatical is **Adolphe Menjou** (1890–1963; section 8, lot 11, by the road, southwest of the lake), suave character actor of the 1930s and 1940s, as well known for his impeccable fashion taste and distinctive mustache as for roles in *The Front Page* and *A Star Is Born.* Speaking of which, **Janet Gaynor** (1906–1984; Garden of Legends, section 8, lot 193, north of the lake), the lead in the 1937 version of that movie, was a famous actress of the 1930s. She is buried beside two small cypresses next to her first husband, famous MGM costume designer **Gilbert Adrian** (1903–1959; same location).

A nearby tenant is actor-tenor **Nelson Eddy** (1901–1967; section 8, north of

the lake), who co-starred with Jeanette MacDonald in a series of operetta-like adventure romances in the 1930s and early 1940s. Bandleader and jazz clarinetist **Woody Herman** (1913–1987; Court of the Apostles, grounds, unit 10, crypt 6689) is here, but his incredible jazz clarinet is now silent.

Also present for a final roll call are film director **Victor Fleming** (1883–1949; Abbey of the Psalms, Sanctuary of Refuge, crypt 2081), whose biggest hits were *The Wizard of Oz* and *Gone With the Wind,* and **Jesse Lasky** (1880–1958; Abbey of the Psalms, Sanctuary of Light, corridor G-3, crypt 216), movie producer and Hollywood pioneer. Free at last from the clutches of King Kong, actress **Fay Wray** (1907–2004; section 8, lot 2300) has a small stone in the ground, under her married name, Rothenberg.

Character actor **Peter Lorre** (1904–1964; Cathedral mausoleum, corridor C, tier 1, niche 5), whose first major role was in *M,* ranged from "menacing" to "benign" in *The Maltese Falcon, The Mask of Dimitrios,* and scores of other films. **Paul Muni** (1895–1967; Plains of Abraham, section 14, grave 57), star of such films as *The Good Earth*, *I Am a Fugitive from a Chain Gang,* and *The Story of Louis Pasteur* (for which he won an Oscar for Best Actor), and his screenwriter wife, **Bella Muni** (1898–1971), share the same memorial stone in the Beth Olan Jewish section.

Hattie McDaniel (1895–1952; Garden of Legends, section 8), the first African American to win an Oscar (Best Supporting Actress for her role as Mammy in *Gone With the Wind*), had requested but was denied burial here in 1952. Belatedly, she now has a unique memorial prominently located south of the lake. Times change, thank goodness.

A sad reminder of the anything-goes early days of movies is the presence of **Virginia Rappe** (1896–1921; section 8, lot 257), the young actress who died of peritonitis from a ruptured fallopian tube, the result, allegedly, of being raped by comic Fatty Arbuckle at a wild party/orgy. Although he was acquitted of the charge, his career went south thereafter.

Another ill-fated Hollywood actress, **Barbara La Marr** (1896–1926; Cathedral mausoleum, corridor A, crypt 1308, near Peter Finch), was dubbed "the girl who was too beautiful to live." It wasn't her beauty that killed her, it was her lifestyle. Wild parties, drugs, and alcohol, augmented by tuberculosis, did her in before she turned thirty. She was not just extremely good looking, she was talented as well. A real loss.

The most dramatic recent arrival is punk rocker **Johnny Ramone** (1948–2004; Garden of Legends, section 8, south of the lake), aka John Cummings, his birth name. A larger-than-life-size bronze sculpture of the co-founder and lead guitarist of the Ramones is mounted on a matching polished black granite base, with messages and testimonials etched into all four sides. "As good a friend as there ever was—John Frusciante," one side reads. "Please come back, love, Vincent Gallo," reads another. "Forever here today, never gone tomorrow," writes Lisa Marie Presley. Ramone's prominent location near the Cathedral mausoleum is further highlighted by a spotlight on the statue at night.

It is probably fitting that nearby, next to a tree, is the polished black granite monument of **Douglas Glenn Colvin** (1952–2003; Garden of Legends, section 8, lot 2003, space 4), another member of the Ramones. Known as Dee Dee Ramone, Colvin was a co-founder of the punk rock group. His epitaph cuts quickly to the chase: "OK . . . I gotta go now."

Newest kid on the block is actor **Darren McGavin** (1922–2006; section 7, lot 203, grave 4), best known as Ralphie's father in *A Christmas Story* and as Kolchak in the TV movie *The Nightstalker* (1972).

The cemetery's new ownership has expanded the grounds, and in the rear, beyond section 8, near the fence, many people with Spanish surnames lie in peace. Also beyond section 8 are sizable tombs of many Iranians and other Middle Easterners. One of the most unusual non-celebrity grave sites in the new section belongs to **Brigadier General Emmanuel Nicherie** (1913–2000), who, as the memorial notes, "fought Israel's wars for independence and statehood." A polished black granite memorial inside a similar granite base, with scores of black pebbles in front, it has a bench and its very own willow tree. ★ *Grounds and office open 8:30 A.M.–5:00 P.M. weekdays, 8:30 A.M.–4:30 P.M. weekends, but the Beth Olam section is closed Saturday. A new Asian area by the Columbarium (to the right of the entrance drive) features Thai temples and glittery obelisks. Map $5.00; restroom; flower/gift shop. Check with the office for scheduled showings of Cinespia films ($10 fee/donation).*

> ## LUNCH BREAK
> With so many good restaurants a few blocks away in Hollywood, it is hard to single out one or two, but we like **Bice** (6801 Hollywood Boulevard; 323-962-3474) for its casual, reasonable Italian fare. Another favorite is **Vert** (6801 Hollywood Boulevard; 323-491-1300), Wolfgang Puck's moderately priced French bistro.

DON ADAMS 1923–2005

Born Donald James Yarmy in New York City, Don Adams often said that he borrowed the voice for his colossally inept, not-so-secret Agent 86, Maxwell Smart, from William Powell as Nick Charles in the Thin Man series of detective films. Perhaps, but viewers of the 1960s hit television show *Get Smart!* realized that Agent 86 was all Adams.

Adams's Smart contributed many catch phrases to our cultural lexicon: "Sorry about that, Chief!" "Would you believe . . .?" ". . . and loving it!" Equipped with his shoe phone and a booby-trapped apartment (which more often than not caught him rather than his nemeses from CHAOS), Smart might have been a forerunner of our contemporary "intelligence agencies."

Trained as an engineer, Adams joined the U.S. Marines during World War II and saw action on Guadalcanal, where he was the only survivor of his platoon. Later he was a Marine Corps drill instructor. It's ironic that a man who really could kill another with his bare hands became famous as a lamebrained spy who foiled himself at almost every turn.

During the 1950s he did stand-up comedy, adopting the last name of his first wife, ostensibly to be at the beginning of the line at alphabetical auditions. His act landed him guest spots on *The Steve Allen Show,* and he became a regular on *The Bill Dana Show,* on which he played the bumbling detective Byron Glick, a precursor of Agent 86.

Adams's portrayal of Maxwell Smart won him three Emmys. He later starred in several short-lived television series, such as *The Partners,* and in *Check It Out,* a Canadian sitcom that was successful there, but failed to gain a toehold with U.S. audiences.

His distinctive voice made Adams a natural for cartoon characters; he played the memorable penguin Tennessee Tuxedo in the early 1960s and Inspector Gadget in the 1980s. But for most of us, he will always be Agent 86. He now resides in his permanent "cone of silence" in the Garden of Legends, section 8, northeast of the pond.

MEL BLANC *1908–1989*

As a child in Portland, Oregon, Melvin Jerome Blank was the class clown, always mimicking accents. A teacher said, "You'll never amount to anything. You're like your last name: blank." Mel began spelling his name Blanc and later changed it legally.

After time in radio as a young man, he was hired by Warner Brothers to do the voice of a drunken bull in a 1937 Porky Pig short. This led to being Porky himself. Porky's final line, "That's all folks!" was supposedly a Blanc ad-lib that took. "What's up, doc?" was another Blanc idea, this one for Bugs Bunny. In time, Blanc's was the voice of Daffy Duck, Elmer Fudd, the Road Runner, Yosemite Sam, Sylvester the Cat, and Tweety Pie, and the original voice and irritating laugh of Woody Woodpecker.

In a lifetime of voices, Blanc did more than 3,000 cartoons and was the first

such actor to receive on-screen credit for his work. He had other jobs from time to time: on Jack Benny's radio and television shows, small roles in films, and as a coach of accents for Warner Brothers actors. But he preferred working behind the scenes. His headstone (Garden of the Exodus, section 13, lot 149, next to the road) reads "That's all folks." Too bad there's no soundtrack to go with it.

HARRY COHN *1891–1958*

Cofounder, with his brother Jack and Harry Brandt, of Columbia Pictures, Harry Cohn ruled his studio with a steel fist inside a steel glove, as actors and actresses quickly found out if they crossed him. It wasn't a joke that he was called King Cohn. One employee called him as absolute a monarch "as Hollywood ever knew" (and that was saying something, with Louis Mayer and Jack Warner around) who ran Columbia "like a private police state." Rita Hayworth wasn't the first or the last actress to find that out, though hers were among the most publicized struggles with his iron will.

From his beginnings in a lower-middle-class New York Jewish family, Cohn worked his way up the ladder, first as a streetcar conductor, then a promoter for a sheet music publisher, finally maneuvering a job, through brother Jack, with Universal Pictures. In 1924 he, Jack, and Brandt struck out on their own with Columbia.

Cohn managed film production in Hollywood, while Jack handled the finances from New York. Eventually, after many disagreements, the Cohns bought out Brandt. It is believed Harry Cohn was able to do so with the help of Mob money. At first Columbia was the king of B movies, but eventually, after adding Hayworth, Glenn Ford, Kim Novak, director Frank Capra, and other stars to its roster, the company upgraded its product with more prestigious films. While never losing money, Columbia scored with classics like *Mr. Deeds Goes to Town, Mr. Smith Goes to Washington, Lost Horizon, On the Waterfront, All the King's Men,* and *Born Yesterday,* accruing some forty-five Oscars along the way.

Cohn tightened the screws on his stars, refusing to lend their services to other studios without exacting a heavy price. Stars feared he spied on them, planting listening devices on their sets. If he heard something unpleasant about himself, he would roar his displeasure over a loudspeaker. After noting the crowd that attended Cohn's funeral service (held on a converted Columbia soundstage), the comic Red Skelton supposedly said, "Give the people what they want, and they'll come out." The crowd, wags said, consisted of people wanting to be sure he was really dead.

Harry Cohn holds court in the Garden of Legends, section B, opposite the Cathedral mausoleum. Up three steps is his imposing white marble sarcophagus and, on the left, that of his wife, **Joan Cohn** (1911–1996). Cohn relatives lie in the ground in the front of his ostentatious memorial.

MARION DAVIES *1897–1961*

In Hollywood lore, Marion Davies is usually delegated a footnote that describes her as the longtime mistress of publisher William Randolph Hearst, which she was. But more than just a rich man's toy, she was actually a gifted comedienne, showing her comic flair first on Broadway, then in silent films such as *Tillie the Toiler* (1927) and *The Patsy* and *Show People* (both in 1928). She had a flair for on-the-mark imitations of other stars: Mae Murray, Pola Negri, and Lillian Gish.

Fearful of sound, she overcame a stutter to make several delightful comedies and musicals in the early 1930s: *Not So Dumb, The Floradora Girl, Five and Ten* (with

Leslie Howard), *Polly of the Circus* (with Clark Gable), *Going Hollywood* (with Bing Crosby), and *Operator* (with Gary Cooper). Hearst hampered her career by wanting her in romantic costume dramas, when she was better suited to comedy.

Despite allegedly having several flings on the side, she was devoted to Hearst and he to her until he died. He supposedly tried to get a divorce, but his wife's settlement demands were too high. He and Davies lived lavishly at San Simeon and Ocean House in Santa Monica.

Davies was a shrewd businesswoman, but was also known for her generosity: When Hearst was having money problems, she sold many expensive gifts he had given her to help him out. "The gold digger had fallen in love," she later explained. Her generosity manifested itself after Hearst's death when she donated $1.9 million to UCLA for a children's clinic.

To the world's surprise, ten weeks after Hearst died she married for the first time—at age fifty-four—Horace G. Brown, a former stuntman-seaman-policeman years younger than she, who her friends said looked like a young Hearst. The marriage wasn't a success; she filed for divorce twice, but never finalized the deal.

Davies resides in splendor in an imposing white marble mausoleum (Garden of Legends, section 8, east side of the lake), which has the name DOURAS (her birth name) over the entrance and a bench by it. Sharing posthumous quarters with her is Brown, as well as two surprise guests: **Arthur Lake** (1905–1987), who played Dagwood Bumstead in the twenty or more Blondie movies made between 1939 and 1949, and his wife, **Patricia Van Cleeve Lake.** Long after Davies's death, it came out, according to Patricia's family, that she was the daughter, not a niece as previously announced, of Davies, the result of her liaison with Hearst. While this has never been verified, it makes sense—and a good plot twist.

CECIL BLOUNT DEMILLE *1881–1959*

From the 1930s through the 1950s, when it came to movie extravaganzas, one name leaped out at you: Cecil. B. DeMille. His big-budget films were made with "a cast of thousands," as the ads proclaimed. While his movies began larger-than-life and grew from there, his personal beginnings were sedately middle class. Both his parents had theatrical leanings, and Cecil became an actor and then managed his mother's theatrical agency.

Through the theatrical agency he met Jesse L. Lasky and Samuel Goldwyn, Lasky's brother-in-law. The three men became partners, and in 1912 DeMille directed their first movie, *The Squaw Man,* on a budget of $15,000. The film made $225,000, and DeMille was off and running. He bought out his partners, and began directing epics with gargantuan sets and lavish props. The list is awesome—and so were the profits—what with *The Ten Commandments, The King of Kings, Cleopatra, The Crusades,* and *The Greatest Show on Earth* (his only film to win an Oscar, for Best Picture). Then there were his panoramic westerns: *The Plainsman* and *Union Pacific.*

Today, with all the electronic wizardry and special effects in movies, DeMille's extravaganzas seem quaintly archaic. Even in their day they were more popular with audiences than with critics. Yet he scored a number of "firsts": first to list the actors' names at the start of a film (in *The Squaw Man*); first to sign Hal Roach, Hopalong

Cassidy, and Gloria Swanson; first to show sneak previews to test audiences; first to use camera booms and artificial "effect" lighting.

Fittingly, the DeMille sarcophagi are among the cemetery's most grandiose (Garden of Legends, section 8, lot 59, north side of the lake by the road). With Cecil Blount DeMille is **Constance Adams DeMille** (1874–1960), his wife of fifty-seven years, who outlived him by a year. Brother **William DeMille** (1878–1955) and their mother, **Matilda DeMille** (1853–1923), are also in attendance.

DOUGLAS FAIRBANKS SR. *1883–1939*
DOUGLAS FAIRBANKS JR. *1909–2000*

When the golden-curled Mary Pickford married leading man Fairbanks Sr. in 1920, their fans thought the union was made in heaven—but it broke up fifteen years later, proving that nothing, at least in Hollywood, is forever.

Therefore you won't find Mary sharing his classical portico or splendid white sarcophagus (section 11, next to Cathedral mausoleum, by a large reflecting pond lined with cypress trees). The other occupant is Fairbanks's only child, Douglas Jr., also an actor. Senior's bronze profile inside a laurel wreath, with the "Good Night, Sweet Prince" inscription against the white stone, overlooks a sunken garden and reflecting pool thick with deep red water lilies. Talk about a tomb with a view!

Gymnastic training boosted Senior's flashy acrobatic acting style, which worked better on celluloid than in live theater. From 1915 when he signed his first movie contract until talkies arrived, he reigned supreme in high-flying pictures like *Zorro, The Three Musketeers, Robin Hood,* and *The Thief of Bagdad.* Fairbanks père was an even better businessman than an actor. With Ms. Pickford, Charlie Chaplin, and director D. W. Griffith, he founded United Artists Corporation to distribute their own pictures. This proved a bonanza. In 1936 he married Lady Sylvia Ashley, and for his last three years lived the good life socially and financially here and abroad.

Junior, who shares his last "digs" with Dad, was always in his shadow as an actor, but performed well in serious silent films like *Stella Dallas* and *A Woman of Affairs.* When talkies arrived, he showed he could handle both dashing adventure roles, as in *The Prisoner of Zenda, The Corsican Brothers,* and *Gunga Din,* and sophisticated ones in debonair modern comedies like *The Rage of Paris, Having Wonderful Time,* and *The Young in Heart.* He never achieved the superstardom of Fairbanks the First, but had the family charm and proved to be a more versatile actor. Junior also could write: His two-volume autobiography is as engaging as he was.

JOHN HUSTON *1906–1987*

Comparisons may be odious, but after seeing the colossus that is Cecil B. DeMille's memorial, it is ironic to find such a modest marker (Garden of Legends, section 8, lot 6, west side of the lake) for John Huston, whose work spanned decades and continues to live after him. His achievements began with *The Maltese Falcon* in 1941 and ended—as he did—with *The Dead* in 1987. All in all, he directed thirty-eight films, many of them huge hits.

The son of character actor Walter Huston and Rhea Gore, a newspaper reporter, John came upon his multiple talents naturally. He could act, he could write, and he was good at both. When he decided he would rather write words than speak them, his father helped get him a job as a screenwriter, and he worked on scripts for *Jezebel* and *Wuthering Heights*. But he wanted to direct as well, so after one more script, *High Sierra,* he earned the chance. That's where *The Maltese Falcon* came in—and with it a whole new career as a director.

FILM VAULT

It is difficult to single out just one Huston film, but ***The Man Who Would Be King*** (1975) continues to make us laugh, and the tandem performances of Sean Connery and Michael Caine are so much fun and the script so tight and fine, we can't see this film enough.

World War II intervened, but Huston—assigned to Frank Capra's documentary film unit—was able to hone his skills with three U.S. Army films. Back in Hollywood in 1948, he directed Humphrey Bogart in another big film, *Treasure of the Sierra Madre,* which brought him Oscars for screenwriting and directing and his father one for Best Supporting Actor.

Success mostly followed success in the late 1940s and 1950s—with *Key Largo, The Asphalt Jungle, The African Queen* (bringing Bogart an Oscar for Best Actor), *Moulin Rouge, Beat the Devil,* and *Moby Dick.* In 1983 he received a Lifetime Achievement Award from the American Film Institute, which may have spurred him on to direct three more first-rate films: *Under the Volcano, Prizzi's Honor,* and *The Dead.* His crisp, well-made movies were always within budget.

As an actor, Huston appeared in thirty movies and television features, earning a Best Supporting Actor Oscar nomination for *The Cardinal* and playing a pivotal part in *Chinatown.* After wrapping *The Dead,* Huston was in Rhode Island (where he was born), helping his son Danny direct his first movie, when he died. Life had come full cycle. John Huston the scriptwriter would have appreciated the tidy ending.

TYRONE POWER *1914–1958*

With his darkly handsome looks and the fact that he was the third generation of a theatrical family and had family friends to help along the way, Tyrone Power began in movies when he was eleven. He was only twenty-two when he signed a seven-year contract for top billing with 20th Century Fox. That was in 1936, and within seven years he had made twenty pictures, becoming a matinee idol in the process and thriving as a lead in *Lloyds of London, Alexander's Ragtime Band,* and *A Yank in the RAF.*

From 1942 to 1946 he was in the *real* military, as a U.S. Marine Corps flight officer on dangerous missions in the South Pacific. At the war's end, he had a first lieutenant's rank, a new maturity, and some of his best movie roles still ahead. *The Razor's Edge* and *Nightmare Alley* were offbeat films that proved he was more than just a pretty face. A few swashbucklers followed—*Captain from Castile, Prince of Foxes,* and *The Black Rose*—but in *The Sun Also Rises* and *Witness for the Prosecution,* he continued to grow as an actor.

Like his father, who died with his acting boots on, Power suffered a fatal heart attack in the midst of a duel on the set of *Solomon and Sheba* in Madrid. His friend, fellow actor David Niven, said, "He was that great rarity—a man who was just as nice as he seemed to be." Married three times, Power had three children, two daughters and a son.

His monument here, in the Garden of Legends, section 8, next to the pond, is surely more self-important than he was: Three white marble steps lead to a marble funeral urn, marble bench, and marble book—standing upright—with bas-relief masks of the Greek gods of Comedy and Tragedy and Shakespeare's line from *Hamlet* that "there's a special providence in the fall of a sparrow."

BENJAMIN "BUGSY" SIEGEL *1906–1947*

A notorious gangster, Brooklyn-born Benjamin "Bugsy" Siegel has gone underground here, so to speak, in the Beth Olam mausoleum. In the entrance nearest Gower Street, turn right at the second aisle and look in section M2. His crypt 1087 is on the left, third row from the bottom. Note that the marker, in the shape of an open book with raised lettering, states "In loving memory from the family." *Which family?* one wonders. (Maybe we've seen too many Mafia movies.)

Not many mobsters had the good fortune to be played on-screen by charismatic Warren Beatty, as Siegel was in the 1991 *Bugsy,* though Siegel was himself supposedly handsome, with considerable charm. The film's distortion of the real Siegel played down some of the facts: that he was a thug and no-goodnik from childhood, devising his own protection racket as a teenager; that he was a cold-blooded hit man and Murder Inc. killer with a crazy, unpredictable streak (hence the nickname "Bugsy") in the 1930s; that he was sent by the Jewish Mafia (Meyer Lansky was his childhood friend and protector) to the West Coast to help develop gambling rackets for the East Coast Mob. Siegel didn't "discover" Las Vegas and wasn't the visionary who conceived of building his dream hotel-casino, the Flamingo, there, as the film would have us believe. The Flamingo was someone else's dream; Siegel simply took over the project when the originator ran out of money.

Once a crook, always a crook: Siegel was stealing the Mob's money and siphoning it off to Switzerland, using his mistress, Virginia Hill, as a conduit. Hill, by the way, though good-looking, was no Annette Bening but a tough-as-nails Mob courier. Together, Hill and Siegel charmed many Hollywood types, like George Raft, and became part of the local nightlife. Hill even bought the Beverly Hills mansion of opera star Lawrence Tibbett.

Siegel was a notorious womanizer. Though married to his childhood sweetheart, Esta Krakow, who was herself the sister of a hit man (Whitey Krakow), he had affairs with actresses Wendy Barrie and Marie "The Body" MacDonald, socialites, and many other women, in addition to Hill.

In 1939 Siegel, Whitey Krakow, and two other men, on Mob orders, killed Harry Greenberg, a fellow mobster who had become a police stool pigeon. By the time Siegel was arrested and tried for the murder, he had already killed Krakow. As so often happened, Siegel had a reprieve and was acquitted.

He seemed to have a magic life—that is, until his Las Vegas casino enterprise failed in 1947 (and Hill absconded with the money he owed the Mob). Lansky, who had prevented a hit on Siegel years earlier, withdrew his protection. As Siegel was sitting relaxed in Hill's Beverly Hills mansion, a Mob hit man, believed to be one Eddie Cannizzaro, blasted him with an M1 carbine. Siegel died instantly. Supposedly his casket cost $5,000, but only five family members attended the funeral service held at Hollywood Memorial Park before the grounds opened for the day.

RUDOLPH VALENTINO *1895–1926*

Although he took permanent "retirement" here in 1926, Rudolfo Alfonzo Raffaelo Pierre Filibert Guglielmi di Valentina d'Antonguolla—as he was christened in Castellaneta, Italy—is still a magnet for visitors. Foreigners and Americans alike seek him out in the Cathedral mausoleum (turn left at the entrance to the last hall on the left, then at the end, on the upper wall left, is crypt 1205). Bronze flower vases anchor each side of the graceful, curved bronze marker. For years a mysterious "Lady in Black" regularly tucked a fresh red rose here. Valentino would be over 110 years old today, but fans still visit this sexy silent-screen star who died so young. In fact, every August 23, the date he died, a bevy of women in black, carrying red roses, gather at his wall crypt, read poetry, and leave messages.

As a young man, Valentino tried to join Italy's Royal Naval Academy, but was rejected for a chest size *one inch* too small (they evidently were picky in those days). He came to America in 1913, with no English, no money, and minimal skills, armed only with a certificate in scientific agriculture and saturnine "Latin lover"

looks. At first, these led nowhere, but a move to Hollywood got him a few parts as villains in early movies. He soon lucked into the lead in *The Four Horsemen of the Apocalypse,* in which he tangoed his way to instant stardom. *The Sheik* followed, and female fans fantasized about being swept up by sheik Rudy on horseback and carried away to his tent in the desert . . . sigh.

While Valentino was in New York at the premiere of *Son of the Sheik,* he fell ill with a gastric ulcer. Surgery, a ruptured appendix, and peritonitis followed, and at age thirty-one he was dead, leaving millions of women around the world desolate.

MOUNT SINAI MEMORIAL PARK

5950 FOREST LAWN DRIVE;
(818) 905-7600 OR (800) 600-0076;
WWW.MOUNTSINAIPARKS.ORG

At the edge of Burbank, overshadowed by adjacent Forest Lawn Hollywood Hills, this tranquil resting place is the final home of many accomplished Jewish entertainers—actors, comedians, and writers. Perhaps it is a bit of Jewish irony, but the Hebrew name for Mount Sinai, *Bet Ha Hayim,* translates into "House of the Living." While there is a map, it doesn't contain specific grave listings, and the office staff cannot/will not divulge grave locations. What *is* available is a little packet (free) of "Pebbles from Jerusalem," soft limestone pebbles to leave at grave sites—a thoughtful touch and a Jewish cemetery tradition.

Here reside **Herschel Bernardi** (1923–1986; Courts of Tanach, crypt 52250), character actor in many B movies of the 1950s; **Sidney Skolsky** (1905–1983;

Maimonides 2, lot 9840, space 2), Hollywood gossip columnist in filmdom's Golden Era and author of the autobiographical book *Don't Get Me Wrong, I Loved Hollywood;* and **Billy Halop** (1920–1976; Garden of Shemot, crypt 6418), best known as one of the Dead End Kids in both the Broadway show and later in the 1937 movie of the same name.

Actor **Norman Fell** (1924–1998; Garden of Heritage, Columbarium of Tradition, niche 1601A) was in many movies but is best known for his role as Stanley Roper, the landlord in television's popular, long-running sitcom *Three's Company,* for which he won a Golden Globe for Best Supporting Actor. His gravestone reads "A greatly talented and romantic man."

Dawn Steel (1946–1997; Psalms 7, Companion Estate 101, space 1), whose name sounds like a heroine in a romantic novel, was a tough-minded movie executive, one of the first women to head a major Hollywood studio. Waiting for Gabriel to blow, Gabriel blow, is jazz trumpeter **Ziggy Elman** (1911–1968; Courts of Machpelah, wall crypt 121), sideman and soloist with Benny Goodman and Tommy Dorsey, known for his heaven-sent recording of "And the Angels Sing."

Bruce Geller (1930–1978; Garden of Shemot 2A, small family plot across the lawn from the mosaic) may not be a household name, but his creations were: *Mannix* and the original *Mission Impossible* television action-thriller series, for which he was writer and producer. Who knows what else he might have done had he not died in a plane crash at age forty-eight?

Lee J. Cobb (1911–1976; Garden of Shemot, lot 42), star of *Death of a Salesman* on Broadway, made a number of movies despite being blacklisted for a

time in the 1950s. His last film was *The Exorcist* (1973). Facing the Roman-style mosaic in the ground, you'll find his grave to the far left, under a large tree.

Brandon Rick Tartikoff (1949–1997; Ramah 12-2, lot 2056) is now at rest in the stress-free ambience of a gardenia and hydrangea–bordered garden, surrounded by weeping willow, laurel, and a comforting waterfall—quite a change from his high-pressure life as a wunderkind television executive at NBC, then ABC, and later as chairman of Paramount Pictures. His gilt-edged gravestone reads, after his name, "The last great ride." ★ *Grounds and office open 8:00 A.M.–5:00 P.M. daily, except Saturday. Map; restrooms.*

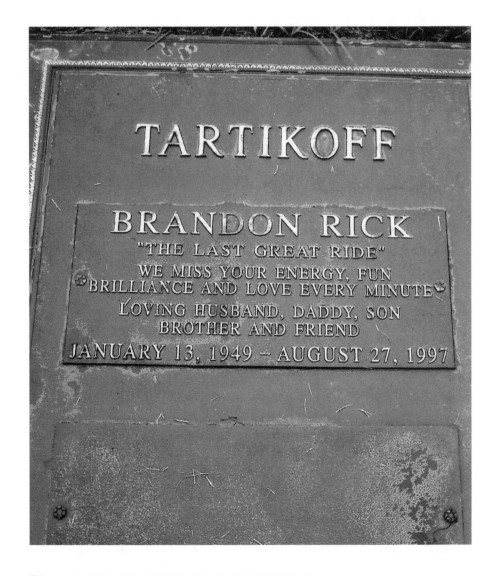

CASS ELLIOT *1941–1974*

Cass Elliot (born Ellen Naomi Cohen, in Baltimore, Maryland) is remembered for two things: She was the outstanding female vocal talent of the Mamas and the Papas, and she died by choking on a ham sandwich. The first is as true as the second is false. She actually died in bed of a heart attack.

Her velvety voice rounded out the sound of the popular 1960s group when she joined as its fourth member in 1965. The Mamas and the Papas promptly rose to fame when the single "California Dreamin'" was released that November. Their place in pop history was cemented by the 1966 releases of albums containing the hits "Monday, Monday" and "I Saw Her Again Last Night."

Too much success too fast and internal strife tore the band apart after only four albums were released, but Cass went on to a successful solo career that included numerous guest appearances on television musical variety shows, in addition to her own specials. She even headlined in Las Vegas. She had a solo hit, "Dream a Little Dream," on the album of the same name.

After a successful performance at the London Palladium Theater, she died later that night in the same room and bed that The Who's Keith Moon would also expire in four years later—a weird coincidence. Oh yes, the ham sandwich story: Apparently there was a half-eaten ham sandwich in the room where she died, metamorphosing through the rumor mill that it was the cause of death, but the coroner's verdict was heart failure, with no choking involved. She died far too young, at age thirty-three.

Cass was married twice and left a daughter, Owen Vanessa. She never revealed the identity of the father. Her crypt is in Court of Tanach (lot 5600, space 2) under her birth name, Ellen Naomi Cohen.

PHIL SILVERS *1911–1985*

With his large black-framed glasses, beady eyes, and expression of supreme conniving, Phil Silvers *was* Sergeant Ernie Bilko, a role he played to such hilarious perfection in the 1950s television series *The Phil Silvers Show* that most people called the show "Sergeant Bilko." This clever comic actor perfected the role of an artful schemer, playing it again as a slave in *A Funny Thing Happened on the Way to the Forum* (1966).

As the youngest in a Brooklyn, New York, family of eight children, he had to call attention to himself. He did so with gusto from age eleven, when he sang in theaters whenever the projector broke down (back in those days, it often did). At thirteen, young Silversmith (the family name) left school entirely to sing and then play a stooge in vaudeville.

After a long vaudeville career, he graduated to Broadway, where he was in several minor shows. He then made a splash with *Top Banana* in 1952, winning a Tony for his freewheeling performance.

From his first movie, *Hit Parade of 1941,* Silvers appeared in supporting roles or as comic relief for the next two decades, in everything from *Lady Be Good* (1941) and *Cover Girl* (1944) to *Summer Stock* (1950) and *It's a Mad, Mad, Mad, Mad World* (1963). Few of the films made use of his tremendous talent, so it's no wonder Bilko was like a breath of fresh air. Through the years Silvers made guest appearances on many TV shows, *The Carol Burnett Show, Rowan & Martin's Laugh-In,* and *The Dean Martin Show* among them.

One never thinks of Bilko caught napping, but Silvers died in his sleep, after a long illness, and remains peacefully at rest in vault 1004 in the Heritage Gardens, in front of the Heritage mosaic on the far right. His marker bears a six-pointed star, his name, and beneath it the single word "Comedian," an understatement if ever there was one.

NORTH HOLLYWOOD

PIERCE BROTHERS VALHALLA MEMORIAL PARK

10621 VICTORY BOULEVARD AT CAHUENGA; (818) 763-9121

Surrounded by brick walls, this lovely little old-fashioned cemetery is mostly flat, with many graves flush with the grass. A few private mausoleums and statuary dot the grounds. A lovely art deco fountain, a vintage gem, is the centerpiece at one road intersection. This restful park is enhanced by a super-friendly office staff. Don't be surprised, if they aren't busy, if one of them offers to drive you around the grounds in a golf cart. It happened to us (and we didn't even mention we were writing a book).

Valhalla has a unique asset: At the far end of the grounds is the spectacular Portal of the Folded Wings, subtitled "a shrine to aviation." It is a magnificent round gateway with ornate Spanish churrigueresque portals and a tiled dome covered with colorful mosaics. Built in 1924 and once the main entrance to the cemetery, it is now on the National Register of Historic Places. Inside the portal are many plaques honoring people who made important contributions to aviation.

A plaque on the Portal's right (as you enter from the cemetery grounds) honors aviator **Amelia Earhart** (1898–1937), who is believed to have crashed her plane in the Pacific, but her body was never found. A persistent rumor is that she was scouting the prewar Far East for the U.S. government, to see what Japanese activity was going on in the region. This has never been proved.

Also commemorated in the Portal is **Bert Kinner** (1882–1957), the builder of Earhart's first plane and inventor of the compound folded wing. Another aircraft pioneer is here: **John Moisant** (1868–1910), who designed and built the first all-metal plane and was the first to fly it across the English Channel with a passenger.

High-flying in the Portal are pioneer test pilot **James Smith** (1884–1956), who invented a freestyle manually operated parachute; **Charles Taylor** (1868–1956), who helped the Wright brothers build their first engine and plane; **Carl B. Squier** (1893–1967), the thirteenth licensed pilot in the United States and co-founder of Lockheed Aircraft, who sold planes to Earhart and Charles Lindbergh, among others; and **Hilder Smith** (1890–1977), an aviation pioneer and the first female parachutist.

Like many cemeteries in the Los Angeles area, Valhalla has its share of movie professionals, most of whom constitute a superior B-list of films from their earliest silent days until recent times, including stuntmen, backstage pros, and a stellar cast of hundreds of working stiffs. Notable among the many actors are **Mae Murray** (1889–1965; section 6328, block G, lot 6); **Barton MacLane** (1902–1969; Hope section 5460), with roles in *The Maltese Falcon, Treasure of the Sierra Madre,* and scores more; **Mae Clarke** (1910–1992; section C, lot 2424); character actor **Melville Cooper** (1896–1973; Adoration section 6602); **Gail Russell** (1924–1961; section 4887, block E, lot 2); and **Nels P. Nelson** (1918–1994; section 10640, block IJ, lot 3), one of the Munchkins in *The Wizard of Oz.*

Joe DeRita (1909–1993; section 338, block D, lot 19) joined the Three Stooges as Curly Joe after Joe Besser left. Character actress **Mary Gordon** (1882–1963; section 333, block A, lot 5) played Mrs. Hudson, Sherlock Holmes's housekeeper, in all the Holmes movies of the 1940s, while actress **Lita Grey** (1908–1995; Garden of Remem-brance, rose garden, unmarked grave) may be best remembered as Charlie Chaplin's first wife, married when she became pregnant at age fifteen; the marriage lasted three years.

LUNCH BREAK

For Mexican food, try **Mucho Mas** (10405 Burbank Boulevard at Clybourn; 818-980-0300), recommended by several Valhalla office personnel. The quesadillas are especially tasty.

Other permanent residents include **Chief Yowlachie** (1891–1966; Prayer section 6519, block G), a Native American who played Indians, always Indians, in many

films, but was also a trained opera singer, performing under the name Daniel Simmons. **Edward Ludlum** (1920–2000; Niches of Remembrance, row J, niche 8) was a stage director and one of the founders of professional theater in Los Angeles, but also directed movies and episodes of television's *Gunsmoke* and *Death Valley Days*. He was influential in the careers of several actors, including Paul Newman, Sally Field, and Audie Murphy.

Here too is **Bud Westmore** (1918–1973; section 931, block L, lot 4), of the famous Westmore makeup family (comprised also of Perc, Ern, Wally, Monte, and others), who helped generations of movie actors put their best faces forward.

Two who were more actors than athletes are here: **Max "Slapsie Maxie" Rosenbloom** (1904–1976; section 9820, block J, lot 3), who held the light heavy-weight title from 1930 to 1934, but made more of a mark in films playing himself as a genial, slightly goofy sidekick, and **"Gorgeous George" Wagner** (1915–1963; section 9370, block J, lot 4), a highly popular professional wrestler better known for his bleached hair, mincing style, and the flimsy, feminine robes he wore into the ring than for his wrestling skills.

A real athlete, **Vincent DiMaggio** (1912–1986, Garden of Remembrance, lot 111), older brother of Joltin' Joe, had a commendable ten-year career with five different major-league baseball clubs, but never matched his kid brother's record or fame. ★*Grounds and office open 8:00 A.M.–6:00 P.M. daily. Map; restrooms.*

OLIVER NORVELL HARDY *1892–1957*

Visualizing Oliver Hardy without Stan Laurel is akin to imagining Chang without Eng. If ever there were a pair that made up a whole, these were the guys. Although Hardy had appeared in over 300 films before Hal Roach Studio director Leo McCarey paired him with Laurel, "Babe," as he was known to friends, is only remembered for being the larger half of the most popular film comedy duo ever.

And that's no slight. Ollie was the beloved screen ignoramus who never recognized his own stupidity because his inseparable friend Stanley was ostensibly the dimmest light on the planet—only the contrivances of the story would reveal that even Stanley's childlike mentality was superior to Ollie's. They were first linked under their own names in 1927's silent flick *Sugar Daddies,* but made the transition to sound effortlessly as their voices perfectly reflected their on-screen personas. They first co-starred in a feature-length film in 1931, *Pardon Us,* and followed it with a steady assortment of shorts and features, to ever-increasing popularity. After all, no matter who and where you were, you could feel superior to Stan and Ollie.

Norvell Hardy was born in Harlem, Georgia, in 1892. His father died when Norvell was just ten months old, and years later he adopted his dad's name, Oliver, as his own. Young Norvell originally wanted to pursue a singing career, as he had a mellifluous natural tenor voice, which can be heard in several of his films (*Way Out West* for example). Ollie's physical talent is visible on-screen: at 6-foot-1, weighing in at over 300 pounds, dancing and performing many of his own athletic stunts.

Ollie's most famous recurring on-screen lines would have made appropriate epitaphs: "Why can't you do something to help me?" and "Here's another fine mess you've gotten me into!" The lovable pair won an Academy Award for 1932's *The Music Box,* in which their film personas were never more perfectly defined and encapsulated. Can anyone today view this film and not find kinship with the blissfully ignorant pair?

Ollie and Stan were partners in over thirty films, many of them timeless and without cultural boundaries. Their popularity was responsible for the formation of Sons of the Desert, a fan club named for their still-hilarious 1933 film of the same name. It's that fan club that upgraded Hardy's simple wallet-size bronze grave marker in the Garden of Hope to a plaque set into a wall behind it. The plaque reads: "A Genius of Comedy. His Talent brought Joy and Laughter to All the World." A heartfelt amen to that.

Oliver Norvell Hardy succumbed to heart failure at age sixty-five.

GLENDALE

Whenever someone in another part of the United States hears the
words "California cemetery," only one comes to mind: Forest Lawn.
So much has been written about this mammoth parklike burial
ground—including English satirist Evelyn Waugh's wicked spoof,
The Loved One—it has come to epitomize the very word cemetery.
And despite the profusion of Forest Lawns, the one in
Glendale is the one everyone thinks of. It is so vast, so full of
luminaries, that it is a chapter by itself.

FOREST LAWN MEMORIAL PARK–GLENDALE

1712 SOUTH GLENDALE AVENUE; (323) 254-7251

Forest Lawn as it is today was made in one man's image, that of **Hubert Eaton**
(1881–1966). Actually, the cemetery was founded in 1906 by a group of San Francisco
businessmen. But in 1912 Eaton and another man, C. B. Sims, entered a sales contract with the cemetery, and in 1917 Eaton alone took over the management.

It was Eaton who discarded the traditional view of the cemetery as a mourn-
ful place with rows of upright gravestones. In its stead he took the concept of the
parklike cemeteries of the East and adapted them to California. A trendsetter among
graveyard pioneers, he became a master of landscaping, so that the many graves
embedded in the grass are scarcely visible in the distance on what look like perfect

hillsides of emerald green, with names like Haven of Peace, Eventide, Vale of Memory, Memory Slope, and Brotherly Love. Eaton also was the first to open a mortuary on cemetery grounds.

Eaton's euphemistic name for a cemetery as a "memorial park" is now dominant throughout California, and his idea of a funeral as a joyful "celebration of a life," not a sorrowful mourning of a death, has taken hold throughout the country. He rewarded himself with a burial spot in the select Great Mausoleum, sequestered with movie stars of the most incandescent magnitude.

Forest Lawn's 300 acres are a tribute to Eaton's vision. Rolling hillsides are graced with mausoleums bearing names like Freedom Mausoleum, courtyards lined

with wall and ground graves (Court of Freedom, Court of David, Court of the Christus), and eclectic statuary that runs the gamut from Grecian maidens and Michelangelo replicas, to weeping Victorian family scenes and art deco fountains. Monumental sculptures bear religious, classical, and patriotic themes. There is even a 1,000-seat auditorium (Hall of the Crucifixion).

The office, on the right as you enter the gates, is in a half-timbered building that would be at home in England's Cotswolds. The entrance lounge is as warm and inviting as a living room, with a gas fireplace and comfortable furnishings.

Across from the office is a pond with ducks and geese. The immaculate grounds contain Wee Kirk o' the Heather church, a stone building that wouldn't look out of place in the Scottish countryside. In fact it was modeled on a 14th-century church at Glencairn, Scotland. Church of the Recessional and Little Church of the Flowers are two other nondenominational churches on the vast grounds. Both are copies of centuries-old English churches

There are now at least six Forest Lawns, but this one is the mother church, so to speak—the burial ground for so many stars, it can take days to hunt them all down. And we mean *hunt,* for the map lists no celebrity graves, and office person-nel are instructed not to divulge where anyone famous is buried. "It's a privacy issue," we were told. Grounds workers are not so discreet, and they are your best bet for finding special favorites.

But don't get your hopes up about visiting **W. C. Fields, Clark Gable, Jean Harlow**, or **Carole Lombard.** They are all sequestered in the Great Mausoleum. The closest you can get, unless you are friend or family (don't even think about it—there's a huge penalty for false claims), is to peer into the various roped-off halls when you visit "The Last Supper," one of the public attractions in the Great Mausoleum.

Also sequestered in the Great Mausoleum are **Irving Thalberg** (1899–1936), the producer called the "boy genius," who died young, and his wife, actress **Norma Shearer** (1902–1983), who won an Oscar for *The Divorcee* (1930) and later starred in *The Women*. They might be peered at from the roped-off Sanctuary of Benediction, reposing at the very end on the left, next to a stained-glass window.

Another producer in a place of honor in the Great Mausoleum is **David O. Selznick** (1902–1965), who is at the far end on the left, next to a stained-glass win-dow, in the Sanctuary of Trust, inside the Columbarium of Prayer. Selznick was one of the major players in the Golden Age of films. Among his coups were producing *Gone With the Wind, Rebecca, A Star Is Born,* and *Duel in the Sun.* In classic Hollywood tradition, he married *Duel's* star, Jennifer Jones.

Content yourself with the beautiful plantings, ponds, and hilltop grounds, offering the best of all possible views of Los Angeles spreading below. Forest Lawn is not your little old-fashioned neighborhood burial ground, but big business. It is also a mega tourist attraction. More than 60,000 people have come here to be married, as Ronald Reagan and Jane Wyman did in Wee Kirk o' the Heather. Regis Philbin did, too. The names of permanent guests could fill a book on the history of the entertainment industry. At last count there were more than 300,000 perpetual inhabitants.

Here's a sampling of who, with some persistence, can be unearthed: **Clara Bow** (1905–1965; Freedom Mausoleum), the "It" girl of silent movies, whose wall niche is shared with her husband, **Rex Bell** (1903–1962), cowboy actor and onetime lieutenant governor of Nevada; "Man of a Thousand Faces" **Lon Chaney Sr.** (1880–1930; Great Mausoleum, Sanctuary of Meditation, C-6407, unmarked), horror-film actor best known for *The Hunchback of Notre Dame* and *Phantom of the Opera;* and **Theda Bara** (1885–1955; Columbarium of Memory, niche 1955), vamp supreme in silent movies.

Later arrivals include **Dorothy Dandridge** (1922–1965; Freedom Mausoleum, Columbarium of Victory, niche 32269), the beautiful singer and actress who starred in *Carmen Jones* and *Porgy and Bess,* and **Dan Dailey** (1915–1978; Court of Freedom, plot 7065, space 4), a popular actor for over three decades, nominated for an Oscar in *When My Baby Smiles at Me.*

Three members of two famous movie comedy teams reside in the Freedom Mausoleum: **Chico Marx** (1887–1961; Sanctuary of Worship, right side, sixth row up from the floor), the Marx Brother with the fake Italian accent; **Gummo Marx** (1893–1977; Sanctuary of Brotherhood, left side, third row up from the floor), who was his brothers' agent and longtime manager; and **Larry Fine** (1902–1975; Sanctuary of Liberation, left side, first row up from the floor), the wild-haired, violin-playing member of the original Three Stooges.

Best known for her role in *The Member of the Wedding* (1952), singer-actress **Ethel Waters** (1896–1977; Ascension Garden, lot 7152) later sang in the Billy Graham Crusades and in Richard Nixon's White House. Also in Ascension Garden is **Ted Knight** (1923–1986; lot 9127), the comic actor who was a favorite as the obtuse anchorman on television's *Mary Tyler Moore Show.* Acrobatically gifted **Harold Lloyd** (1893–1971; Great Mausoleum, Begonia corridor), one of the great silent-film comedians, is silent still.

Though billed as "The Perfect Fool," **Ed Wynn** (1886–1966; Columbarium of the Dawn) could do serious drama (*The Diary of Anne Frank*) as well as the silly com-

GENE RAYMOND
BELOVED HUSBAND
1908 – 1998

Jeanette MacDonald Raymond

BELOVED WIFE
1907 – 1965

edy routines with crazy hats he was known for. His son, **Keenan Wynn** (1916–1986; same location, the crypt above his father's), was a supporting actor in movies and television who could play comedy and drama with equal aplomb. The gravelly, crushed rock voice of **Lionel Stander** (1908–1994; Garden of Honor, crypt 7246) made him a natural for comedy, a role he played in scores of movies and the television comedy-mystery series *Hart to Hart.*

Matinee idol **Robert Taylor** (1911–1969; Garden of Honor, Columbarium of the Evening Star) is also in residence. He was a handsome leading man in almost seventy films over three decades, including *Magnificent Obsession, Waterloo Bridge,* and *Johnny Eager.* He was also married at one time to Barbara Stanwyck. Nearby is **Joan Blondell** (1906–1979; Garden of Honor, Columbarium of the Evening Star, between the Freedom mausoleum and Court of Freedom), who played brassy, bottle-blond "best friend" in countless movies, but in real life often got her man. Her second husband was actor Dick Powell; her third, producer Mike Todd.

Final credits here go to soprano **Jeanette MacDonald** (1903–1965, though she claimed to be born in 1907; Freedom Mausoleum, Sanctuary of Heritage, right wall), the actress-singer paired with tenor Nelson Eddy in many movie musicals of the 1930s and 1940s. She is at rest with her husband, **Gene Raymond** (1908–1998), an actor in *Flying Down to Rio* and other 1930s films.

Piquant French actress **Lilli Palmer** (1914–1986; Commemoration section) has checked in across from the Freedom mausoleum. Known for *The Diary of Anne Frank, The High Commissioner,* and many other films, she was also once married to actor Rex Harrison.

Tom Mix (1880–1940), popular cowboy actor, has been put out to pasture in Whispering Pines, lot 1030, space 8, at the top of the hill. **Charles "Charlie" Ruggles** (1886–1971; Garden of Memory, lot 1007), comic character actor who played in more than a hundred films, is here as well. British-born **Victor McLaglen** (1886–1959; Gardens of Remembrance, Columbarium of Eternal Light, next to Humphrey Bogart) played in scores of 1930s films and won a Best Actor Oscar for *The Informer* and Best Supporting Actor nomination for *The Quiet Man*.

Perhaps the most grandiose memorial belongs to the comedian **Joe E. Brown** (1891–1973), who played in many films but whose most memorable role was as the wealthy man who pursued Jack Lemmon, thinking he was a woman, in *Some Like It Hot*. The best line in a film of good lines was the last, and it belonged to Brown:

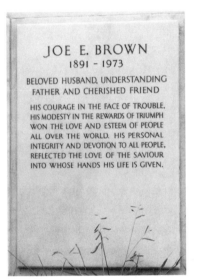

"Nobody's perfect." His monumental memorial resides in Sunrise Slope, on the grass behind the Great Mausoleum. To reach it you have to navigate a serpentine road.

If not eternal youth, charming **Bob Cummings** (1908–1990; Great Mausoleum, Columbarium of Serenity, niche 21505) has found an eternal home, where he might contemplate his many movie roles (*Saboteur* and *Dial M for Murder*, for starters) and his lead in television's *The Bob Cummings Show*.

Playwright **Clifford Odets** (1906–1963; Garden of Honor, Columbarium of Honor) had his works first produced by the Group Theatre and later on Broadway; they include *Golden Boy, Waiting for Lefty,* and *The Country Girl*. He went west to write screenplays for *The Big Knife, The Sweet Smell of Success,* and other films.

A recent arrival is **Ralph Edwards** (1913–2005; Ascension Garden, lot 7190), master of ceremonies of two of the most popular radio and television shows in history, both Emmy winners: *Truth or Consequences* and *This Is Your Life*.

Not everyone at rest in Forest Lawn had movie ties, to wit: **L. Frank Baum** (1856–1919; section G, next to narrow road), author of the Oz books, and **Don Drysdale** (1936–1993; Great Mausoleum, Utility corridor), Hall of Fame pitcher with the Los Angeles Dodgers. **Gutzon Borglum** (1867–1941; Great Mausoleum), sculptor of Mount Rushmore and other monumental works, lies below "The Last Supper" stained-glass window.

Evangelist **Aimee Semple McPherson** (1890–1944) was as famous in her day as Billy Graham is today. Her show-stopping, monumental sculptural memorial of white marble, with an angel on both ends, resides on Sunrise Slope, the lawn behind the Great Mausoleum, reached by the same winding road that passes the Joe E. Brown memorial a short distance farther along.

In the third garden alcove to the right of the entrance to the Great Mausoleum is the wall grave of **Louis L' Amour** (1908–1988), who wrote over a hundred western novels, forty-five of which were turned into movies.

Opposite the Great Mausoleum entrance is the dramatic mausoleum of Danish actor and humanitarian **Jean Hersholt** (1886–1956). "Riding" the top is a bronze figure of a horseman, modeled on Hans Christian Andersen's Clods Hands character. Hersholt made a number of films, including *Grand Hotel* and *Dinner at Eight,* and received many awards for his myriad good works.

One might think that **Sam Cooke** (1931–1964; Garden of Honor, right side, private) received his smooth voice straight from heaven. From singing gospel music

LUNCH BREAK

For tasty burgers, fries, and sandwiches, **In-N-Out Burger** (310 North Harvey Drive; 800-786-1000) is just the ticket. It's a chain, but offers a big bite for your buck.

JEAN HERSHOLT
1886 — 1956

(with four of his seven siblings) in his father's Chicago Baptist church, he went on to perform with the gospel groups Highway QC's and Soul Stirrers, but was kicked out for recording popular music. His 1957 hit "You Send Me" sold a million copies and was followed by many other hits: "Only Sixteen," "What a Wonderful World," "Chain Gang," "Twistin' the Night Away," "Bring It on Home to Me." In a bizarre incident in a south Los Angeles motel, Cooke was shot to death at age thirty-three in what an inquest jury ruled justifiable homicide. His posthumous hit, "A Change Is Gonna Come," became an unofficial civil rights theme song. ★*Grounds and office open 8:00 A.M.–5:00 P.M. daily. Map; restrooms; gift shop; flower shop; museum; three churches.*

GRACIE ALLEN *1902–1964*
GEORGE BURNS *1896–1996*

The best thing that ever happened to small-time vaudeville comic George Burns—as he was the first to admit—was meeting Gracie Allen, an unemployed actress. She was seventeen, he was twenty-seven, and they soon began a partnership and mar-

GRACIE ALLEN AND GEORGE BURNS
1902 - 1964   1896 - 1996
TOGETHER AGAIN

riage that lasted until her death forty-one years later. Their schtick as a comedy team was for George to play straight man, Gracie—as a dizzy dame—to get the laugh lines (written by him).

Their act was so popular, they soon had their own radio show, which lasted twenty-one years, followed by eight years on television and a number of movies for Paramount Studios. After Gracie died, Burns went on solo, in movies—*The Sunshine Boys, Oh God!* and *Going in Style* among them—in Las Vegas as a single act, and writing his memoirs. He made growing old look like fun and seemed to enjoy it to the hilt.

Burns scheduled his hundredth-anniversary shows at the London Palladium and Caesar's Palace in Las Vegas, joking that he couldn't die because he had these engagements to keep. He made one hundred all right, but his confinement in a wheelchair made him miss all his birthday parties. Three months later, he joined Gracie. Their crypt in the wall in the Freedom Mausoleum reads "Together Again." How appropriate.

HUMPHREY BOGART *1899–1957*

To look at Humphrey Bogart's early movies, you'd think he grew up on grim city streets. His low-life demeanor in *Kid Galahad, Dark Victory,* and *Brother Orchid*—all made in the mid-1930s—was so effective, it seemed hard to believe that "Bogie" was born Humphrey DeForest Bogart, son of a prominent New York doctor and his artist wife, and that he attended the exclusive Phillips Academy in Andover, Massachusetts.

At age seventeen he enlisted in the U.S. Navy and served briefly in the military police. While serving, he was hit in the mouth by a handcuffed prisoner trying to escape. This left Bogart with a faint scar and a slight lisp, both of which made him a natural for bad-guy roles. His breakthrough part as an actor was as a killer with

some sensitivity in *High Sierra,* followed by *The Maltese Falcon,* in which he played Sam Spade, a hard-boiled detective with integrity. *Casablanca* gave a new dimension to his acting skills.

By the time he met Lauren Bacall, his co-star in *To Have and Have Not* in 1944, he had been through three tumultuous marriages. His fourth—to her—turned out to be his lucky number, leading to two children and a settled life. Their two later films together, *The Big Sleep* and *Key Largo,* conveyed the same magnetic attraction as the first.

FILM VAULT

Casablanca (1942) tops the list of most people's favorite golden oldies. As a romantic tale of doomed lovers, espionage, and wartime intrigue in an exotic setting, it's unmatched. Add a superb cast headed by Bogart, Ingrid Bergman, Paul Henreid, and Claude Raines ("I'm shocked, shocked!") and that says it all.

The early 1950s were the golden years of his career, showing more range and versatility—with *The African Queen* (for which he won an Oscar), *Beat the Devil, The Caine Mutiny, Sabrina,* and *The Desperate Hours.* Cancer caught up with him in 1957, and he died just after completing *The Harder They Fall.* All in all, he made more than seventy movies. Look for his marble wall crypt in the Columbarium of Eternal Light inside the Gardens of Remembrance.

NAT "KING" COLE *1919–1965*

Like Louis Armstrong, Nathaniel Adams Cole had versatility. He played a seductive jazz piano and sang in a husky, sexy voice. Unlike Armstrong, who used both his vocal and trumpet talents throughout his life, Cole largely gave up the piano to focus on a singing career. Born in Montgomery, Alabama, he grew up in Chicago after his minister father moved the family north. Nat played the organ and piano in his father's church, then graduated to his own band, the King Cole Trio, which soon began recording for Capitol Records.

He later became Capitol's most successful recording artist. "Straighten Up and Fly Right" was the trio's first big hit in 1943. "Get Your Kicks on Route 66," "It's Only a Paper Moon," "Nature Boy," " Mona Lisa," and "I Love You for Sentimental Reasons" followed as a few of his megahits. There were more photogenic singers around, but Cole was blessed with a resonant voice, fine diction, and an engaging personality.

Though he was the first major African-American musical artist to have his own sponsored radio series, he was plagued by racism: first when he bought a home in an upscale white Los Angeles neighborhood, later when his work in civil rights led to an attack while he was performing in Birmingham, Alabama, in 1956. Cole was the first African American to have a weekly television series, but it was cancelled—in spite of being popular—for lack of sponsorship; a black show was considered too "controversial" at the time (1956).

Nat King Cole made a few movies—*St. Louis Blues* and *Cat Ballou* among them—but it was as a mellow singer that he really scored. Look for his crypt on the pale pink marble walls of the Freedom Mausoleum.

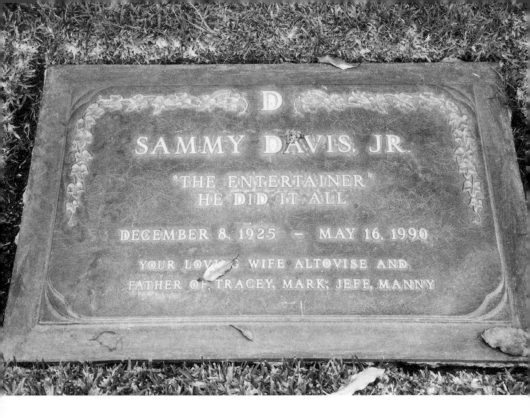

SAMMY DAVIS JR. *1925–1990*

What made Sammy Davis Jr. run? Presumably his dad, a show business father. Young Sammy spent his childhood on the road, learning early to sing, dance, play drums, do impersonations, and ingratiate himself with an audience. For years he was part of the Will Mastin Trio, which included his father and Mastin. After a brief time in the army during World War II, where racism nagged him as it did throughout his life, Davis rejoined the act and scored a big hit in Las Vegas doing imitations of other performers—Jimmy Cagney, Jimmy Durante, and Edward G. Robinson among them.

While recovering from a near-fatal car crash, in which he lost an eye, he sought solace in religion and converted to Judaism, later cracking that he was "the only colored, one-eyed Jewish entertainer in show business." Through Frank Sinatra, Davis became part of the Rat Pack, which in turn led to six movies with the group. He made other films as well, including the successful *Cannonball Run* and *Tap*.

Davis was both talented and energetic, but his obsequiousness around Sinatra, Dean Martin, and the other Rat Packers brought criticism in the black press, accusing him of trying to be white. In 1961 Davis married Swedish starlet May Britt— his second of three wives—and had two children and adopted a third, but the hate mail and blatant racism forced him to hire bodyguards. The tension eventually eroded the marriage. A frenzied schedule—television, concerts, and best-selling records—and his hard-drinking, superfast lifestyle caught up with him, leading to kidney and liver problems, a mild heart attack, and eventually throat cancer and death.

Inside the Court of Freedom, to the left of the large mosaic depicting the signing of the Declaration of Independence, Sammy Davis is at rest at last, beneath a decorative headstone that proclaims "The entertainer—he did it all." Next to his grave is that of his father and other family members. Behind Davis's stone, by the wall, are two white marble, classically-garbed, Greek-style lovers embracing on a pedestal.

WALT DISNEY *1901–1966*

With Disneyland and Disney World; the cartoon land of Mickey and Minnie Mouse, Donald Duck, and Goofy; and all the films produced by Walt Disney Productions, it sometimes seems there never was a time B.D.—Before Disney. But the fact that much

of the world is now Disneyfied didn't just happen by chance. The genius behind it all was Walt Disney, a Chicago-born, Missouri-raised farm boy with talent as a commercial artist, who was a pioneer in cartoon animation and a genius in marketing.

Disney moved to Hollywood in 1923, and soon his Mickey Mouse starred in the first synchronized sound cartoon, a breakthrough that led to other cartoons and, in short order, his own studio. Other "firsts" followed: the first cartoon in full color; the first full-length animated film, *Snow White and the Seven Dwarfs* in 1937 (followed by scores of others, among them *Pinocchio, Fantasia, Dumbo, Bambi,* and *Cinderella*); and Disney being the first major studio to enter television—with *Walt Disney's World.*

Disneyland and Disney World have been around so long, it is hard to realize they were the world's first theme parks, created by Disney's yearning for amusement parks that could be wholesome entertainment for the entire family. (One wonders what he would think of some of the decidedly unfamily-type films produced these days under the Disney aegis.)

Walt Disney won scores of awards, including an honorary Oscar, four Academy Awards, and the Presidential Medal of Freedom. The California Institute of the Arts (Cal Arts) was endowed by Disney. With all of this, his final address is surprisingly discreet. On the far right side of the long Court of Freedom, near a life-size statue of George Washington by John Quincy Adams Ward, is a secluded, flower and vine–bedecked Disney corner. Its wall crypt's plaque lists Walter Elias Disney and various family members.

W. C. FIELDS *1880–1946*

A Fields film character once said, "The world's a funny place; you're lucky if you get out of it alive." He needn't have worried. Through his films and adoring fans, W. C. Fields guaranteed his own immortality.

Born William Claude Dukenfield in Philadelphia, Pennsylvania, his youth was anything but happy-go-lucky. Forced to work in his father's grocery store, young William escaped stern reality by practicing juggling, for which he had an innate talent. But practicing with the produce, often dropping and bruising fruit, exhausted his father's patience, prompting the youth to flee and seek his own way.

By the time Fields was in his late teens, billed as the "World's Most Famous Comic Juggler," he charmed European royalty with his act. He hit domestic stardom as a regular in the Ziegfeld Follies, soon becoming one of the highest-paid men in the country. As such, he earned much more than the president of the United States; deservedly so, as his acts *always* satisfied his audiences. Using W. C. Fields as his stage name, he segued into film roles that embodied his curmudgeonly, put-upon, heavy-drinking persona. He started in silents, then effortlessly slipped into talkies, in which his nasal delivery perfectly fit his screen character.

First there were shorts, notably *The Barber Shop, The Dentist, The Pharmacist,* and *The Fatal Glass of Beer* (produced by Mack Sennett), and then his popularity led to features, which included *Tillie and Gus* (1933) and *It's a Gift* and *The Old Fashioned Way* (both 1934), all featuring darling Baby Leroy. This prompted many Fields one-liners about his aversion to children, such as "I love children . . . if they're properly cooked."

His favorite author was Charles Dickens. Watching his films with that in mind, W. C.'s characters often seem as though they were transplanted from a Dickens story to modern times. In fact, the only straight role he played on film was Mr. Micawber in Dickens's *David Copperfield* (1935). It's pure Fields.

More classic Fields films followed: *Poppy* (1936), *You Can't Cheat an Honest Man* (1939; with Edgar Bergen and Charlie McCarthy), *My Little Chickadee* (1940; co-starring Mae West), and *The Bank Dick* (also 1940), considered by many his masterpiece. Fields broke into abstract comedy in his last starring role, playing himself in 1941's *Never Give a Sucker an Even Break,* in which he hilariously attacks the impersonal, artificial Hollywood studio system. Heavy drinking caused failing health, virtually ending his film career, but he managed to connect with fans via radio, where he had a famous "feud" with Charlie McCarthy, the wise-guy dummy of popular ventriloquist Edgar Bergen.

A nonreligious man, Fields was surprised in what turned out to be his deathbed by friends who caught him reading a Bible. "Just looking for loopholes," he explained.

He resides currently off-limits in the Hall of Inspiration's Columbarium of Nativity in the Great Mausoleum.

ERROL FLYNN *1909–1959*

Swashbuckling on the screen, this dashingly handsome, athletically built, Tasmanian-born, English-trained actor conveyed a self-deprecating manner and wry humor that added to his enormous appeal. In his first Hollywood movie role in 1935 in *The Case of the Curious Bride,* he played a corpse, leading him to comment, "Some say it was my best role." By his third movie, *Captain Blood,* he was a star.

He made some marvelous adventure films—*The Charge of the Light Brigade, The Adventures of Robin Hood* (which many critics consider his best), and *The Sea Hawk* among them. Yet, according to his daughter Deidre, as reported in a *Los Angeles Times* interview in 2005, "When he first started out in theater in England, he

had his mind set on being a serious actor, but Jack Warner kept him in tights."

Not all the time, by any means. Flynn's fifty movies covered a surprisingly wide range of subjects: historical dramas (*The Private Lives of Elizabeth and Essex*), westerns (*Santa Fe Trail, They Died With Their Boots On*), romantic comedies (*Never Say Goodbye*), biographies (*Gentleman Jim*, about boxer James Corbett), comedy (*Footsteps in the Dark*), wartime thrillers (*The Dawn Patrol, Edge of Darkness*), and romance (*Let's Make Up, Four's a Crowd*). He made eight movies with Olivia de Havilland (and supposedly had an affair with her during one of them) and two with Bette Davis (with whom he feuded furiously).

Off camera, he lived almost as recklessly as in some of his films. He had three wives (Lily Damita, Nora Eddington, and Patrice Wymore), scores of affairs, and a sex scandal with two underage (but worldly) girls, which led to a rape trial and acquittal (though "in like Flynn" was a catch phrase and widespread joke long after the trial ended). Bouts with drugs and liquor, along with several financial disasters, were part of his considerable personal baggage.

Flynn's career dipped disastrously by the late 1940s, but he did make the serious *That Forsythe Woman* in 1949, playing the demanding role of Soames Forsythe. "He went against type," his daughter Deidre said, "It was his favorite picture." The last two years of his life were almost pathetic—gallivanting the globe and making a silly movie with his teenage mistress. Yet in 1957 he gave a fine supporting performance in *The Sun Also Rises,* and the next year he managed a masterly portrayal of his old drinking pal John Barrymore in *Too Much, Too Soon.* In both films he played a drunk, a role he knew well.

A Peter Pan who never really grew up, Flynn died at age fifty of a massive heart attack. His gravestone, in the grass in the Garden of Everlasting Peace, seems guarded by a demure half-dressed nymph on a pedestal. It figures. The stone reads, after his name and dates, "In memory of our father from his loving children." Buried with him, supposedly, are six bottles of whiskey, a final housewarming gift, as it were, from some of his drinking cronies. His autobiography, *My Wicked, Wicked Ways,* was published posthumously.

CLARK GABLE 1880–1946

Back in the 1930s, if you heard "the King of Hollywood," you'd darn well know who it was: Clark Gable. His good looks, manliness, wry humor, and incredible sex appeal made him a standout. It also didn't hurt that he had some fantastic roles: as the cocky reporter in *It Happened One Night* (for which he won a Best Actor Oscar), as Fletcher Christian in *Mutiny on the Bounty,* and as Rhett Butler in *Gone With the*

Wind, all three of which won Oscars for Best Picture. Both his roles as Christian and Butler earned him Oscar nominations as well.

Appealing to both men and women, Gable could seemingly do no wrong. In picture after picture in pre–World War II Hollywood, he was a presence that almost guaranteed success. Whether romantic comedy, adventure, historical drama, action films, whatever—*Men in White, The Call of the Wild, San Francisco, Parnell, Saratoga, Too Hot to Handle, Test Pilot, Idiot's Delight, Strange Cargo, Boom Town, Somewhere I'll Find You*—Gable could handle them all with vigor, charm, and wit.

He almost didn't become an actor. The son of a German-American couple, he was born in Cadiz, Ohio. His mother died when Clark was six months old. His father remarried, and the family moved to a suburb of Akron. After high school Clark had trouble settling down, so he worked in a tire factory in Akron.

FILM VAULT

Gone With the Wind is an epic that never gets old or dated. It has everything: a great cast (Gable, Vivien Leigh, Olivia de Havilland, Leslie Howard, Thomas Mitchell, Hattie McDaniel, Victor Jory, Ward Bond); an exciting story set in a cataclysmic period of history; a torrid, tumultuous romance; a splendid script; and scenic spectaculars. What's not to like? No wonder it scooped up every Oscar in sight in 1939.

Seeing a play stirred in him the desire to act, a pursuit he followed for several years, touring with second-string companies. In Portland, Oregon, he dropped out and started selling neckties at a department store. His acting coach, Josephine Dillon, an older woman with some money, suggested they head for Hollywood, with her as his manager and new wife (his first of five). An appearance in the play *The Last Mile* led to a screen contract with MGM in 1930. The rest, as is often said, is movie history.

Less well known is his time in the U.S. Army Air Force. In 1942, shortly after the tragic death in a plane crash of Carole Lombard, his third wife, Gable joined the military. In three years of service, he flew several missions in raids over Nazi Germany, earned a Distinguished Flying Cross and an Air Medal, and retired with the rank of major.

By then Hollywood had moved on, and Gable never recouped the stunning roles he had during the 1930s. There were some hits—*The Hucksters, Command Decision,* and *Mogambo* among them—but he was increasingly bored and dismayed by the scripts he was offered. *The Misfits,* with Marilyn Monroe and Montgomery Clift, in 1961 was possibly the last straw. Monroe's tardiness, in which she kept the cast and crew waiting endlessly, irritated him. He died at the end of filming.

On a personal level, the love of his life was Carole Lombard. His fourth wife was Sylvia Ashley, widow of Douglas Fairbanks Jr., and his fifth was Kathleen Spreckels, with whom he had had a thirteen-year affair. She was the mother of his only legitimate child, a son who was born after Gable's death. It says a lot that he chose Carole to be his companion in his final habitat.

Off limits, Gable's wall crypt can be glimpsed if you go inside the Great Mausoleum to see "The Last Supper" window. Facing the window, off a corridor to the right, is the Columbarium of Prayer. Inside it on the far left is the Sanctuary of Trust. It is roped off, but if your eyesight is good, you'll see on the left side, eight crypts in from the wall, two up from the bottom, Gable's crypt, opposite a marble bench. Lombard is to his left, seventh in from the entrance. That's as close as you'll get.

JEAN HARLOW *1911–1937*

Surprisingly, Jean Harlow's background was the opposite of the type of role she often played on screen: a loud, bleached blond, often sluttish and barely couth. The reality: She was the only offspring of a successful Kansas City, Missouri, dentist. Born Harlean Carpenter (her first name made up from parts of her mother's maiden name), she attended a private girls' school, Ferry Hall, in Lake Forest, Illinois, after her mother remarried (having divorced her father) and moved there.

At age sixteen Harlean eloped to Los Angeles with Charles McGrew Jr., a young stockbroker. The marriage lasted just two years, but she tried out for movie work and snared a few bit parts. Her career began to take off with a part in a Laurel and Hardy short, *Double Whoopee* (1929). This led to a breakthrough role in Howard Hughes's lavish 1930 production, *Hell's Angels*.

Harlean, by now Jean Harlow, proved to be a gifted comedienne and a better actress than her bimbo looks suggested. A cluster of films—*The Public Enemy* (with Jimmy Cagney), *Goldie, The Secret Six* (with Clark Gable)—were all made in 1931. The next year brought even bigger roles in *Red-Headed Woman* and *Red Dust* (with Gable again). Gable and Harlow worked well as a team and made six films together.

On the brink of major stardom, Harlow married Paul Bern, an MGM producer, but apparently the marriage was unconsummated. When Bern was found dead in her bedroom under weird circumstances (drenched in her perfume), MGM chief Louis Mayer did everything possible to hush up the suicide and paid for the funeral.

This uncomfortable event didn't hamper Harlow's career. In 1933 her comic turn in *Dinner at Eight* stole the show from bigger names. *Libeled Lady* (1936) was another strong comic performance. After an affair with boxer Max Baer, a suspected fling with Bugsy Siegel and another mobster, and a brief marriage to cinematographer Harold Rosson, Harlow was engaged for two years to actor William Powell. While she was making *Saratoga* in 1937 with Clark Gable, she was rushed to the hospital with uremic poisoning and died of kidney failure. An understudy had to take over half of her *Saratoga* scenes; the result was surprisingly seamless. In her brief twenty-six years, she made twenty-three films, enough to secure for her a major place in cinema history.

Strictly speaking off-limits, Jean Harlow's wall crypt can be glimpsed, barely, if you turn right at the end of the long hall where visitors are instructed to turn left to "The Last Supper" window. Down the hallway is the Sanctuary of Benediction on the right side. The first crypt on the left side belongs to Red Skelton, the second to Sid Grauman, and at the far end on the left is Harlow's. Powell supposedly paid for her niche, adding the words "Our Baby" to her name. Even with X-ray vision, though, you can't possibly read this.

ALAN LADD *1913–1964*

Once you know Alan Ladd's history, you can better understand his expressionless face on-screen. His family was so poor, as a young child he had to pick fruit, deliver newspapers, sweep floors in stores, and do other menial jobs. He was also malnourished and so small for his age that he was called "Tiny." Even as an adult he never grew beyond 5 feet, 6 inches.

After high school he worked for two years as a grip in films, and tried acting but was told he was too small and too pale. He had bit parts in more than fifteen films but was going nowhere, so he tried radio instead.

In 1939 a talent scout, Sue Carol (who became his second wife in 1942), discovered him and got him a role as a psychotic killer in *This Gun for Hire* (1942). What made this an important film for Ladd was that he was playing against type. Up to that time, movie killers were pugs, usually physically unattractive. Ladd was good-looking, with even features and a nice baritone voice. For that reason, his impassive face was all the more menacing. He changed the stereotype of "tough guy" forever.

FILM VAULT

One of the top westerns ever made, *Shane* (1953) remains one of our favorites. A great cast, led by Ladd, Van Heflin, Jean Arthur, Jack Palance, and Brandon De Wilde, with an experienced director, George Stevens, *Shane* has terrific cinematography (for which Loyal Griggs received an Oscar) and a hard-to-beat story.

Alan Ladd

1913 — 1964

BELOVED HUSBAND AND FATHER

Sue Carol Ladd

IN THIS HEART OF MINE..
YOU LIVE ALL THE TIME...

From then through the 1940s (with less than a year out for army service, during which he contracted an ulcer and double hernia), he starred in numerous films: westerns, crime and war dramas, and others, including *The Great Gatsby.* The best was probably *The Blue Dahlia,* in which he co-starred with Veronica Lake. In all, he made seven films with Lake. Not only did they have on-screen chemistry, but she was shorter than Ladd. In films with other women, he often had to stand on a box or the actress walked in a shallow trench beside him. This wasn't necessary with Lake.

He got the part of a lifetime as the loner gunslinger in *Shane* (1953), one of the all-time great westerns. But from then on his career steadily declined with roles in B films. Difficult as it is to believe, Ladd lobbied hard for the title role in *Lawrence of Arabia* (1962). Casting him as Lawrence would have been like Ronald Reagan playing Rick in *Casablanca,* though Reagan was actually the first choice for that role.

In 1964 he played an aging, faded movie star in *The Carpetbaggers.* It was his last film. He died soon after, apparently a suicide.

Ladd's last stand is with his wife, **Sue Carol Ladd** (1907–1982) in a wall crypt in the Sanctuary of Heritage in the Freedom Mausoleum, with the words "In this heart of mine . . . you live all the time." In front of their crypt is a bronze bust of Ladd by sculptor Lia Di Leo, with a bronze plaque beneath it that includes an eight-stanza poem by Edgar A. Guest that begins "I hold no dream of fortune vast . . ."

CAROLE LOMBARD *1908–1942*

In her short life (thirty-four years), Carole Lombard made an astonishing number of films—many shorts, but more than thirty full-length features—and established herself early on as a major comedienne. In *Twentieth Century* (1934) with John Barrymore, *My Man Godfrey* (1936) with William Powell, *The Princess Comes Across* (also 1936) with Fred MacMurray, and *Nothing Sacred* (1937) with Frederic March, she defined the meaning of screwball comedy. Not only that, but she was a class act, with even features, blond hair, and a svelte figure.

She began life as Jane Peters (that name is on some of her early credits in short films) in Fort Wayne, Indiana. On her mother's side, the family emigrated from England in 1634. Her father's family came somewhat later, the nineteenth century, from Germany. The story goes that Carole was discovered at age twelve playing baseball by a film director. True or not, she made tons of shorts (where she probably honed her comic timing) throughout the 1920s and moved easily into talkies.

FILM VAULT

Lombard excelled in lighthearted sophisticated comedy, and **My Man Godfrey** (1936), with William Powell and an all-star supporting cast, was the epitome of the screwball genre—a Great Depression film that still delights. No wonder she was nominated for a Best Actress Oscar for her ditsy performance.

In 1930 Lombard married William Powell, sixteen years her senior. The marriage lasted less than two years, but the friendship continued until her death. Later she met and eventually married Clark Gable (in 1939). They bought a ranch in the San Fernando Valley and seemed sublimely happy.

Some three years later, with the United States at war, Lombard went with her mother back to Indiana to appear at a war bond rally. Flying back to Los Angeles on a clear night, the plane refueled in Las Vegas, then began the last lap of the flight. Shortly after takeoff, the plane inexplicably crashed into a mountain 30 miles west of town. All twenty-three passengers were killed. President Franklin Roosevelt later declared Lombard the first female war casualty killed in the line of duty and awarded her the Presidential Medal of Freedom.

When she died, Lombard had just finished making *To Be or Not to Be* with Jack Benny, a comedy-thriller directed by Ernst Lubitsch. Before it was released, one of her lines was edited out of the film. It was this: "What can happen in a plane?"

Carole Lombard resides for eternity next to Clark Gable in the Great Mausoleum's Sanctuary of Light. Although Gable married again twice, he chose to be with Carole in his final act.

WILLIAM MULHOLLAND *1855–1935*

Mulholland Drive the road and *Mulholland Drive* the movie are well known in Los Angeles—but who the heck was Mulholland? William Mulholland was an Irishman (born in Belfast) who came to the United States to make his fame and fortune. He did both in California, and earned infamy as well. A self-taught engineer, he became the head of the Los Angeles Department of Water and Power.

So? So this was a power position that led to the creation of a metropolis from a hick desert town. Along with Frederick Eaton, an engineer and mayor of Los Angeles, Mulholland brought water from the Owens River via an aqueduct and a series of tunnels to a reservoir in the San Fernando Valley. The project was completed in 1914 at a cost of $24 million. For a time, Mulholland was so popular that some urged him to run for mayor. His reply was one of the most scorching political rejections of all times: "I'd rather give birth to a porcupine."

HOUSE CALL

Mulholland Drive isn't a house, but it is William Mulholland's best legacy (other than water). In 1924 he oversaw the completion of this almost-50-mile-long drive from North Hollywood to the Malibu coast. Winding along the ridge of the Santa Monica Mountains, the tortuous, serpentine road is famous for its spectacular views of Los Angeles below and of the San Fernando Valley. Wooded, natural, and beautiful, with deer and other wildlife romping at will, it makes it easy to forget that a city the size of L.A. is just a hop-skip away.

When the aqueduct drained the river dry, Owens Valley farmers dynamited it, forcing Los Angeles to negotiate for water rights. (Some of the story, fictionalized, can be gleaned in *Chinatown*.) Mulholland supposedly said at the time that he "half-regretted the demise of so many of the valley's orchard trees, because now there were no longer enough trees to hang all the troublemakers who live there."

Mulholland rode high, despite suspicions of graft connected with the water rights, but fifteen years later, in 1928, he had his comeuppance. The St. Francis Dam, a project of his that he had just inspected, broke, flooding the Santa Clara Valley, destroying the town of Santa Paula, and swamping parts of Ventura County, killing 450. Mulholland took full responsibility for the worst civil engineering disaster in U.S. history and resigned. Later at the inquest, he said tearfully, "I envy the dead."

In seven years he joined them. Mulholland need envy no one these days. He is in the Great Mausoleum, Memorial Terrace, Sanctuary of Meditation.

MARY PICKFORD *1893–1979*

Don't let those golden curls fool you, nor the soubriquet "Little Mary." Mary Pickford, née Gladys Smith, developed from a six-year-old unschooled Canadian child performer to one of the most successful film actresses of her time, a scenario writer, and film producer with her own studio.

Her career began in 1898 acting in melodramas. Years of arduous one-night stands led finally to Broadway and stardom—at age fifteen. Two years later she began making movies, hundreds of them over the next twenty-four years, well into the sound era. By 1917 she was earning $1 million or more a year, no small sum for that era. One of her four talkies, *Coquette,* won her an Academy Award in 1929. Meanwhile she and her second husband, popular actor Douglas Fairbanks, reigned as Hollywood's royal couple at Pickfair, their Tudor mansion in Beverly Hills.

Their sixteen-year marriage ended in 1936, but Mary rebounded, married (happily) actor-bandleader Buddy Rogers, produced movies, and thrived on her shrewd investments. But by 1976, when she received a special Academy Award, she was an eighty-four-year-old alcoholic recluse. Three years later "America's Sweetheart" was gone. Her imposing white marble tomb—lavish with cherubs, doves, and grandiosity—speaks of another age; she reclines in the Garden of Remembrance, along with her mother, sister, brother, aunt, and two cousins.

CHARLES DILLON "CASEY" STENGEL *1890–1975*

There have been better baseball players—and probably better managers—than Casey Stengel, but few as colorful. When Charles Dillon Stengel began playing major-league ball as an outfielder for the Brooklyn Dodgers in 1912, he was nicknamed K.C., partly because of his hometown (Kansas City, Missouri), but also because of the poem "Casey at the Bat," which was popular at the time. Thus K.C. soon became Casey forever. Known for his pranks, practical jokes, and disjointed speech, Casey would divert fans by catching fly balls behind his back or tipping his cap, out of which a sparrow flew.

After playing sporadically for fourteen seasons, then managing and coaching in the minor leagues, he became manager of the Brooklyn Dodgers in 1934 and later of the Boston Braves. In 1949, after twenty-five years of managing some of baseball's best and worst teams, Stengel won his stripes, pinstripes that is: as manager of the New York Yankees. In his first season the Yankees won the World Series, and during his twelve-year reign they played in ten Series and won seven.

This gave Stengel baseball's best record as a manager, with sixty-three World Series games played and thirty-seven wins. His tortured language, known as Stengelese, made good copy, so the press and Yankee fans doted on him. When he was finally fired in 1960 because of his age, Stengel had the last word: "I'll never make the mistake of being seventy again."

Four years later he agreed to manage a new National League team, the New York Metropolitans, saying "Most people my age are dead at the present time." The Mets were so bad that during Stengel's four-year tenure, they won 194 games and lost 452, a fact that prompted him to dub them "my amazin' Mets." The Mets later improved and eventually even won two World Series titles; they are still called the "Amazin's," but no longer ironically. After Stengel retired, the Baseball Writers' Association immediately and unanimously elected him to the Hall of Fame, waiving the usual five-year waiting period.

The inscription on his marker on the left wall of the Court of Freedom, beyond a statue of Justice by Daniel Chester French, is pure Stengelese: "There comes a time in every man's life and I've had plenty of them." Amazin'.

JIMMY STEWART 1908–1997

Nice guys don't make the front page of tabloid newspapers. And if anyone in Hollywood fit the definition of Mr. Nice Guy—with no irony intended—it was surely James Maitland Stewart, known throughout his long career as Jimmy. His "aw, shucks," charming, boy-next-door screen persona wasn't just acting—it seems to have been his real-life personality. His was a privileged life, but he never flaunted it. He was the real deal.

Born into a prosperous Indiana, Pennsylvania, family, he graduated from Princeton University, tried Broadway without much luck, then headed west, follow-

ing his friend and fellow actor Henry Fonda, whom he had met in a theater group in Falmouth, Massachusetts. An MGM screen test prompted Stewart's first movie, *The Murder Man,* in 1937, which led to twenty-four films in a five-year period. One was *You Can't Take It With You.* Another, *Mr. Smith Goes to Washington,* garnered him the New York Film Critics best actor award, and in 1940 he won his first and only Oscar for best actor in *The Philadelphia Story.*

Honesty, integrity, and common sense were written all over him in dozens of screen roles, both as contemporary and western heroes. His own heroism was real: From 1941 to the end of World War II, Stewart served in the U.S. Army Air Corps as commander of a bomber squadron. He flew twenty-five missions, earning a Distinguished Flying Cross and the rank of colonel. (Years later, in 1959, his rank was upped to brigadier general in the Air Force Reserve.) When he returned to filmmaking, he refused to let his studio exploit his heroism for publicity purposes.

HOUSE CALL

Though not open to the public, Stewart's house (918 North Roxbury Drive) at the lower end of the canyons off Mulholland Drive can be glimpsed from the road.

Stewart's first postwar movie, *It's a Wonderful Life,* has become a Christmas holiday classic. It is the film most people remember him by, but it wasn't a box office success. Whether through the ability to choose the right scripts or just plain luck, Stewart made many memorable movies—*Destry Rides Again, Call Northside 777,*

Harvey, Vertigo, Rear Window, Anatomy of a Murder, The Man Who Shot Liberty Valance, and *How The West Was Won* among them.

Married late—at age forty-one—Stewart was an anomaly, a star who stayed married to the same woman for forty-five years, raised a family of four, and lived outside the spotlight. Even as he aged, the shy chuckle, slight stutter, and soft-spoken charm remained.

His modest brown bronze gravestone is located in the grass near Wee Kirk o' the Heather churchyard. Follow the direction of the arrow in the bow of the horseman statue at the top of the hill; Stewart's grave is directly in the arrow's path. It reads "James Maitland Stewart—For he shall give his angels charge over thee to keep thee in all thy ways." To his right is the gravestone of his wife, **Gloria Hatrick Stewart** (1918–1994), who preceded him by three years. His message on her grave reads "In our most loving memories, she will always be with us, she made life better."

SPENCER TRACY *1900–1967*

Anyone who has enjoyed Spencer Tracy in such films as *Test Pilot, Adam's Rib,* or *Bad Day at Black Rock,* with his rugged looks and manly appeal, might be surprised to learn that when he went to Hollywood after a few big hits on Broadway, 20th Century Fox studio bosses thought he was too "ugly" to be a leading man. His eighteen films for Fox, as a bad guy or gangster, were mostly discards. A perfectionist, given to fierce arguments over script changes, and a heavy and belligerent drinker, he was finally released by Fox, which may have been the best thing that ever happened to him.

It was when he signed with MGM—and stayed with them for twenty years—that his career took off. Three roles really did it: *San Francisco* (1936), Fritz Lang's *Fury,* and the comedy *Libeled Lady.* From then on, he was able to demonstrate his range—acquired in his early training at New York's American Academy of Dramatic Arts, and before that at Ripon College in Wisconsin—in a variety of films. These included roles as a Portuguese fisherman in *Captains Courageous* (for which he won an Oscar), a priest in *Boys Town* (a second Oscar), a newspaperman in *Stanley and Livingstone,* and an explorer in *Northwest Passage.*

Tracy's style was so natural, it didn't look like acting, about which he once said, "Know your lines and don't bump into the furniture." But in reality, he was known for his painstakingly careful preparation.

It was the nine films he made with Katharine Hepburn that put him—and her—in the superstar class, especially *Adam's Rib, Woman of the Year, State of the Union,* and *Pat and Mike*. Through working together professionally, they developed one of Hollywood's most enduring personal relationships. It lasted twenty-five years, until Tracy's death. Although he was long separated from his wife, Louise, they never divorced. He was a practicing Catholic, and as a young man and onetime Jesuit student, even considered becoming a priest.

When MGM dropped him, mostly because he could be a pain to work with, his career seemed over. But he went on to give fine performances in four Stanley Kramer films in the 1960s: *Inherit the Wind; Judgment at Nuremberg; It's a Mad, Mad, Mad, Mad World;* and, though he was deathly ill during the filming, *Guess Who's Coming to Dinner.* Ever the trouper, he finished the film, though he died before receiving a Best Actor nomination for it (his ninth).

> **FILM VAULT**
>
> Tracy made a lot of movies still worth seeing today, but a sleeper that holds up beautifully is **Libeled Lady** (1936), a madcap comedy with Jean Harlow, Myrna Loy, and William Powell. All four stars dazzle in their frenzied and fun performances.

Outside the Freedom Mausoleum, in the Garden of Peace, to the right of the George Washington statue, Spencer Tracy's mottled gray granite marker (with the word TRACY) is embedded in a tan limestone wall, with a bench in front of it—as low-key and unpretentious as his acting style.

NORTH OF LOS ANGELES

Like so many communities clustered around Los Angeles, the towns in the San Fernando Valley, to the northeast and even as far west as Santa Barbara, have more than their share of departed notables. Most of these were connected to the area's prime industry: filmmaking. Scoping them out, because they are in so many different towns, involves travel, which can be daunting even to intrepid grave explorers. We've summarized alphabetically by town to make it easier for you.

ALTADENA

MOUNTAIN VIEW CEMETERY AND MAUSOLEUM

2400 NORTH FAIR OAKS AVENUE;
(626) 794-7133 OR (800) 468-1095

With hedges all around, Mountain View has sections with such names as Valley View, Royal Oak, Founder's Lawn, and Serene Pastures. Founded in 1882 by Levi W. Giddings (who put himself where his money was—and resides here) and still family-owned, the sprawling grounds look as though they may have seen better days. The graves are well-kept, but the roads are cracked, and the neighborhood might be questionable at night (it's fine in the daytime, though, when the grounds are open). Signs throughout the grounds urge visitors to keep their cars locked and valuables in the trunk. Yet the office is a handsome old building with a gas fireplace in the entrance room and a chapel next door. There is a map, but it is none-too-helpful.

One of founder Giddings's descendants, **Jae Carmichael** (1925–2005), who is now on the premises herself (in Founder's Lawn, lot 1610, grave 19), initiated a cemetery "first": the installation in several dozen historic gravestones of computer chips called Memory Medallions. These chips enable anyone with a handheld or laptop computer to view five-minute silent films on luminaries, even while standing by their grave sites. Carmichael herself was an artist, writer, and independent film-maker, who did much to update the old cemetery.

Full-time residents here cut a wide swath among Civil War generals and Congressional Medal of Honor recipients, U.S. congressmen and diplomats, early governors, scientists, silent-screen stars, musicians, and other entertainers. The most colorful character on the premises may be **Thaddeus S. C. Lowe** (1832–1913; Royal Oaks, lot 761, grave 1), a balloonist and entertainer who claimed provenance all the way back to a baby born on the *Mayflower—after* it landed.

Prominent media types here include **Dr. Frank Baxter** (1896–1982; ashes in vault), who was one of the Public Broadcasting System's earliest stars, host of a series on Shakespearean plays and later a series on science. Also on the premises are radio pioneer **Ted Husing** (1901–1962; Valley View, lot 2258), famous as a play-by-play sportscaster, and religious leader and publisher **Herbert W. Armstrong** (1931–1986; Founder's Lawn, lot 2110), whose *The World Tomorrow* radio and television broadcasts were aired for over fifty years. **J. Vernon McGee** (1904–1988; Radiant Meadows, lot 1726, grave 3) is also present. He founded the Through the Bible radio network, which broadcast over 600 radio stations in the United States and Canada and in thirty-five languages around the world.

Actors at rest here include **Hugh Sanders** (1911–1966; Pompeian Court, crypt 45), who appeared in television and movies, notably as the doctor in *To Kill a Mockingbird,* and **William Wagner** (1883–1964; Sunset Lawn, lot 951, space 4), who played on stage and in film from the 1920s to 1950s.

Look here for such athletes as tennis player **Maurice McLoughlin** (1890–1957; Alpine Meadow, grave 105), who introduced the aggressive serve way back in the early 1900s, when he won many singles and doubles matches and helped make tennis a popular sport. **Mildred Singleton** (1933–2004; Pasadena mausoleum, wall 59, row D1) is also here. The top female athlete of the 1950s, she was a gold medal winner for high jump in the 1956 Olympics and was also great at track and basketball.

Matthew Robinson (1914–2000; Vista del Monte garden crypt), baseball great Jackie Robinson's older brother, was a silver medal winner in the 200-meter race in the 1936 Olympics. Like Jesse Owens, who won multiple gold in the same Olympics, he was an in-his-face African-American winner in Hitler's Aryan Germany.

Scientists in this restful place include seismologist **Charles Richter** (1900–1985; Mountain Meadow, lot 3852, grave 14A), who invented the measuring device by which the magnitude of an earthquake is calculated (the Richter scale), and physicist **Samuel Wesley Stratton** (1861–1931; Royal Oak, lot 704), the first director of the Federal Bureau of Standards. China-born **Mary Stone** (1873–1954; Radiant Meadow, lot 466, grave 2) was a missionary doctor in China who organized that country's first Red Cross and first Women's Christian Temperance Union. She also founded a modern nursing school there.

Once here, but now spirited away, was **Earl Derr Biggers**

LUNCH BREAK

City Thai (48 South Fair Oaks Avenue, Pasadena; 626-577-1500) is an attractive little place in the center of Pasadena, with many Thai specialties. We like the green curry and Kang Ped (red curry) especially, but everything is good value.

(1884–1933), a popular mystery writer and playwright early in the twentieth century. His first mystery was *Seven Keys to Baldpate* (1913), but it was his six mysteries about Charlie Chan, based on a Honolulu Chinese detective he read about on a vacation trip to Hawaii, that made his name; all were adapted to movies. Chan was depicted as wise, honorable, and with a strong moral center. While the Charlie Chan books and movies seem dated today, Biggers intended them as a rebuttal to the rampant racism that existed in an era of fear about "the yellow peril." He liked to lace his stories with Chan aphorisms like "Only very brave mouse makes nest in cat's ear" and "Careless shepherd make excellent dinner for wolf." ★*Grounds and office open 8:00 A.M.–5:00 P.M. daily. Map; restrooms. Walk Through Times, a costumed tour with horse-drawn carriage, is held annually; check at the office for the date.*

ELDRIDGE CLEAVER *1935–1998*

In 1968 California governor Ronald Reagan said, "If Eldridge Cleaver is allowed to teach our children, they may come home one night and slit our throats." As evinced by that quote, Cleaver provoked strong feelings in many Americans with his militancy and inflammatory rhetoric.

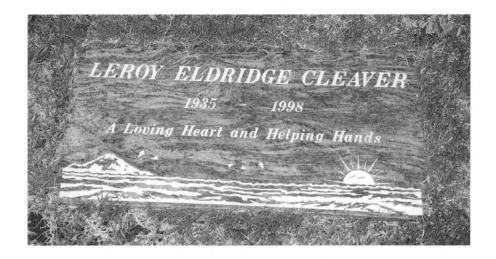

Born in Wabbaseka, Arkansas, as Leroy Eldridge Cleaver, he and his family later moved to Watts, a predominantly black section of Los Angeles. There, as a teenager, he drifted into a life of petty crime. He was imprisoned in 1954 for marijuana possession, and his 1957 release was followed by a conviction for assault with intent to commit murder that same year, earning him a two-to-fourteen-year sentence. While a guest of the state, he penned essays that later became a book, *Soul on Ice,* in 1968.

Politicized in prison, Cleaver, upon his release in 1966, joined the radical Black Panthers and served as its spokesman. The Panthers' militant profile, advocating violence against the white "system," guaranteed they would be clouded in controversy, and Eldridge was one of the lightning rods. While advocating Marxism and encouraging revolutionary and violent behavior, the Panthers also ran some highly visible social programs, such as providing food and shelter to the needy in Oakland.

Cleaver became a legendary figure among some African Americans, gaining admiration for his defiant stance regarding social inequalities and his contempt for the path of change through nonviolent resistance, as advocated by the Reverend Martin Luther King. In 1968 Cleaver ran for president of the United States on the Peace and Freedom Party ticket. Later that turbulent year he was wounded in a gunfight the Panthers had started with the Oakland police.

Charged with attempted murder, Cleaver skipped bail and fled the country, ending up in France. While there he experienced a religious conversion to Christianity. He returned to the United States in 1975, renounced the Panthers, and faced his attempted murder charge. This was eventually reduced to assault, earning him a sentence of probation and community service.

His memoir, *Soul on Fire*, detailing his various conversions, was published in 1978. Still seeking religious guidance, he became a follower of the Reverend Sun Myung Moon. In the early 1980s Cleaver alienated many of his followers when he unsuccessfully ran for a Republican senate nomination in California and supported Ronald Reagan for president. By the mid-1980s he was addicted to crack cocaine and was convicted for burglary and cocaine possession. In 1994 he was hospitalized for injuries inflicted by another addict, but recovered with the support of his family and his immersion in Christianity.

On May 1, 1998, Eldridge Cleaver died at age sixty-two at Pomona Valley Hospital; his family refused to reveal the cause of his death. His simple mottled-gray granite grave stone (#4599 in the ground) is in the rear of the Valley View section, near the hedge, in front of an upright headstone bearing the name LAUGHARN. It is next to a sprinkler, between two trees. For one whose life was filled with tumult and rebellion and restless searching, he may have found peace here at last.

RICHARD PHILLIPS FEYNMAN *1918–1988*

The most famous scientific name on the premises belongs to Richard Phillips Feynman, a man, or now shade, of many parts: physicist, mathematician, author, co-winner of the 1965 Nobel Prize in physics for quantum electrodynamics, professor for most of his career at California Institute of Technology.

A graduate of M.I.T., with a doctorate from Princeton, Feynman was a prodigy at age twenty-three. He worked on the atomic bomb project at Princeton and later at Los Alamos, New Mexico.

His unprepossessing gray granite stone, with a darker border, #1617, lies flush with the grass in the Founder's Lawn section, across the road from the curb stenciled with #4460. His wife, **Gweneth M. Feynman** (1934–1989), is beneath the same stone that bears his name and the words "In loving memory."

GEORGE REEVES *1914–1959*

Although his 1950s television alter ego, Superman, could do so, actor George Reeves wasn't able to move faster than the speeding bullet that ended his earthly life.

Film buffs will recognize Reeves as one of the Tarleton twins wooing Scarlett O'Hara in *Gone With the Wind*, but his place in history will forever be linked with his role as TV's Man of Steel. Born George Keefer Brewer, Reeves put his budding film career on hold when he joined the U.S. Army Air Corps, where he appeared in training films. After his discharge, he took off-screen menial jobs and sporadic bit roles in mostly B films, before he somewhat reluctantly assumed the role of Superman.

Reeves was frustrated that he became so identified with the role, he found it almost impossible to get serious film work.

Mere days before his wedding, late on a night when he and his fiancée, Lenore Lemmon, entertained friends at his home, he retired while the others were still downstairs. A shot was heard, and Reeves was found in bed with a fatal gunshot wound through his head. Officially, a ruling of suicide was rendered, but subsequent investigations clearly challenged that finding and raised the question of whether or not he was actually murdered. His quick demise remains one of Hollywood's unsolved mysteries; however, no kryptonite was found at the scene, effectively clearing Superman's nemesis, Lex Luthor.

Reeves's last known residence is in the Pasadena mausoleum, Sunrise corridor.

C H A T S W O R T H

OAKWOOD MEMORIAL PARK

22601 LASSEN STREET;
(818) 341-0344

Located in a pleasant residential neighborhood, Oakwood (which opened in 1924) is a little bower, with rolling hills, an abundance of trees, private mausoleums, several terra-cotta grottoes, gardenlike areas with religious statues, a chapel, and a pretty steepled church. Sections have names like Oak Glen, Acacia, Vale of Memory, Sequoia, and Willow Heights. The Anglican church, we learned, was saved from destruction and moved to the Oakwood grounds, courtesy of Roy Rogers, who lived nearby. Several signs on the grounds in October offer this advice: CAUTION: RATTLESNAKE SEASON. Let the stroller beware.

Star quality among numerous actors who have found final peace at Oakwood belongs to **Gloria Grahame** (1923–1981; Pioneer section, lot 242, grave 8), who played many good-hearted "bad" girls. She won a Best Supporting Actress Oscar for her role in *The Bad and the Beautiful* (1952).

Other actors here include **Adele Jergens** (1917–2002; Pioneer section, lot 533, grave 1), Brooklyn-born model, chorus girl, and B-movie bombshell. Her films included some with Red Skelton and Abbott and Costello. Her husband, **Glenn Langan** (1917–1991; same location), was in *Fury at Furnace Creek, Treasure of Monte Cristo,* and other films spanning thirty years.

Actress **Grace Cunard** (1893–1967; section C, lot 870) appeared in more than

120 silent films and wrote some 30 as well. **Trinity Loren** (1963–1998; Pioneer section, lot 441, grave 2) was a porn star in films such as *The Wild, Wild Chest.* Enough said.

Here, in the mausoleum, wall niche 357, is **Stephen Boyd** (1931–1977; mausoleum 1, north wall, niche 257), who acted in movies for over twenty-five years but never had star billing. Historical epics were his specialty, like *The Bible* and *Ben-Hur,* in which he won praise for his role as Messala.

Also riding the Oakwood range is **Alphonso "Al" Jennings** (1863–1961; Vale of Memory section, lot 29, grave 2), who had an amazing life, first as a lawyer, then as an outlaw who robbed banks. He was caught and jailed for five years. When he came out, he practiced law again, then became an actor (considered the first cowboy actor in western films of the silent era) and producer of a film about his own life, *Al Jennings of Oklahoma* (1951).

Other actors here are Chicago-born **John Samuel "Jack" Ingram** (1902–1969; section F, lot 140, grave 5), who appeared in more than 200 movies, most of them westerns, and **Russell "Lucky" Hayden** (1912–1981; section H, lot 174, grave 5), actor in the Hopalong Cassidy serial (playing Lucky Jenkins) and other cowboy films. **Roger Raymond Greenleaf** (1892–1963; section D, lot 295, grave 1) acted in thirty-one television series (from *The Lone Ranger* to *Dragnet* and *Perry Mason*) and fifty-six movies (including *All the King's Men* and *Birdman of Alcatraz*).

Frank Kelly Freas (1922–2005; Sequoia section, lot 458, grave 1) is here, too. As a magazine and science-fiction book illustrator, he was most responsible for *MAD Magazine*'s Alfred E. Neuman image.

Ted Snyder (1881–1965; section H, lot 223, grave 6), composer of "The Sheik of Araby," "Who's Sorry Now?" and other songs, earned his place in history by giving Irving Berlin his first break, in 1909, as a pianist for a music publishing company. Together they wrote many songs, with Berlin providing the lyrics, Snyder the music.

Also somewhere on the premises is **Dorothy Mackaye** (1899–1940; ashes in unknown, unmarked grave), stage and film actress whose major role was in a scorching real-life murder. She and her lover, actor Paul Kelly, were convicted of manslaughter in the killing of Mackaye's husband, fellow actor Ray Raymond (Kelly did the actual deed). After serving time, the guilty lovers eventually married.

Bob Crane (1928–1978) of *Hogan's Heroes* fame, another victim of True Crimes, *was* here, but his final address has been changed to Pierce Brothers Westwood Village Memorial Park in Los Angeles. ★*Grounds open 8:30 A.M.–5:00 P.M. daily. Office hours: 8:30 A.M.–4:30 P.M. daily, except Sunday. Map; restrooms.*

FRED ASTAIRE *1899–1987*

"Can't act. Can't sing. Balding. Can dance a little." Not much of an appraisal of a budding Hollywood wannabe. What happened to the Paramount executive who wrote that report of a screen test is unknown, but the potential failure he was writing about? Fred Astaire.

While it is rumored that Astaire was born in tails and a top hat, he was actually a regular baby, born in Omaha, Nebraska, to a family named Austerlitz. The name Astaire was borrowed from an uncle, whose last name was L' Astaire, when Fred and his sister, Adele, were developing their dancing act for vaudeville. The team was so successful that they appeared in top Broadway shows in the 1920s—*Lady Be Good, Funny Face, The Gay Divorcee,* and *The Band Wagon* among them.

Adele broke up the act in 1932 when she left to marry an English lord, Charles Cavendish. Astaire's first movie was *Dancing Lady* in 1933, in which he danced with Joan Crawford. He really began to soar, though, the same year in his first film with Ginger Rogers, *Flying Down to Rio,* in which they introduced the carioca.

From then on, through ten Astaire-Rogers films, Fred showed the range of his dancing virtuosity, from tap to tangos, waltzes, and variations of ballroom. He worked hard to make his dancing look easy. Most of their 1930s films had simple, often silly, plots, in glamorous settings with sophisticated gowns for Rogers and tux and top hat for Astaire; they had enormous appeal to Depression audiences.

The films also introduced songs by some of the best composers of the time—George Gershwin, Cole Porter, Irving Berlin, and Jerome Kern. Such hits as "They Can't Take That Away from Me" (Gershwin), "Night and Day" (Porter), "Cheek to Cheek" (Berlin), and "The Way You Look Tonight" (Kern) were sung by Rogers and Astaire. Somehow, Astaire's light, reedy voice was good enough to carry the tunes and, with his winsome, effervescent charm, added to the appeal of each film.

When Rogers left to test her wings in dramatic roles, Astaire soldiered on, making a total of forty-four films in his long career, all but a handful of them musicals. Each was as charming as the previous. He had other dance partners, among them Eleanor Powell, Rita Hayworth, Joan Leslie, and Cyd Charisse. Two standout films were *Funny Face* (1953) with Audrey Hepburn and *Silk Stockings* (1958) with Charisse. His last musical was *Finian's Rainbow* in 1968 (he was sixty-nine), and his dancing/singing partner was Petula Clark.

His roles in two serious films, *On the Beach* (1959) and *The Towering Inferno* (1974), earned high critical praise. The latter film won him his only Oscar nomination, though his work with Helen Hayes in *A Family Upside Down* on television (1978) earned him an Emmy.

Awards were many: an honorary Academy Award (in 1950), Emmys (1961 and 1978), Kennedy Center Honors (1978), American Film Institute's Lifetime Achievement Award (1981). In 1980, at age eighty-one, Astaire married for the second time (he had a son, Fred Jr., and daughter, Ava, by his first wife, Phyllis Baker Potter, who died in 1954). His new wife, Robyn Smith, was an actress-turned-jockey. She was almost fifty years younger than he, but they had seven, presumably happy, years together.

Near the Oakwood entrance, down a slight slope from the curb in G of the Sequoia section, lot 82, is the Astaire grave. His simple stone, set into the grass, reads "I will always love you my darling * THANK YOU." Resting three graves above his, to the right, are those of his mother and of his sister, **Adele Astaire Douglass** (1897–1981).

GINGER ROGERS *1911–1995*

Rogers and Astaire together again—here in Oakwood. As part of the most famous ballroom dancing team in movie history, Ginger Rogers is often cited by feminists who claim "she did everything Astaire did but backwards and on high heels."

She could act. She proved it by quitting her career as a dancer and lead in musical comedies in order to try to make it as a serious actress. She not only made it—in such films as *Stage Door* (1937), *Primrose Path* (1940), *I'll Be Seeing You* (1944), and *Perfect Strangers* (1950), among others—but won an Oscar for her role as a working-class girl in *Kitty Foyle* (1940).

Let's flash back to the beginning. Virginia Katherine MacMath was born in Independence, Missouri. The name Ginger came from the way a cousin mispronounced Virginia, and Rogers was the last name of her mother's second husband. Her family moved to Texas when Ginger was a toddler, her parents divorced soon thereafter, and her father died a few years later when she was eleven.

Meanwhile, Ginger and her mother were vagabonds, moving frequently and ending up in Fort Worth, where Ginger attended high school. Single-mindedly, she knew she wanted to be on the stage, so heading for Broadway was a "given." From a small role in *Top Speed,* she got a screen test and was Hollywood-bound. While Rogers had bit parts and several decent secondary roles, especially in *42nd Street* and *Gold Diggers of 1933* (with her key number "We're in the Money"), it was the pairing with Astaire that made her famous. Though the plots were often flimsy, their chemistry was not, and their graceful dancing and easy repartee helped Depression audiences forget their problems.

In her solo career, Rogers made comedies as well as serious films, with some of her comedies, like *Roxie Hart* (1942) and *It Had to Be You* (1947), proving what a light, deft touch she had. All in all, she made more than sixty movies; *Harlow* in 1965 was her last. That year she continued on to Broadway as the lead in *Hello Dolly!* and later starred in *Mame* in London for fourteen months. She then directed an updated version of the Rogers and Hart musical comedy *Babes in Arms*. She finally retired in 1984.

A multitalented woman—she won several tennis trophies, played golf, was a good swimmer and skeet shooter, owned a dairy farm, and bred Guernsey cows—Rogers may have been too formidable for the men in her life. She was married and divorced five times.

Her final abode is to the right of the main entrance on Valley Road, the E part of the Vale of Memory section, lot 303, grave 1. Her bronze plaque has a rose in bas-relief in the top two corners. It seems only fitting that Ginger's gravestone is shared with her mother, **Lela Rogers** (1880–1977), who was her lifetime promoter, booster, confidante, and best friend.

EDEN MEMORIAL PARK

11500 SEPULVEDA BOULEVARD; (818) 361-7161

The Jewish Eden Memorial Park is across the road from Catholic San Fernando Mission Cemetery, making it easy to visit both on a single trip. The terrain is steeply hilly with a few pine trees; most graves are noted by markers in the ground. There are few headstones, but three modern, utilitarian mausoleums. Cypresses line the road by the uppermost mausoleum. Benches near the road are thoughtful touches, designed for meditation. The map is of little help in finding the graves, and the office personnel will not divulge locations.

As in most Los Angeles–area graveyards, Eden has its share of film folk. They include actor **John Brown** (1904–1957; Akiba section, 17-55), best known for his reprise of Digger O'Dell, the friendly mortician on the television show *The Life of Riley*; **Harvey Lembeck** (1923–1982; Mount Jerusalem section), actor in the Beach Blanket movies, plus

> ## LUNCH BREAK
> With the smoky aroma and sawdust on the floor, **The Bear Pit Bar-B-Que** (10825 Sepulveda; 818-365-2509) is a casual spot for a touch of barbecue. We like the sandwiches best.

many others; and child actress **Mitzi Green** (1920–1969; Garden of Love section), who played in many 1930s films. ★*Grounds open 8:00 A.M.–5:00 P.M. daily, except Saturday. Office hours: 9:00 A.M.–5:00 P.M. daily, except Saturday. Map; restrooms.*

LENNY BRUCE *1925–1966*

Talking dirty and influencing people was what Lenny Bruce excelled at, and his influence still reverberates today. A New York City native, he served in the U.S. Navy and after his 1946 discharge moved to Hollywood to pursue an acting career. With the move, he changed his name from Leonard Alfred Schneider to Lenny Bruce. Without much luck in Hollywood, he wound up back in New York nightclubs performing stand-up comedy and impressions for ever-growing crowds.

His act differed from a lot of contemporary comics: He didn't rely on one-liners and jokes about his mother-in-law but incorporated social commentary and improvisational riffs that pointed out idiosyncrasies in politics, religion, race relations, and social mores. His frankness dealing with adult subjects was provocative and won him a following among young people of the baby boomer generation and intellectuals, but also attracted the ire of those not ready for his cutting-edge topics and full-frontal vocabulary.

He said things in his act that at the time, the 1960s, were shocking and considered blasphemous, such as "Since they condone capital punishment, I want them to stop bitching about Jesus getting nailed up," or "If something about the human body disgusts you, complain to the manufacturer."

In 1951, while doing stand-up on the nightclub circuit, Bruce met and married a stripper with the stage name of Hot Honey Harlowe (Harriett Jolliff was her real name); they divorced in 1957. (Their relationship was dramatized in the 1974 biopic *Lenny*.) He released some comedy records and appeared on *The Arthur Godfrey Show* and *The Steve Allen Show,* among others. He was a favorite guest of Hugh Hefner, who championed Bruce as a defender of the First Amendment. Beginning in 1963, Hefner released Bruce's autobiography, *How to Talk Dirty and Influence People,* in installments in *Playboy* magazine. It was published as a book in 1965.

Bruce was arrested for obscenity in San Francisco in 1961 after a nightclub performance. He was later acquitted, but he had become a target for the authorities, who repeatedly arrested and harassed him for his use of forbidden language onstage. Long before the "f" word became common coinage on the comedy circuit and cable television, Bruce used it constantly as part of his act to accentuate various points he was making.

Soon, nightclub owners stopped hiring him because they didn't want a performer in their clubs arrested for obscenity; also, his act was becoming increasingly preoccupied with his legal cases and less about his comedy. Some "performances" consisted of Bruce reading from his court transcripts. Needless to say, audiences (and club owners) were less than thrilled. As if he didn't have enough difficulties, in 1963 he was busted for drug possession.

In 1964 Bruce was convicted of obscenity in New York City. He was publicly supported in his fight for free speech by literati such as Norman Mailer, James Baldwin, John Updike, and William Styron. He appealed his conviction. Two years later Bruce was found dead of a drug overdose at home in Hollywood; he was forty years old. In 2003 he was pardoned posthumously by New York governor George Pataki.

Bruce can be found in the Mount Nebo section, plot 298-C in the ground. His stone, surrounded by grass, states "Lenny 'Bruce' Schneider * Beloved Father * Devoted Son * Peace at last." Who can argue with that?—even though it sounds too conventional for the man.

GROUCHO MARX *1890–1977*

Groucho (born Julius Henry Marx in New York City) was the Marx Brother whose show business career continued beyond the highly successful partnership with his brothers. He and three of his four brothers—Chico, Harpo, and Gummo (Zeppo joined later)—had a variety of vaudeville acts managed by their mother, Minnie, which led to Broadway comedy success in *I'll Say She Is, The Cocoanuts,* and *Animal Crackers.* Each brother had a well-defined persona. Groucho's was that of an unprincipled, wisecracking schemer, wearing a greasepaint mustache and smoking a large cigar, quick on the puns and double entendres, delivered slyly in rapid fire.

The brothers' anarchic comedy style lent itself to rampant ad-libs, to the delight of audiences and the chagrin of writers. This led George S. Kaufman (co-author of *The Cocoanuts* and *Animal Crackers*) to say during one of their stage performances, "Wait, I thought I heard one of my lines." In 1929 a film version of *The Cocoanuts* introduced the Marx Brothers to world-wide audiences (Gummo dropped out of the act and was replaced by Zeppo as the "straight man"). *Animal Crackers, Monkey Business, Horse Feathers, Duck Soup,* and *A Night at the Opera* followed and delivered outrageous comedy that is still fresh.

Invariably Groucho was paired with a wealthy dowager, played by the stout Margaret Dumont, whose money, not her person, attracted him. Dumont was his virtual "straight man," allowing him to bounce insults and puns off her with impunity; she seemed oblivious of every rude crack he threw her way. Behind the scenes, Groucho asserted that Dumont really didn't get the gags. Some famous Groucho-isms directed at Dumont: "Marry me and I'll never look at another horse"; "Will you marry me? Did he leave you any money? Answer the second question first"; "We're fighting for this woman's honor, which is probably more than she ever did"; "I've had a perfectly wonderful evening, but this wasn't it"; "I never forget a face, but in your case I'll make an exception."

The later Marx Brothers films (*A Day at the Races, Room Service, At the Circus, Go West, The Big Store, A Night in Casablanca,* and *Love Happy*) lacked the caliber of writing of the early films, and the brothers seemed as tired as the gags. After *Love Happy,* except for guest appearances and bit parts, Chico and Harpo virtually retired (Zeppo had left the group after *Duck Soup* to open a successful theatrical agency), but Groucho was just gathering steam.

First, he acted in several unremarkable films (*Copacabana, Double Dynamite, Will Success Spoil Rock Hunter?*), but his next big success was hosting the radio and then television quiz show *You Bet Your Life.* This allowed Groucho (with a real mustache) to ad-lib and be the center of attention, which fit him like a glove. A classic example of his sly wit on the show was this exchange with a female contestant who said she had eight children: GROUCHO: "Eight children! Eight?" WOMAN: "Well, I love my husband." GROUCHO: "I love my cigar, but I take it out every now and then."

The show aired through 1961, then Groucho "retired." However, through television film festivals, the Marx Brothers were introduced to a new generation of fans. In 1972 Groucho performed in a one-man show, culminating in a sold-out performance at Carnegie Hall. This was recorded and released on a double album called *An Evening With Groucho*. In 1974 he received a special Oscar at the Academy Awards.

In his later years Groucho descended into senility; he died of pneumonia at age eighty-six. Regarding his death he once said, "I wish to be cremated. One tenth of my ashes shall be given to my agent, as written in our contract."

Here are a few favorite Groucho-isms: "Time flies like the wind, fruit flies like bananas"; "Now there's a man with an open mind, you can feel the breeze from here"; "One morning I shot an elephant in my pajamas. How he got in my pajamas I'll never know."

Woody Allen described Groucho as "the best comedian this country ever produced," saying, "he is simply unique in the same way that Picasso or Stravinsky are." A famous French witticism was "Je suis Marxiste, tendance Groucho." ("I'm a Marxist of the Groucho variety.")

It seems appropriate that one of comedy's most famous cutups would have capacious final digs, but that's not the way it is—and for a reason. Five years after his death, Groucho's ashes were stolen and later recovered at another cemetery (Mount Sinai Memorial Park, 12 miles away). Whether the theft was a disgruntled agent's revenge, a fan's whim, a collegiate's idea of humor, or an attempt at ransom, Eden did the ultimate, treating the ashes as a matter of high security with security devices installed throughout the grounds. Look in the Court of the Tribes mausoleum (the first one up from the office, facing the Hills of Judea section). Inside the second door on the left, there is a very small room, about 10 by 12 feet. In the center of the right wall is Groucho's bronze marker, with his name, dates, and a Star of David. While not quite Fort Knox or a metropolitan airport, Eden is wired. Groucho might be amused.

SAN FERNANDO MISSION CEMETERY AND MAUSOLEUM

11160 STRANWOOD AVENUE; (818) 361-7387

In this eighty-six-acre Catholic graveyard, the terrain is level, with most tombstones flush with the ground. Religious statues are interspersed among a few tall palms and olive and pine trees. The tan brick walls and buildings with red tile roofs are in the Spanish mission style, which echoes the authentic old San Fernando Mission adjacent to the cemetery.

Many of Mexican and other Hispanic descent are buried here, and at Christmastime the graves are decorated with ornaments, candy canes, tinsel, tiny artificial Christmas trees, and even wrapped gifts. The saddest graves are those of babies; during the holidays they are often piled high with gifts and toys.

There were no superstars resting here until Bob Hope's arrival in 2003, but a number of remarkable character actors who were the joy of many devout movie fans of Hollywood's Golden Age. One of our favorites was **Edward Arnold** (1890–1956; section D, lot 132, grave 9), born Gunther Edward Arnold Schneider. Portly and imposing, he embodied steely bankers, corrupt politicians (as in *Meet John Doe*), and pompous white-collar villains in more than 150 movies. The list includes *You Can't Take It With You, Diamond Jim, Mr. Smith Goes to Washington,* and *The Great Ziegfeld.*

William Bendix (1906–1964; section D, lot 241, grave 10, by a large tree) is known to movie lovers mostly for his roles as none-too-bright palookas, sometimes brutal, sometimes with a heart of gold. But he was a much better actor than such roles suggested and could do tragedy as well as comedy. Among the more than fifty movies he played in: *Lifeboat* (maybe his best performance), *Woman of the Year, The Babe Ruth Story,* and *Detective Story*. His biggest bid for immortality was as Riley in the movie, radio show, and television series *The Life of Riley.*

Others you will encounter here are **William Frawley** (1887–1966; section C, lot 66, grave 4), who played Fred Mertz on television's *I Love Lucy* and later appeared in *My Three Sons,* and **Henry O'Neill** (1891–1961; section C, lot 124, grave 7), who appeared in more than 200 movies.

Ed Begley Sr. (1901–1970; section C, block 8, lot 401, halfway to the wall) won a Best Supporting Actor Oscar for *Sweet Bird of Youth* and also appeared in *12 Angry Men, Boomerang!* and *Sorry, Wrong Number,* among other films. He was the father of actor Ed Begley Jr.

Gerald "Jerry" Colonna (1904–1986; section B, lot 848, grave 7) is here. This trombone-playing musician and comic actor with intense brown eyes and a walrus moustache is best known as Bob Hope's sidekick in three of the Hope-Crosby "Road" pictures. Another comic "between engagements" here is **George Gobel** (1919–1991; section D, lot 191, grave 3), aka "Lonesome George," the Emmy award–winning stand-up comedian who once had his own television show.

Actor **Kevin Joseph "Chuck" Connors** (1921–1992; section J, lot 20, grave 123) played in movies (*Pat and Mike, Flipper*), but was best known as the star of television's *The Rifleman* and *Branded.* He may be the only actor who played both professional basketball and baseball for two major-league teams (Chicago Cubs and Brooklyn Dodgers).

Another notable resident is **Ritchie Valens** (1941–1959; section C, lot 248, grave 2), the first Latino rock star, whose hit recordings were "Come On, Let's Go,"

"Donna," and "La Bamba." He died while on a national concert tour during a blinding Iowa snowstorm in the same plane crash that killed Buddy Holly. Valens's family name, Valenzuela, is on his ornately etched headstone, which he shares with his mother, **Concepcion Reyes** (1915–1987). A 1987 movie, *La Bamba,* tells the story of his short life. ★*Grounds open 8:00 A.M.–5:00 P.M. daily. Office hours: 8:00 A.M.–5:00 P.M. Monday–Friday, 8:00 A.M.–4:00 P.M. Saturday, 10:00 A.M.–3:00 P.M. Sunday. San Fernando Mission (the only entry to Bob Hope's grave) is open 9:00 A.M.–4:30 P.M. daily, except Thanksgiving and Christmas. Map; restrooms; Sunday mass 9:00 A.m. and 10:30 A.M.*

WALTER BRENNAN *1894–1974*

Character actors may not bring you to a movie theater, but they are often the ones you remember when you leave. Look at all the great westerns—most were ensemble works, dependent on a cast of believable characters. Walter Brennan was one of the best. In a forty-five-year career, he appeared in over 450 movies and won a Best Supporting Actor Oscar three times (for *Come and Get It, Kentucky,* and as Judge Roy Bean in *The Westerner*), the first actor to do so.

When he was only forty-one he created the role of a scruffy, obstreperous codger and played a similar part many times over. He had scores of other

characters—comic and tragic—in his versatile repertoire. Much of his best work was for director Howard Hawks and with Gary Cooper, a close friend. Directors liked Brennan's work ethic and reliability as much as his talent, and he worked for many top-notch ones—Hawks, Fritz Lang, John Ford, Henry Hathaway—holding his own with actors like Cooper, Henry Fonda, Spencer Tracy, John Wayne, Jimmy Stewart, and Gregory Peck. Married for fifty-four years to his high school sweetheart, Brennan continued to work into his seventies, moving easily into television—and the sitcom *The Real McCoys*—when movie roles dried up. No question about it, *he* was the real McCoy.

Brennan's grave, in section D, lot 445, grave 8, is two to the left of the 445-marked curb.

BOB HOPE *1903–2003*

The indefatigable Bob Hope made it all the way to his hundredth birthday, one of the longest runs in show business. He was over ninety when he co-hosted his last television special, *Laughing With the Presidents,* and still made up to 300 appearances a year. He was *almost* ninety when he entertained U.S. troops in the first Gulf War and eighty-five when he made a cameo appearance in *Spies Like Us*.

Hope, born Leslie Townes Hope in Eltham, England, moved to Cleveland, Ohio, when he was three years old. It's hard to see him as a boxer, but he tried his hand as an amateur, under the name Packy East (sounds like a Hope character). He later made a joke of it: "Some fighters are carried back to their dressing rooms. I'm the only one who had to be carried both ways."

He had better luck in vaudeville as a dancer (a pretty good one), with a little singing and a lot of jokes thrown in. His debut Broadway show was the musical *Roberta* in 1932, which also featured Fred MacMurray and George Murphy. It was Murphy who introduced him to Dolores Reade, a nightclub singer. Hope and Reade were married the same year, a union that lasted until his death. They later adopted four children, Linda, Tony, Nora, and Kelly.

Next, career-wise, came *The Ziegfeld Follies of 1935* and in 1936 the Cole Porter Broadway hit *Red, Hot and Blue,* in which Hope shared top billing with Ethel Merman and Jimmy Durante. The audience loved Hope's ad-libbing onstage, but Merman hated it, saying, "If that so-called comedian ever behaves like that again, I'll use my shoe to remodel his ski nose." He did, but she didn't. (The nose was just one of many things that Hope used as grist for his comedy.)

Then it was bye, bye Broadway, hello Hollywood. His first movie was *The Big Broadcast of 1938*, followed by *Some Like It Hot* and one of Hope's best ever, *The Cat and the Canary* (both in 1939), which moved him up into stardom. *Ghost Breakers* in 1940 continued a successful formula that worked again and again for him in the "Road" pictures: a plot that splices spooks and mystery with laughs. Hope's movie persona was often the amiable goofball, often a scaredy-cat, always personable. In all, he made more than sixty films. The biggest hits were the "Road" pictures with Bing Crosby and Dorothy Lamour: *Road to Singapore, Road to Morocco,* and the like, seven in all.

Radio was a natural medium for him—but then everything was, it turned out. From the late 1930s to mid-1950s, his rapid-fire monologue (abetted by a huge stable of joke writers) and wisecracks on *The Pepsodent Show* had a huge audience. "Thanks For the Memory," which he sang at the end of each weekly show, became forever associated with him.

At the beginning of World War II, Hope joined a Victory Cavalcade of Stars traveling the United States to raise $1 billion in war bonds. This soon led to a USO tour of combat zones abroad, first in North Africa and Italy, later in the Pacific. The gratitude and laughter of the troops gave Hope such a buzz, it started a practice that carried him to almost every continent through every war in every decade of the rest of his life.

The man never stopped. On television he was master of ceremonies at the Academy Awards and host of endless charity golf tournaments and other charitable events. He was honored by Congress, which adopted a resolution on his ninety-fourth birthday, with a resolution making him an honorary veteran of the armed forces. He was also knighted by Queen Elizabeth with an Order of the British Empire and was the recipient of more than fifty honorary college degrees.

Though the address of Hope's grave is the cemetery, it can only be reached by going outside the cemetery grounds around the block to San Fernando Boulevard and the Mission of San Fernando. Enter the mission church (a minuscule admission charge), which dates back to 1804. It in itself is worth a visit to see the ornate six-teenth-century gold leaf–covered reredos behind the altar. Behind the church is a pretty garden, with a fountain, palms, pines, orange and kapok trees, and poinsettias.

Past this garden is a second one called the Bob Hope Memorial Garden. When his wife asked Hope where he wished to be buried, he replied, "Surprise me!" and this lovely private garden might surprise and delight anyone who visits. A rosy beige marble walkway leads past a memorial wall of bas-reliefs on the right, highlighting important aspects of Hope's long career. A centerpiece of the garden is a replica of a famous Our Lady of Hope statue in Pontmain, France.

On the left side of the garden, up several steps, are Bob Hope's and his family's Spanish limestone sarcophagi in a marble alcove (Dolores's is not yet occupied). In this alcove is a bronze replica of Anna Hyatt Huntington's *The Holy Family Resting.* To the left of Hope's grave is that of his son, **Anthony J. Hope** (1940–2004), and Dolores's mother, **Teresa Kelly Da Fina** (1890–1977).

CHURCH OF OUR SAVIOUR CEMETERY

601 NORTH ROSES ROAD;
(818) 282-2764

As you enter the grounds, the cemetery is on the left, and to the right, beyond a magnificent jacaranda tree, is the simple and lovely Anglican Church of Our Saviour. You might drop by the church first to see the luminous stained-glass window depicting St. George slaying the dragon, which was donated in memory of General George Smith Patton Jr., a long-standing church member. Behind the church in a quiet garden is a large bronze statue of the general, with a stone proclaiming him "a son of the parish."

The pretty little cemetery is marked by private mausoleums, obelisks, scores of gorgeous old trees—birches, palms, a row of shiny avocados and an ivy-covered fence. The homey one-person office is inside an attractive old frame house, to the right of the front parlor. The pace here is agreeably slow.

Certainly the best-known residents are the Patton family, to be found just next to the curb in section G. While **General George Smith Patton Jr.,** "The Liberator," (1885–1945) has a gravestone near his father's, mother's, and sister's, he was, as the stone says, "buried with his men of the U.S. Third Army in Hamm, Luxembourg."

An imposing Celtic cross in gray granite honors him with a quote from Psalm XIV that begins "Lord who shall dwell in thy tabernacle . . ." Patton—a brave, irascible, hard-fighting military man (as the 1970 movie *Patton* reveals)—was a hero, flawed certainly, of World War II.

Family members who *do* reside here are **George Patton Sr.** (as his gravestone states, "born in Charleston, Virginia 1856, died in Lake Vineyard, California 1927"); his wife, **Ruth Wilson** ("born Lake Vineyard, California 1861, died Lake Vineyard 1928"); and their daughter, **Anne Wilson Patton** (1887–1971).

LUNCH BREAK

Pasadena is just a few blocks away and has scores of good places to eat. **Kansai** (36 South Fair Oaks Avenue; 626-564-1560), a small, inexpensive Japanese restaurant, offers hearty noodle soups and other tasty dishes. For something a bit fancier, yet still casual, there's **Crocodile Cafe** (140 South Lake Street; 626-449-9900) for well-prepared eclectic food. The grilled dishes are especially well done, as are the pizzas (from the wood-burning oven) and salads.

HENRY MATHER GREENE *1870–1954*

To admirers of early modern California architecture, Greene & Greene is a familiar name. Together, Henry and his older brother, Charles Sumner Greene, designed and built scores of homes in the Los Angeles–Pasadena area in eleven years. Like so many who found fame and fortune in California at the time, the Greenes were eastern transplants. They were born into a Cincinnati, Ohio, family with venerable New England pedigrees on both sides. But the family soon moved to St. Louis, where their father practiced medicine.

The brothers attended the School of Architecture of the Massachusetts Institute of Technology, and later apprenticed with Boston architectural firms. While in Boston, they visited exhibits of Japanese arts and handcrafts, something new to Americans at the time. Charles, the more artistic of the brothers, was especially susceptible to the beauty and simplicity of Japanese design, concepts on which the brothers drew in their own work.

Following their parents to California in 1893, the Greenes opened their own architectural office in Pasadena. Success, mostly by word of mouth, came quickly. Charles, the artist-designer, and Henry, the practical manager whose forte was construction, made a perfect team. Their highly prolific partnership lasted until 1916 when

HOUSE CALLS

Taking a tour of **The Gamble House** (4 Westmoreland Place, Pasadena; 626-793-3334) is a wonderful way to see the Greene brothers' work. The 1908 house and its integrated furnishings were designed by the Greenes with impeccable taste. It is essential to reserve ahead for the one-hour tour. Another nearby example of the Greenes' work is a room with their furniture and interiors on display in the Huntington Library, Art Collections, and Botanical Gardens (1151 Oxford Road, San Marino; 626-405-2141).

Charles and his family moved to Carmel. The brothers died three years apart, Henry first, then Charles in 1957.

Unfortunately, they lived long enough to see many of their houses demolished, including their parents' 1921 home in Carmel. All told, sixty-three Greene & Greene buildings (not just houses) have been destroyed. The good news is that seventy-four

Greene houses still exist, along with an elementary school, studio, and store, most of them in Pasadena.

While the Greenes were never big national names like Frank Lloyd Wright, they worked with a similar approach, using natural materials, earthy colors, and deceptively simple designs. Because the Greenes did mostly domestic architecture, they lacked the bold impact of Wright. Yet, like Wright, they believed an architect should have control of the entire building environment, inside and out.

Henry Greene's simple gravestone in two tones of gray, with floral motifs surrounding his dates, is in section S, 871. Look for the curb marking S226. To his right is the similar stone of **Emeline Dart Green** (1876–1935), his wife of thirty-six years.

S A N   M A R I N O

HUNTINGTON LIBRARY, ART COLLECTIONS, AND BOTANICAL GARDENS

1151 OXFORD ROAD;
(626) 405-2141;
WWW.HUNTINGTON.ORG

This vast 207-acre estate is beautiful by any standards. The 150 acres of gardens alone are among California's jewels. The property was the home of Henry Huntington and his wife, Arabella. In keeping with the beauty of the surroundings is the white marble mausoleum where both Huntingtons lie in stately and perpetual rest. It is at the opposite end of the property from the entrance—a pleasant walk.

Designed in the round, with a double colonnade, modeled on an amalgam of Roman temples and other monuments, it was the work of architect John Russell Pope, who used it as a prototype for his Jefferson Memorial in Washington, D.C. Carved in high relief on the circular walls are neo-classical panels depicting biblical and poetic scenes, the work of sculptor John Gregory. Considering that both Henry and Arabella were avid art collectors (with his and her collections on the grounds), it is no

LUNCH BREAK

There's a self-service snack shop at the **Patio Restaurant** on the grounds. For something more elegant, make reservations (required) for a complete English tea, with sandwiches, scones, tarts, and fresh fruits served in the **Rose Garden Tea Room** (818-683-8131), also on the grounds.

wonder that the mausoleum is a work of art. It's a pity that it wasn't completed until two years after Henry Huntington died, five years after Arabella. ★*Open 1:00–4:30 P.M. Tuesday–Friday, 10:30 A.M.–4:30 P.M. Saturday and Sunday; closed Monday and major holidays. Map; restrooms. Admission is charged; free the first Thursday of the month.*

HENRY EDWARDS HUNTINGTON *1850–1927*
ARABELLA DUVAL HUNTINGTON *1850–1924*

Henry Huntington was not born a wealthy man, but he died one. It didn't hurt that he was the nephew and heir of Collis P. Huntingon, a founder of the Southern Pacific railroad and one of the "Big Four" powerhouses of early California history.

Henry did all right, too. Born in Oneonta, New York, he went west to work on his uncle's railroad enterprises. Spurred on by his uncle's success, Henry made his money in the Pacific Electric Company, a street railway system of Los Angeles, building the most extensive interurban rail system in the United States. His "big red cars" ran from Los Angeles to Long Beach, covering more than 1,100 miles of track and linking hundreds of southern California towns.

Divorced in 1902, he married Arabella Duval Huntington, the widow of uncle Collis (but thirty years younger), thirteen years after Collis's death in 1900. Henry and

Arabella made a formidable cultural team. Although they were both sixty-three years old when they married and were together only eleven years, they spent that time burnishing their legacies. Arabella was an important art collector in her own right; together they amassed an impressive art and furniture collection.

Henry Huntington said as early as 1906, "I am going to give something to the public before I die." When you visit this property, you'll see firsthand what a rich treasure he has bequeathed in British, French, and American art; hosts of botanical beauties; a priceless collection of rare books; and a major archival research center.

When Huntington was attracted to this part of the San Gabriel Valley in 1902 and bought the property, it was called San Marino Ranch. At first he planned to have citrus orchards, but later built a splendid Beaux-Arts mansion (now the Huntington Art Gallery) to house the enormous book and art collections he had been accumulating.

The Huntingtons, in their beautifully carved sarcophagi in their magnificent mausoleum, have good reason to be proud.

S A N T A   B A R B A R A

SANTA BARBARA CEMETERY

901 CHANNEL DRIVE; (805) 969-3231

With sweeping views of the Pacific Ocean—situated amid beautifully groomed green lawns, punctuated by native Monterey cypresses, stately pines, coastal live oaks, towering palms, eucalyptus trees, and a Romanesque-style chapel (where the office is located)—this lovely burial ground encompasses fifty-seven acres and dates back to 1867. Scattered on the graceful grounds are obelisks and private mausoleums shaped like pyramids and Greek temples. The precious cliff-top location must be the envy today of local Realtors. It is choice property.

It is also the address of a number of notable people who made Santa Barbara their final destination. They include several U.S. congressmen, mayors, a U.S. senator, Congressional Medal of Honor recipients, and a goodly share of movie professionals. Actress **Jeanne Crain** (1925–2003; central section, block N, near marker 154) is one. She was nominated for an Oscar for *Pinky* and is best remembered for *Leave Her to Heaven* and *A Letter to Three Wives*. Along with her is her husband and fellow actor, **Paul Brinkman** (1918–2003; central section, block N, grave 101), who died two months before she did.

Other actresses include **Heather Angel** (1909–1986; mausoleum, Sanctuary of Life Eternal, bay A, tier 5, niche 13), whose major role was in television's *Peyton Place,* and **Norma Varden** (1898–1989; mausoleum, room 3, group F, row 14, niche 74), who had many small parts in big films—*Random Harvest, Casablanca, National Velvet, Strangers on a Train,* and *Gentlemen Prefer Blondes* among them.

Virginia Cherrill (1908–1996; chapel, bay A, niche 51) is best known for the company she kept: first, as Charlie Chaplin's discovery and her role as the blind flower girl in his *City Lights,* then as a onetime wife of Cary Grant.

Czech figure skater turned Hollywood actress, **Vera Ralston's** (1921–2003; Sunrise Urn Garden northwest, grave 73) biggest glory moment came when she won a silver medal in the 1936 Olympics and met Adolf Hitler and insulted him. Her twenty-six B films couldn't top that. Look for her under her married name, Alva.

A big name in her day was **Suzy Parker** (1932–2003; Island section, lot 186), the best-known model of the 1950s. She later appeared in several movies, among them *Funny Face, Kiss Them for Me,* and *Ten North Frederick.*

British actor **Laurence Harvey** (1928–1973; Ocean View addition, C-132) had a meteoric career with several choice movie roles—*Butterfield 8, Walk on the Wild Side, Darling, Room at the Top* (for which he was Oscar-nominated), and best of all, *The Manchurian Candidate.* But his life was tragically curtailed by cancer. Resting with him, to the left of a huge Monterey cypress, is **Domino Harvey** (1969–2005), his

daughter by wife Pauline Stone, a *Vogue* model. Domino, a model turned bounty hunter, of all things, drowned in her bathtub in a possibly drug-related death. Her short life, the stuff that movies are made of, was made into one called *Domino* in 2005.

Other actors on (or in) the boards here are **Christopher Bernau** (1940–1989; Mausoleum in the Pines, courtyard, row 6, niche 43), with roles in two long-running television soaps, *Dark Shadows* and *The Guiding Light;* **John Ireland** (1914–1992; Mausoleum in the Pines, block C4, tier 6, crypt 9), whose fifty-year career was highlighted by an Oscar nomination for Best Supporting Actor in *All the King's Men;* and **Leslie Fenton** (1902–1978; Sunset section, block C, lot 25), who appeared in *The Public Enemy* (1931), but was more successful as a director and producer (*Tomorrow the World, Saigon, Whispering Smith*). Director **Byron Haskin** (1899–1984; Montecito Urn Garden west, grave 114) was best known for his science-fiction films (*The War of the Worlds, Conquest of Space, Robinson Crusoe on Mars*), but also scored with *The Naked Jungle* and *Treasure Island,* among others.

Lewis T. Burton (1809–1879; Summit section, addition L, lot 351) served in the army under John Fremont and was the first *American* mayor of Santa Barbara. His land holdings contained all of Lompoc Valley, including what is now Vanderbilt Air Force Base.

Also taking to this field is **Edwin "Eddie" Lee Mathews** (1931–2001; Ocean View Triangle, lot 151, south half), baseball Hall of Famer and top third baseman of his era, playing the hot corner for the Braves (Boston, Milwaukee, and Atlanta) for fifteen years. He set a record for homers (486) in his position, which was unmatched until broken by Mike Schmidt. Playing the outfield for the Pittsburgh Pirates and other teams was **Albert Francis Gionfriddo** (1922–2003; section M, lot 51), whose biggest achievement may have been as a Brooklyn Dodger, robbing Joe DiMaggio of a tying home run in the 1947 World Series.

Here too is **Marcela Zabala Howard** (1903–1987; Sunset section, block C, lot 25), widow of Charles S. Howard, owner of Seabiscuit, the horse of the century (last century, that is).

Certainly two of the most distinguished residents here are nature writer and botanist **Donald C. Peattie** (1898–1964; Central section, block D, lot 168) and medical pioneer **William David Sansum** (1880–1948; Ridge section, lot 376), maker of the first synthetic insulin.

Avant-garde poet **Kenneth Rexroth** (1905–1982; Sunset section, block C, grave 18) helped launch the concept of the "Beat Generation" through his poetry readings. **Frederick Forrest Peabody** (1858–1927; Central section, lot 163, boulder near the road) began his career selling Arrow shirts in 1915, as a partner in one of the first major nationwide advertising campaigns, and ended it as a wealthy philanthropist. ★*Grounds open 8:00 A.M.–5:00 P.M. daily. Office hours: 8:30 A.M.–4:45 P.M. Monday–Friday. Map; restroom.*

RONALD COLMAN *1891–1958*

It takes a fan of old movies to remember Ronald Charles Colman nowadays, but in his 1930–1940s heyday he was the romantic lead in such movies as *A Tale of Two Cities, Lost Horizon, The Prisoner of Zenda, If I Were King, The Light That Failed,* and *Random Harvest.*

Colman's upper-middle-class English family, prep school, years in an exclusive British regiment in World War I (during which he was wounded, decorated, and medically discharged), his training for the diplomatic corps—all were fodder for his acting career. This began somewhat unceremoniously, however. His first role was as a mute Indian herald (played in blackface) in a forgettable play.

RONALD COLMAN
1891 — 1958

OUR REVELS NOW ARE ENDED.
THESE OUR ACTORS,
AS I FORETOLD YOU,
WERE ALL SPIRITS,
AND ARE MELTED INTO AIR,
INTO THIN AIR.
WE ARE SUCH STUFF
AS DREAMS ARE MADE ON;
AND OUR LITTLE LIFE
IS ROUNDED WITH A SLEEP.

After minor successes in London and on Broadway, he arrived in Hollywood in 1925. A few silent films followed, but it was talkies that made him. Some silent stars failed in talkies because of poor voices and vocal training. But Colman's distinctive, plummy voice and upper-class English accent were naturals in the new medium. His voice was ideally suited to nuanced roles of experienced, sometimes world-weary heroes. Ironically, he ended his career as he began it: as an Indian train conductor in a cameo in *Around the World in Eighty Days*.

Colman's final curtain came down with a bout of pneumonia. His large, upright, polished black granite headstone, in the Ridge section, near marker 309, features a theater curtain half-opened to reveal a quote from Prospero's speech in *The Tempest:* "Our revels now are ended . . . We are such stuff as dreams are made on; and our little life is rounded with a sleep." A long peaceful sleep, we hope, although only half of Colman's ashes are here; the rest were returned to his homeland, England.

ROBERT MAYNARD HUTCHINS *1899–1977*

Little remembered today outside academic circles, Robert M. Hutchins was a star of higher education during the mid-twentieth century—tall, handsome, articulate, witty, brilliant. Look at these stats: He graduated from Yale in 1921, was named secretary of the Yale Foundation, earned a law degree, and became dean of Yale Law School two years after graduation—at age twenty-eight. Within two years, as an educational reformer and shaker-upper, he brought in new faculty, including William O. Douglas (later of the U.S. Supreme Court), and altered (for the better) the law school's direction.

Two years later, the University of Chicago's trustees, taking a "gamble on youth and brilliancy," made him their president. Hutchins, scion of a long line of college-educated clergymen, lived for innovation. He promoted a core curriculum of "great books" for undergraduates, favoring a general liberal arts education over narrow vocational specialties. (Even today his "great books" canon is followed and read in book groups all over the United States.)

His most controversial decision, for a Midwest school, was to abolish football. As he put it, "A student can win twelve letters at a university without learning how to write one." Some of his other audacious proposals were modified or rejected. Even so, during his tenure the University of Chicago was a place of high-energy intellectualism.

When he left Chicago in 1951, his major personal goal had been thwarted: He had hoped that Franklin Roosevelt would appoint him to a seat on the U.S. Supreme

Court. It didn't happen. Hutchins, a committed liberal politically, opposed Roosevelt's rearmament policies in the early 1940s, thus incurring the president's permanent disfavor.

From 1951 onwards, Hutchins established, with Ford Foundation assistance, the Fund for the Republic, operating in Montecito, California, as the Study of Democratic Institutions. It was his aim to run a "great academy," an idealistic learning center unrestricted by the limitations of a university. Its goal was to study foreign policy decisions, examine the nuclear arms race, and analyze the major political and social issues of the day. In a halcyon setting, scholars were invited, papers were given, and ideas were discussed. But at the end of the day—i.e., two years after Hutchins's death—the center closed with world issues unresolved.

During his lifetime, Hutchins wrote more than 300 essays on education. For all his cerebral smarts, his most often quoted line, ironically, is this: "Whenever I feel like exercise I lie down until the feeling passes." In today's intellectual climate, he'd probably host a talk show.

Robert Hutchins's black granite gravestone lies flat in the ground. It features him and his wife, **Vesta Sutton Hutchins** (1918–1994).

S I M I   V A L L E Y

RONALD REAGAN PRESIDENTIAL LIBRARY AND MUSEUM

40 PRESIDENTIAL DRIVE;
(805) 522-8444 OR (800) 410-8354;
WWW.REAGANFOUNDATION.ORG

On a hilltop, a Spanish mission–style building with a courtyard houses the museum and library of the fortieth president of the United States, with a collection of Reagan memorabilia, photographs, a full-scale replica of the Oval Office, and a portion of the Berlin Wall. President Ronald Reagan lies in repose on the other side of the infamous wall. ★*Open 10:00 A.M.–5:00 P.M. daily, except January 1, Thanksgiving, and Christmas Day. Admission is charged.*

RONALD WILSON REAGAN *1911–2004*

Critics of President Reagan like to belittle his movie career with sly remarks about *Bedtime for Bonzo,* the comedy with a chimp that he made in 1951. But, in fact, in the 1940s prime of his movie career, Reagan was a personable and charismatic actor, in such films as *Brother Rat; Knute Rockne, All American; John Loves Mary;* and *The Hasty Heart.* Most of his fifty-plus films were light-hearted romantic comedies; many were B movies. His one real blockbuster, *Kings Row,* brought out the best in him as an actor, proving that he was more than just a pretty face and athletic physique.

I KNOW IN MY HEART THAT MAN IS GOOD
THAT WHAT IS RIGHT WILL ALWAYS EVENTUALLY TRIUMPH
AND THERE IS PURPOSE AND WORTH TO EACH AND EVERY LIFE

RONALD WILSON REAGAN
FEBRUARY 6, 1911   JUNE 5, 2004

As his career was downsized in the 1950s, he turned to television's *General Electric Theater* as host and frequent star, later serving the same dual role on *Death Valley Days*. His final movie was a 1964 remake of *The Killers*. By then he was putting his considerable "people skills" to work as GE spokesman and speechmaker.

Most of Reagan's early life has been well documented: his upbringing in Dixon, Illinois; his baptism in his mother's Disciples of Christ church; his seven summers as a lifeguard, saving seventy-seven lives; his happy college days at Eureka College; his years as "Dutch" Reagan, Iowa radio sportscaster, during which he honed his natural storytelling skills; his chance visit to Hollywood, resulting in a screen test and contract with Warner Brothers; his eight-year marriage to actress Jane Wyman and subsequent marriage in 1952 to another actress, Nancy Davis.

Many credit Reagan's conversion from liberal Democrat to conservative Republican to the influence of Nancy and her right-wing stepfather. That may be, but during his two separate terms (1947–1952, 1959–1960) as president of the Screen Actors Guild (SAG), he was already becoming an ardent anti-Communist, partly because he deplored the Communist influences in SAG. He was a friendly witness before the House Un-American Activities Committee, and later, it is believed, was an FBI informant on actors he considered disloyal Americans.

Reagan's political career began in 1964 when he made a dramatic convention speech supporting Barry Goldwater for president. It so impressed Republican leaders, they urged him to run for governor of California. In 1966 he did, and beat two-term governor Edmund "Pat" Brown. Four years later he was reelected.

Reagan ran for president in the 1976 Republican primary against Gerald Ford and lost; four years later he was the nominee. The Iran hostage crisis, double-digit inflation, and other factors led to his victory over Jimmy Carter. He was, at age sixty-nine, the oldest man ever elected president. Running for reelection in 1984, he routed Walter Mondale.

Opponents underestimated Reagan for most of his political career. He was often portrayed as lazy, little more than an amusing raconteur. Being a master storyteller was part of his considerable charm and how he often disarmed his political opponents. He was much given to anecdotes, some of them dubious (like his campaign stories about "welfare queens" using food stamps to buy liquor—a legal impossibility), and one-liners, which sometimes backfired and got him into trouble.

We'll leave a full assessment of our fortieth president to historians. That Reagan contributed to the end of the cold war is unquestionable; that he personally single-handedly ended it is highly disputed. His second term was clouded by the Iran-Contra scandal. There is some question as to when he developed Alzheimer's disease, which he officially acknowledged having in 1994, six years after he left office. In 2001 a fall shattered part of his hip, leaving him virtually immobile. Within three years, in the final stage of Alzheimer's, he died at ninety-three. It was a life made for a movie.

W E S T L A K E   V I L L A G E

PIERCE BROTHERS VALLEY OAKS MEMORIAL PARK

5600 LINDARO CANYON ROAD;
(805) 495-0837

Located near the Lindaro Canyon Road exit off Highway 101, this Elysian burial ground seems quite countrified and peaceful. Canada geese waddle about the well-kept grounds among profusions of flowering plants and shrubs. There are gently sloping hillsides, dotted with private mausoleums, fountains, and statuary, and secluded garden sanctuaries. The office is on the right of the main road that leads into the grounds. To the left of the same road is the Beth Olam Garden, a section of Jewish graves, bordered on two sides by rows of towering cypress trees.

Valley Oaks's off-the-beaten-track location may attract few groupies, but it does shelter several people of note. Prominent among them is comic book artist **Jack Kirby** (1917–1994; near the cypresses at the top of the Beth Olam Garden) who co-created Captain America, the Hulk, and other Marvel Comics super-characters.

In the same area is **Ronald Goldman** (1968–1994; Beth Olam Garden, plot 63, grave D). Here by chance and bad timing, young Goldman happened to be in the wrong place at the wrong time. He was a waiter at a Brentwood restaurant and was returning eyeglasses to Nicole Brown Simpson at her home when he and she were brutally murdered.

Elsewhere on the Valley Oaks grounds is the "Father of Fitness," **Victor Tanny** (1912–1985; mausoleum). He preceded Jack LaLanne as an exercise and push-ups guru.

For musical moments, there are country music singer **Jerry Scoggins** (1911–2004; Columbarium of Peace, #19, back wall, middle of bottom row) and classically trained **Marty Paich** (1925–1995; plot 640, grave D), whose fifty-year career as composer, arranger, conductor, pianist, and producer gave him work in jazz, popular music, and movies.

Michael O'Shea (1906–1973; Garden of Gethsemane, plot 313) was a movie actor (*Jack London* and *Man from Frisco,* among others) and husband of beautiful

> ### LUNCH BREAK
>
> **Marmalade Cafe** (Promenade at Westlake, 140 Promenade Way; 805-370-1331) doesn't feel like a chain, its soups, sandwiches, baked goods, and desserts are so fresh-tasting. It's also possible to take out rather than eat in. **Rosti** (160 Promenade Way; 805-370-1939) offers hearty northern Italian dishes that are both satisfying and well-priced.

Virginia Mayo (1920–2005; same location). More a lovely presence than a great actress, Mayo starred in *The Secret Life of Walter Mitty* and *The Best Years of Our Lives,* among other high-profile films of the 1940s and 1950s. ★*Grounds open dawn to dusk daily. Office hours: 9:00 A.M.–5:00 P.M. daily. Map; restrooms.*

KAREN CARPENTER *1950–1983*

Karen Carpenter grew up in New Haven, Connecticut, and took band in high school to avoid gym class. She gravitated to the drums and percussion, and later joined her older brother, Richard, a pianist, in forming a group with a friend, Wes Jacobs, on bass and tuba. It was called the Richard Carpenter Trio.

They didn't make much of a wave, but later, as a brother-sister duo, a demonstration tape with Karen on vocals attracted the attention of Herb Alpert at A&M Records. They signed in 1969, and it only took them a few months to score a No. 1 hit with "Close to You," followed rapidly by another, "We've Only Just Begun."

They were hot! Between 1970 and 1976 they won three Grammy Awards and charted sixteen consecutive Top 20 Billboard singles, making them one of the most popular American groups of the time. In 1976 their tour of Japan was the highest grossing of a musical act up to that time.

During this period, Karen was battling anorexia nervosa, her weight fluctuating and affecting her private life. In 1980 she married a man almost a decade older, but it didn't take, resulting in a separation. At her parents' home in Downey, California, Karen Carpenter died of heart failure attributed to strain brought on by anorexia.

At the top of a gently sloping hillock, past a little stream rolling over rocks, is a sumptuous mausoleum with the word CARPENTER above the metal door. Made of rose-black polished granite, this spare-no-expense memorial contains Karen's sarcophagus, with the words "Star of earth—a star in heaven." Small palms in granite planters do "guard duty" at each side of the mausoleum door. (The mausoleum was moved from its original site in Forest Lawn Cypress in Orange County.)

ARTIE SHAW *1910–2004*

Few celebrities quit while they're ahead, but Artie Shaw did—to the astonishment of the jazz world. Born Arthur Jacob Arshawsky in New York City, Shaw excelled at almost everything he undertook—and that was plenty. In fact, Shaw was almost as famous for being fickle as for his prodigious musical talent. He turned his back on his musical career, yet revisited it several times, but it was his many marriages that made his name a punch line of nightclub comedians.

Shaw grew up in New Haven, Connecticut, and taught himself to play the saxophone and then the clarinet. At age fifteen he was touring with Johnny Cavallero's dance band and became adept at arranging and conducting. In the late 1930s he organized his own swing band, featuring the vocalist Billie Holiday. He was the first white bandleader to hire a black singer as a full-time band member. Shaw had many bands and many hits, including "Frenesi," "Stardust," "Nightmare," and "Summit Ridge Drive." But for all the hits and all the bands he would lead, nothing came close to the attention and adulation created by Cole Porter's "Begin the Beguine." It catapulted Shaw past Benny Goodman as the "King of Swing" and forever enshrined him at the top of all swing bandleaders of that era. It also brought riches in the form of his band's weekly paycheck of $60,000 in 1938 dollars.

Restless intellectually, he didn't mask his contempt toward his audiences who were stuck on his past accomplishments while he continued to move forward musically. When his contemporaries were happily signing autographs for adoring fans, he refused. Often when asked for his signature, his response was "What's in it for me?" Not a way to endear yourself to your fans.

After Pearl Harbor, Shaw joined the U.S. Navy. He was asked to form a band to entertain the troops, often playing as many as four shows a day while traveling

Artie Shaw

May 23, 1910 – Dec. 30, 2004

The Soul Of The Song
(For A.S.)

He taught the clarinet to think
Not just to sing.
To explore the music it was making,
To let the fingers probe and find
The hidden places,
The crevices of meaning and emotion
a good song has –
But must be found and captured
By some divinity or other,
A melody that cannot just be played,
For nuances and grace notes
can't be chartered,
The secret tempos and their keys
Can only be discovered.
By a mind that is listening for the soul
The manuscript does not display.

A. C. Greene

through the Pacific war zones. They played on ships, at bases, and even at Guadalcanal.

After a medical discharge, Shaw formed yet another band. His virtuosity on the clarinet was legendary. He was arguably the best ever to play jazz, but he wasn't content to rest on his laurels. Influenced by the classics, especially Stravinsky, Debussy, and Bartok, he added string sections in his bands. This influence can be heard in his composition "Interlude in B Flat" (1935), which combined symphonic and jazz forms and came to be known as "Third Stream." This "stream" involved blending a large string section with jazz horns—a wonderful marriage (maybe his best).

Speaking of marriage, Shaw had almost as many as he had bands. In all, he was married eight times, most famously to actresses Lana Turner, Ava Gardner, and Evelyn Keyes (his last wife), all ending in divorce.

One of Shaw's most highly regarded later bands, which had several incarnations, was the Gramercy Five, which had him again pushing the boundaries of jazz. In 1954 he retired his jazz clarinet for good, never to play it publicly again, feeling that he had accomplished all he could on it.

Shaw then turned his attention to writing. In 1952 he published the loosely autobiographical *The Trouble With Cinderella* to critical acclaim. Over the next thirty years, he was involved in various pursuits: He became a devoted and expert fly fisherman; a competitive marksman ranked fourth in the United States, who made his own rifles and loaded his own ammunition, even owning a gun manufacturing firm; and made his own chess sets, collected art, practiced wood carving, and was a gourmand.

He produced and distributed films and continued writing, publishing two more books, *I Love You, I Hate You, Drop Dead!* (1977) and *The Best of Intentions, and Other Stories* (1989). At various times he owned and lived in houses and/or farms in Pennsylvania, New York, Connecticut, and Spain. Returning to the United States, he finally settled in Newbury Park, California, where he spent the last years of his life.

Shaw did return to music briefly, after a thirty-year absence, arranging and conducting the Artie Shaw Orchestra. While spending many of his later years working on his final, unfinished book, he also lectured and gave college seminars on art, music, culture, and divorce, on which he considered himself an expert.

He lived most of his last years as a curmudgeon. Never having been fond of his fellow man, Shaw, when asked by *Who's Who in America* to write his own epitaph, came up with "He did the best he could with the material at hand." But a few years later, he offered a revision: "I've cut it down to two words: 'Go away.'"

Artie Shaw died at ninety-four. He left two sons from different marriages. His final gig is in the Tranquility section, 7-E, near the road, opposite a beautiful gnarled tree surrounded by a small garden and within tootling distance of the Karen Carpenter mausoleum. His gray-flecked granite gravestone has a black inset and gilt-colored border. The wording contains a sixteen-line poem, "The Soul of the Song," by A. C. Greene, which begins "He taught the clarinet to think not just to sing . . ." He couldn't have put it better himself.

CULVER CITY

Los Angeles segues into Culver City as smoothly as in any good movie, and as in such a movie there are scores of surprises. As the second-largest cemetery in the entire Greater Los Angeles area (Holy Cross) is here, with another starring attraction nearby (Hillside Memorial Park), it is easy to spend a spectrally rewarding day in this single town.

HILLSIDE MEMORIAL PARK AND MORTUARY

600 CENTINELA AVENUE;
(310) 641-0707

On fifty well-kept grassy acres that roll and dip, this Jewish sacred ground has been the final home, since its beginning in 1942, of many prominent Hollywood bigwigs—actors, entertainers, producers, comedians, composers—with grave sections named Valley of Remembrance, Garden of Rachel, Mount Sholom, Court of the Matriarchs, Mount of Olives, and the like.

The well-named site couldn't be better for a final repose: high above the fray of the thunderous Los Angeles throughway traffic of Interstate 405, reaching upwards, with a hillside of olive trees. Heavenly! Beyond the office is a tumultuous waterfall that seems to spill forth from the monumental mausoleum of Al Jolson. Note the benches throughout the grounds.

Many notable residents are to be found in the wall crypts and private rooms of the three-story mausoleum that hugs the hillside. Among the marble wall crypts

are numerous comedians like **Eddie Cantor** (1892–1964; Hall of Graciousness, niche 207, second floor), a singer and comedian dubbed "Banjo Eyes." He was a staple of stage, movies, radio, and television for thirty-five years.

Here too are **George Jessel** (1898–1981; Memorial Court, niche 516), vaudeville, radio, and movie comedian who received an Oscar for his humanitarian work; **Allan Sherman** (1924–1973; Columbarium of Hope, niche 513), satiric songwriter ("Hello Mudduh, Hello Fadduh"), comedian, and the voice of Dr. Seuss's animated *Cat in the Hat;* and **Ben Blue** (1901–1975; Columbarium of Graciousness, niche 810), a rubber-limbed comic in vaudeville, later a regular on television in the 1950s and 1960s.

Newcomer **Jan Murray** (1916–2006; Canaan Garden Mausoleum), was a comedian and game show host of *Treasure Hunt,* among others.

David Janssen (1931–1980; Memorial Court, niche 516) was a child actor who succeeded in the business as an adult—a not-too-common situation. His most memorable role was as Dr. Richard Kimble in television's *The Fugitive* series; his marker reads "My Love Is With You Always."

In the vicinity are **Dick Shawn** (1923–1987; Memorial Court, niche 734), a gifted comedian and comic actor, now residing in the same courtyard as Janssen. Shawn's most uproarious performance was as the hippie actor playing Hitler in the 1967 movie *The Producers.* **Irving Wallace** (1916–1990; Isaiah, V, niche 136) was the author of numerous best-selling novels, and **Selma Diamond** (1920–1985; Courts of the Book, Jacob, I, 4004) was a writer on Sid Caesar's pioneering television hit, *Show of Shows.* Later, wearing her actress hat, she played Selma Hacker on NBC-TV's *Night Court.*

Michael Landon (1936–1991; outer rear of mausoleum), a heartthrob as Little Joe on the television series *Bonanza,* later wrote, produced, and starred in *Little House on the Prairie* and later *Highway to Heaven.* He has his own private room, lavish with fresh flowers and messages, visible through a gated glass door. His epitaph reads: "He seized life with joy. He gave to life generously. He leaves a legacy of love and laughter."

In the mausoleum on a high wall near the front is **David Begelman** (1921–1995), talent agent, producer, and studio head. He is best remembered, unfortunately, for his role as instigator in a major movie embezzlement scandal.

Elsewhere on the grounds are **Moe Howard** (1897–1975; Alcove of Love, C-233), the leader (with the bowl haircut) of the original Three Stooges comedy team (with brother Curly and Larry Fine); **Lorne Green** (1915–1987; Lawn crypts, 5-800-8B, behind the mausoleum), famous for his role as Ben Cartwright in TV's *Bonanza;* and **Joe Pasternak** (1901–1991; Laurel Gardens, block 12), movie producer for almost forty years.

Also on call are **Max Shulman** (1919–1988; Eternal Rest, block 4, plot 31, space 9) author of humorous books (*Barefoot Boy With Cheek*), movies, and television series (*The Many Loves of Dobie Gillis*), and **Hal March** (1920–1970; Mount Shalom, 4-144-6), game show host who emceed the popular and later controversial *$64,000 Question.*

Jerry Rubin (1938–1994; Mount of Olives, 14-466-3) is here as well. A 1960s hippie and co-founder of the Vietnam War protest group called the Youth International Party, whose adherents were known as Yippies, he later turned from a Yippie to a Yuppie and became a successful businessman. He was killed while jaywalking, an iconoclast to the end.

Musical notes are sounded aplenty at Hillside by **Percy Faith** (1908–1976; Garden of Memories, Court of Honor), bandleader and popular song arranger, whose biggest hit was the Oscar-nominated "I'll Never Stop Loving You," and by **Nell Carter** (1948–2003; Acacia Gardens, KK-740), cabaret singer, musical comedy actress, and television and movie actress. She was a multiple-award winner for *Ain't Misbehavin'* and *Annie* on Broadway.

Harry Richmond (1895–1972; Alcove of Love, B-319B) is at Hillside, a song-and-dance man in vaudeville's heyday, whose signature song was "Puttin' on the Ritz." **Mickey Katz** (1909–1985; Valley of Remembrance, I-196-2), was a bandleader who began in the Borscht Belt of the Catskills, New York, and became known for his novelty songs. He was also the father of actor Joel Grey (*Cabaret*) and grandfather of actress Jennifer Grey (*Dirty Dancing*).

The name **Sam Lerner** (1903–1989; Laurel Gardens, 18-177-3A) may not resonate with you, but his songs will: "Falling in Love Again, "I'm Popeye the Sailor Man," and his many musical scores for Alfred Hitchcock movies.

Powerful producers who have their final cuts at Hillside include **Irene Mayer Selznick** (1907–1990; mausoleum, Hall of Graciousness), a daughter of Louis B. Mayer (the head of MGM) and first wife of producer David O. Selznick. She produced *A Streetcar Named Desire* and other Broadway hits. **William Goetz** (1903–1969; Devotion, sarcophagus B) was married to Mayer's other daughter, Edith. He was the head of production at 20th Century Fox and Universal Studios in the 1940s, and was the first to pay stars a percentage of the movie's profits instead of a salary.

Newly arrived **Aaron Spelling** (1923–2006; Hall of Reverence, FFJ1) holds the Guiness World Record for "most prolific television producer of all time." Among his many TV series was *Love Boat.*

Lew Wasserman (1913–2002; Canaan, Family Estate, plot 8.4) was the builder and head of MCA, the entertainment colossus that he controlled for more than fifty years. **Arthur Freed** (1894–1973; Honor, lawn crypts, 418) was an MGM producer-

LUNCH BREAK

A better-than-average chain restaurant near Centinela Avenue is **In-N-Out-Burger** (13425 Washington Boulevard; 800-786-1000), which serves double-size hamburgers and fresh-cut french fries that are out of this world. Lots of spirited Italiano fun is **San Gennaro Cafe** (9543 Culver Boulevard; 310-836-0400), with good pizzas, cheap wine, and live music evenings. If you crave authentic Mexican fare, try the modest **Mi Ranchito Family Mexican** (12223 Washington Boulevard; 310-398-8611), where the food is good and the prices el cheapo.

songwriter whose Oscar-winning hits, *An American in Paris* and *Gigi,* were only surpassed by his songs in *Singin' in the Rain,* possibly the best movie musical of all time.

Russian-born **Max Factor Sr.** (1877–1938; Isaiah, niche 314) is also on the premises. A cosmetics master who invented the first makeup for movies, he seemed to be in almost every film credit of the 1930s. His son-successor **Max Factor Jr.** (1904–1996; same location) carried on the family business in film and later in television.

A businessman with movie ties was **Bernard Schwab** (1909–2003; mausoleum, Courts of the Book). With his three brothers, he established in 1932 Schwab's Pharmacy on Sunset Boulevard. Schwab's became an "office"—hangout, answering service, credit agency, and talent spotter—for out-of-work actors, many of whom made it big later. You need more than ten fingers to count the movie stars who reportedly were "discovered" at Schwab's.

Dead last, we should mention the notorious mobster **Mickey Cohen** (1913–1976; Alcove of Love, A-217), bookmaker and bootlegger. He ran the bookkeeping rackets for Bugsy Siegel until his death; he then assumed Siegel's mantle as the rackets czar of Los Angeles. He survived many murder attempts only to die of natural causes. He now reposes in—irony of ironies—the Alcove of Love.
★*Grounds and office open 8:00 A.M.–5:00 P.M. daily, except Saturday. Mausoleum open 8:00 A.M.–4:00 P.M. daily, except Saturday. Map; restroom.*

JACK BENNY *1894–1974*

A comedian with exquisite timing, Jack Benny began his career as a humor monologist and master of ceremonies. He found his natural milieu as the star of his own radio show, which he expanded later into a television series. Benny portrayed himself as a vain miser from Winnetka, Illinois (where he actually grew up), who never admitted being older than thirty-nine, and a would-be violinist whose screechy scratchings with the bow drew countless laughs.

Born Benjamin Kubelsky in Chicago, he played the violin well enough to tour vaudeville. Everything else was invented for laughs, including his radio feud with fellow comic Fred Allen and his reputation

> **HOUSE CALL**
>
> Despite his "poor mouthing" on radio and TV, Benny lived very well, as his house (1002 North Roxbury Drive, Beverly Hills) testifies. Privately owned, it is viewable *only* as a drive-by.

as a penny-pinching cheapskate. One of his gags: A robber says, "Your money or your life," there's a long pause (his forte was that long pause before the punch line), then Benny says, "I'm thinking, I'm thinking."

What gave the Benny program such appeal—besides his own flawless timing—was excellent writing and a superb cast, headed by Eddie Anderson as Benny's valet, Rochester; bandleader Phil Harris as a good-natured drunk; and Mary Livingstone (his real wife) as Benny's sharp-tongued spouse.

Jack Benny's impressive polished black granite sarcophagus (nothing cheap about that) in the rear of the mausoleum's Hall of Graciousness, which he shares with **Mary Livingstone Benny** (1906–1983), notes that he was a "beloved husband, father and grandfather, a gentle man." Is that violin music we're hearing?

MILTON BERLE *1908–2002*

As an entertainer, Milton Berle's career spanned almost every era and venue of the twentieth century, from burlesque, vaudeville, and silent movies to radio, television, nightclubs, Broadway, and Las Vegas. He began his career as a toddler—age five—entertaining neighbor kids for free with his impressions of Charlie Chaplin. A year later, thanks to his relentlessly pushy stage mother, he appeared with Chaplin himself in *Tillie's Punctured Romance,* which also featured Mabel Normand (no slouch at comedy herself).

Never taking time out for an education, Berle, born Berlinger, did everything. He had top billing and made top dollar without ever becoming tops. Other comedians—of vaudeville, radio, and later television—outclassed him. He didn't seem to care. He was well known among other comedians for stealing their jokes. Even this was fodder for his routine, making fun of his ability as a joke thief. No joke was too old, tired, or unfunny—he did them all.

Berle's golden moment came in television's infancy. He had the good luck of timing, appearing in 1948 in a newly minted show called *Texaco Star Theater*. He was just forty, and the show sent him skyward like a rocket. For eight years he was Mr. Television, "Uncle Miltie." But while some comedians wear well, Berle—with his brash humor, mountainous ego, and pilfered and aged jokes—did not. He may not have burned out, but his audience did.

He did other TV shows, personal appearances, and talk shows, but his time had passed. Berle's wall crypt in the Acacia Gardens section, MM354, is next to the edge of the wedding mural. Take a right as you leave the office, and it is just a short walk on the right. His bronze marker is third from the bottom at the end of the row in a garden enclosure. There are benches nearby for contemplation—or perhaps reminiscences about some of Berle's better routines.

HANK GREENBERG *1911–1986*

Bronx-born Henry Benjamin Greenberg was Major League Baseball's first Jewish superstar, known as "Hammering Hank" for his power as a hard-hitting first baseman with the Detroit Tigers. He spent twelve years with the Tigers—with a four-year hiatus during World War II when Captain Greenberg earned four battle stars and took part in a 1944 air raid on Japan.

One of baseball's all-time top hitters—some of his records still stand—he spent his last playing year with the Pittsburgh Pirates, then became part owner and general manager (GM) of the Cleveland Indians and finally vice president and GM of the Chicago White Sox.

In 1956 he was elected to baseball's Hall of Fame, and in 1983 the Tigers retired his uniform #5—a big sentimental honor—and named him their all-time first baseman. He still holds the team's home-run record. No wonder the green-patinaed bronze  marker on his crypt in Isaiah, V-340, on the outer wall of the mausoleum, reads "Loved and admired by so many." Not including, we assume, many of the pitchers he faced.

AL JOLSON *1886–1950*

Eat your heart out, fellow residents—top billing at Hillside belongs to Al Jolson. Visible from the freeway below and illuminated by spotlights at night, Jolson's awesome hilltop memorial, lined by cypress trees, has a bright mosaic ceiling supported by six towering pillars, with a polished black granite sarcophagus inside. A 120-foot waterfall cascades down in front. Beside the memorial (designed by Los Angeles architect Paul Revere Williams) is a large bronze statue of Jolson on one knee, with arms outstretched, as if singing his famous "Mammy." The memorial's ceiling features Moses with the Ten Commandments in the clouds and the words "The sweet singer of Israel, the man raised up high." It's probably no surprise to learn that Jolson conceived the monument as a tribute to himself.

Born Asa Yoelsom in a Russian (later Lithuanian) village, he emigrated to America in 1890 with his family, settling in Washington, D.C. The son of a synagogue cantor, young Al made money early by singing on street corners. By age fifteen he had quit school and, with his distinctive singing voice and agreeably brassy person-

ality, become a fixture on the vaudeville circuit. A solo act followed, often in blackface (a popular convention of white performers in minstrel shows), then Broadway musicals. "California, Here I Come," "Toot, Toot, Tootsie," and "April Showers" became his signature numbers.

When talking movies came along, Jolson was ready, starring in what has been called the first, *The Jazz Singer,* in 1927, which earned him a place in movie history. A series of radio variety shows followed, when he teamed with comics Parkyakarkas and Martha Raye. During World War II Jolson gave freely of his time to USO shows, and in 1946 *The Jolson Story,* a romanticized movie about his life, revived what by then was a sagging career. His personal life had its share of problems, underscored by four marriages.

Ever the entertainer (for forty years), Jolson died of heart failure after a return from a strenuous USO tour to Korea. Toot, toot, tootsie, goodbye.

DINAH SHORE *1916–1994*

Soft-spoken with a big smile and lilting voice, this southern songbird was a steel magnolia in her determination, true grit, and business acumen. Born Anna Stein Shore, she was the daughter of Russian Jews who immigrated to Winchester, Tennessee. As a toddler she developed polio, which left her with a shortened leg. This didn't stop her from dancing, though as a general rule she wore long pants or a full long gown in her public appearances.

After graduating from Vanderbilt University in 1938 with a sociology degree, she headed for New York and a singing career. She recorded with Cuban bandleader Xavier Cugat and sang solo all through the 1940s and early 1950s, recording over eighty hit records and making personal appearances, many with the USO during World War II. During that time she changed her name to Dinah, after one of her favorite songs.

Then came eight, mostly forgettable, movies. In 1951 she landed a television gig, a variety show called *The Dinah Shore Show,* which ran for thirteen seasons on NBC-TV and was probably her greatest success, followed by *Dinah!,* one of TV's first talk shows. It later morphed into *Dinah's Place,* then *Dinah and Friends.* Her television career earned her nine Emmys, a Peabody, and a Golden Globe.

In her personal life, she was an ardent golfer and founded the Colgate/Dinah Shore Winner's Circle Golf Championship (later changed to the Kraft Nabisco Championship). She married twice, first to actor George Montgomery (with whom she had a daughter, Melissa Ann), then, briefly, to Maurice Smith. Later in life, in the 1970s, Dinah made news of another sort: as the older partner in a winter-summer

romance with actor Burt Reynolds, nineteen years her junior. They evidently had a long, warm relationship.

"Loved by all who knew her and millions who never did" seems a fitting epitaph for such a popular and beloved performer. Some of her ashes rest in Isaiah, V, niche 247, outside the mausoleum wall in the rear. The rest are at Forest Lawn Memorial Parks & Mortuaries in Cathedral City.

SHELLEY WINTERS *1922–2006*

No question, as movie stars go, Shelley Winters was an original. Even in her "dumb blond bombshell" days (as she later described them), she was more than a pretty, shapely starlet. She had a distinctive voice (with traces of her Brooklyn youth), a persona as a tough broad with street smarts, and a look in her eyes that promised mischief. In later years, as a frequent guest on late-night talk shows, she revealed a rowdy sense of humor.

She once described her career as a "rocky road out of the Brooklyn ghetto, to one New York apartment, two Oscars, three California houses, four hit plays, five impressionist paintings, six mink coats and ninety-nine films." That's the outline, but the whole story is something else.

Her first big break in Hollywood came in 1947 as a waitress who is strangled in *A Double Life,* which starred Ronald Colman. *A Place in the Sun* followed, with an Oscar nomination for Best Actress. Her two Oscars came for Best Supporting

Actress—as a middle-aged Dutch housewife sheltering Jews from the Nazis in *The Diary of Anne Frank* (1959) and as a vicious mother in *A Patch of Blue* (1965).

For someone rejected by Columbia Pictures after a year as not "movie material," this St. Louis, Missouri–born girl, whose real name was Shirley Schrift, had quite a ride, receiving a fourth Oscar nomination for her role as a former swimming champion in *The Poseidon Adventure* in 1972, for which she gained thirty pounds.

Winters never lost the weight, but continued to live life to the fullest, as zaftig and zesty as many of the diverse roles she played. In a best-selling autobiography, *Shelley, Also Known as Shirley,* and its sequel, *Shelley II,* she wrote candidly about her affairs with the likes of Errol Flynn, Sean Connery, Farley Granger, Sterling Hayden, William Holden, and Burt Lancaster. With Holden, it was a "same time, next year" relationship; they met each Christmas Eve in his Paramount dressing room for five years. With Lancaster, a two-year affair ended when his wife became pregnant with his third child.

She was married three times, the last two to fellow actors—Vittorio Gassman for two years (by whom she had her only child, a girl), then to Tony Franciosa for three. By one of life's curiosities, Franciosa died a week after Winters did. She'd probably have found this amusing.

Her last residence is in block 11, plot 358, grave 8.

HOLY CROSS CEMETERY AND MAUSOLEUM

5835 WEST SLAUSON AVENUE; (310) 836-5500; FAX (310) 836-3560

Forest Lawn is better known, but Holy Cross may surprise you. Its hilly landscape is like a memorial to stars and supporting casts of Hollywood's Golden Age. Fast forward through dozens of 1930s–1950s films, and you'll uncover scores of solid professional actors and actresses having their big sleep.

From the entrance gate, which resembles a filigreed metal altar screen with a cross above it, and the street lights with a cross above each, the grassy lawns and rolling hills of this Roman Catholic burying ground are a backdrop for grottoes, waterfalls, ponds, and an abundance of religious statuary and shrines. Sections have such names as Holy Innocents, Sacred Heart, Mother of Good Hope, and Precious Blood. The well-kept grounds, with a variety of evergreens and other trees, are celebrity hideaways—for good.

As you enter the slowly rising grounds, you will come to a massive white building whose blue-paneled facade is dominated by a crucifixion scene and a chalice

OCTOBER 26
1914

MARCH 1
1984

JOHN LESLIE COOGAN

HUMANITARIAN · PATRIOT · ENTERTAINER

· FOREVER IN OUR HEARTS ·

below it. This is the Risen Christ mausoleum, with a modern chapel in the center and numerous wall crypts. The office is in the rear of a building to the mausoleum's left; a large parking area is also in the rear.

In the ample well-furnished office, which resembles an upscale hotel lobby, a staffer will give you a map but will advise you to take the elevator to the man in the second-floor office for specific grave locations. With a finely detailed map, he pinpoints every grave you may wish to seek, with details on who-is-where-now. The well-marked graves are easy to locate, and unlike certain other star-studded grounds, the office staffers here are extremely helpful and willing to oblige. There is even a list, with all the graves marked, of most of the notables permanently residing on the grounds.

In his own digs is **Jackie Coogan** (1914–1984; section F, tier 56, grave 47), a movie actor from childhood to old age. He was launched as a child star in Charlie Chaplin's *The Kid* (1921), and was most famous at the end of his long career as Uncle Fester in TV's *The Addams Family.*

Dug in for eternity are **Richard Arlen** (1896–1976; section T, tier 157, grave 130), leading actor in silent movies; **Frank Lovejoy** (1912–1962; section P, lot 306, grave 5), actor famous for playing tough-guy roles; and **Frank Albertson** (1909–1964; section P, lot 284, grave 4), stage, television, and movie actor who was in *Psycho* and *Bye Bye Birdie,* among scores of other films.

English-born **Wallace Ford** (1898–1966; unmarked grave) appeared in more than 200 movies, including *Shadow of a Doubt, Spellbound,* and many westerns, thirteen of which were directed by John Ford. **Edgar Kennedy** (1890–1948; section D, lot 193, grave 7), master of the "slow burn" of exasperation, was in comic shorts and features for over thirty years, and character actor **James Gleason** (1882–1959; section D, lot 368, grave 9) received an Oscar nomination for Best Supporting Actor in *Here Comes Mr. Jordan.* Spanish actor and opera singer **Fortunio Bonanova** (1895–1969; section V, tier 9, grave 214) scored in Hollywood films: *Citizen Kane, Five Graves to Cairo, Going My Way, Double Indemnity,* and loads more.

Jean Peters (1926–2000; section AA, tier 22, grave 39) acted in movies for forty years (including *Niagara* with Marilyn Monroe) and was once married to Howard Hughes, while **ZaSu Pitts** (1894–1963; Grotto section, lot 195, grave 1) used her big eyes in many comic turns in decades of movies, from *Greed* (1925) to *Francis* (1949) to *It's a Mad, Mad, Mad, Mad World* (1963).

Polish-born **Gilda Gray** (1901–1959; section S, tier 46, grave 67) was best known as the "Shimmy Queen," a name she acquired from suggestively shaking her chemise (which she called a "shimmy"), quite a risqué act in her day (though pretty mild by today's standards). She was also known for suing Columbia Pictures—and winning—for using her made-up name in *Gilda,* though the film had nothing to do with her life. In fact, the name was suggested to her by entertainer Sophie Tucker—it beat Marianna Winchalaska on a marquee.

In a career that spanned most of the twentieth century, **Ann Miller** (1923–2004; section F, tier 57, grave 58) was still going strong, dancing and singing, near the time of her death from lung cancer. Name a Hollywood musical of the past fifty years and she probably was in it, tap-dancing with élan and a customary smile. Ironically, she began dancing lessons as a kid to help straighten her legs from a bout of rickets, never dreaming it would become her ticket to ride.

Canadian **Gene Lockhart** (1891–1957; section D, lot 279, grave 6) played in more than 300 films, including *Miracle on 34th Street* and *The Man in the Gray Flannel Suit,* in a career than spanned six decades. Today—how soon we forget—he is probably best known as the father of television actress June Lockhart. He is joined here by his wife, actress **Kathleen Lockhart** (1894–1978; section D, lot 280, grave 7) who played in *Blondie, Bewitched,* and other films, but was overshadowed by both her husband and daughter.

Anyone who grew up with radio probably remembers fondly *The Fibber McGee Show,* a perennial favorite of the 1930s and 1940s. Its stars were **James "Jim" Jordan** (1896–1988; St. Ann section, lot 153, grave 2), aka "Fibber McGee," a dreamer who always had fanciful and impractical schemes, and his wife, **Marian**

"Molly McGee" Jordan (1896–1961; same location), whose common sense always brought Fibber down to earth. Another radio personality is here: **Charles Correll** (1890–1972; St. Ann section, lot 144, grave 7), who was Andy on *Amos and Andy,* a popular show of the same period, whose exaggerated black characters were all played by white men.

Actors abound at Holy Cross, among them **Vince Edwards** (1928–1996; section CC, tier 64, grave 29), who starred as Ben Casey in the 1960s television series of the same name and made scores of movies as well. **MacDonald Carey** (1913–1994; Grotto section, lot 196, grave 19), best known as Dr. Tom Horton on NBC-TV's daytime soap opera *Days of Our Lives,* made scores of movies, too, including *Shadow of a Doubt* (1943) and *The Great Gatsby* (1949). **Pat O'Brien** (1899–1983; section F, tier 56, grave 62) was the perennial sidekick, priest, or Irish cop in 1930s–1940s movies. Funnyman **Hugh Herbert** (1885–1952; section D, lot 267, grave 11) is here; his shtick was a "woo-woo" sound of nervous frustration, accompanied by fluttery hand movements.

Londoner **Alan Mowbray** (1896–1969; section N) had the distinction of being in movies with three different Sherlock Holmes, as well as playing the butler in *Topper,* a romantic lead in *Becky Sharp,* and numerous servants and villains. **Bonita Granville** (1923–1988; Grotto section, lot 196, grave 12) had leads in many 1930s and 1940s movies and earned a Best Supporting Actress Oscar nomination for *These Three* (1936), in which she played a hysterical teenager, probably her best role. She later married oil mogul and television producer **Jack Wrather** (1918–1984; same location).

Many filmmakers have sought final refuge on Holy Cross grounds, among them **Henry Hathaway** (1898–1985; mausoleum, block 42, crypt C1), born the Marquis Henri Leonard de Fiennes. He directed sixty-five films in forty-two years, starring the likes of Gregory Peck, Rita Hayworth, Steve McQueen, John Wayne, and Richard Burton, including such hits as *True Grit* and *How the West Was Won.* Director **Henry King** (1886–1982; Grotto section, lot 97, grave 2) boasts such credits as *Stella Dallas, Lloyds of London, Alexander's Ragtime Band, Jesse James, The Black Swan, The Song of Bernadette, The Gunfighter, The Snows of Kilimanjaro,* and *Tender Is the Night.*

Film director-writer-producer **John Farrow** (1904–1963; section P, lot 317, grave 5) was the winner of an Oscar for Best Screenplay for *Around the World in Eighty Days* but is perhaps better known as the husband of actress Maureen O'Sullivan and father of Mia Farrow.

Joe Hamilton (1929–1991; mausoleum, block 73, crypt B6) was the producer of *The Carol Burnett Show* (and married for some years to its star) and other television shows. **Fred DeCordova** (1910–2001; section BB, tier 80, grave 56) was Johnny Carson's producer on *The Tonight Show* for years, but before that was a TV host and film director.

Musical types to be found here include **Jose Iturbi** (1895–1980; mausoleum, block 16, crypt E1), Spanish concert pianist, classical composer, and conductor, who played himself in *Thousands Cheer* and several other 1940s films. Baritone **Johnny Desmond** (1919–1985; section F, lot 44, grave 30) was a vocalist with Bob Crosby's band, then Gene Krupa's, later during World War II with Glenn Miller's Army Air Force Band, and in the 1950s on the television show *Your Hit Parade*. Ever versatile, he appeared on Broadway in *Say Darling* and in *Funny Girl* with Barbra Streisand. His first hit record was "C'est Si Bon," but "Tenderly" is incised on his gravestone.

Other subterranean singers here are heartthrob **Mario Lanza** (1921–1959; mausoleum, block 46, crypt D2, to right of altar), the Italian tenor who died unexpectedly in his musical prime, and tenor **Dennis Day** (1918–1988; section W, tier 53, grave 37), a favorite on *The Jack Benny Show,* who also had his own television show and was featured in many movies.

Look also for **Edward "Kid" Ory** (1886–1973; Grotto section, lot 59, grave 4), one of the fathers of Dixieland jazz, and personable **Helen O'Connell** (1920–1993; section CC, tier 56, grave 55), a singer with the big swing bands of the 1940s. She popularized "Green Eyes," "All of Me," "Tangerine," and "Amapola" while with Jimmy Dorsey's band, often paired with Dorsey vocalist Bob Eberle.

Lindley Armstrong Jones, better known professionally as **Spike Jones** (1911–1965; mausoleum, block 70, crypt A7), began as a serious musician but soon formed a zany outfit called Spike Jones and His City Slickers. They featured goofy songs like "In Der Fuehrer's Face" and "Cocktails for Two" and did parodies of the opera *Carmen,* all played to the accompaniment of auto horns, bells, whistles, and other noisemakers. The band had the skills to be serious, but it was more fun doing parodies.

Though probably a coincidence, it should please *The Wizard of Oz* fans to find two of the famous cast sharing the same final real estate. **Ray Bolger** (1904–1987; mausoleum, block 35, crypt F2), nimble dancer and genial entertainer, will forever be the Scarecrow without a brain. **Jack Haley** (1898–1979; Grotto section, lot 100, grave 2), always the Tin Man who lacked a heart, was a comedian, singer, and actor for many years before he found fame in this great film. Ironically, the character who supposedly lacked a heart died of a heart attack. The film's other stars—Judy Garland, Bert Lahr, Frank Morgan, and Billie Burke—are far away, not in the Emerald City, but at final repose in New York.

Haley's son, **Jack Haley Jr.** (1933–2001; Grotto section, next to his parents), was as famous in Hollywood as his dad, but more as a director-producer than an actor. He won an Emmy in 1967 for *Movin' With Nancy* and Peabodys for the "Biography" and "National Geographic Special" series. Trivial pursuit: He was also Liza Minnelli's first husband.

Movie people besides actors and directors here include screenwriter **Tim Ryan** (1899–1956; section Q, lot 369, grave 5), who wrote forty-two screenplays (*The Asphalt Jungle* and *From Here to Eternity* among them), as well as acted in 139 movies; choreographer **Hermes Pan** (1909–1991; mausoleum, block 127, crypt D5); and stuntman, actor, and makeup artist **Charles Gemora** (1903–1961; section N, lot 303, grave 1), whose on-screen presence was often in a gorilla costume.

Holy Cross seems to be a gathering place for cinematographers, often unsung. Among them are **John F. Seitz** (1892–1979; section F, tier 65, grave 24), a top cameraman-cinematographer who worked with Billy Wilder, Preston Sturges, and other big-name directors, and influenced film noir with his low-key lighting effects; **Harry Stradling Sr.** (1901–1970; mausoleum, block 15, grave 2), whose film triumphs include *Pygmalion, My Fair Lady, Funny Girl,* and *Hello Dolly!;* **George Folsey** (1898–1988; mausoleum, room 15, crypt E2), whose forte was glamorizing stars with softer lighting, and who received thirteen Oscar nominations for such films as *Thousands Cheer, Meet Me in St. Louis, Green Dolphin Street,* and *Million Dollar Mermaid;* and **Joseph A. Valentine** (1900–1949; section B, lot 36, grave 3), whose 1930s–1940s films include *Joan of Arc, Saboteur,* and *Wings Over Honolulu.*

Hollywood luminaries aren't the only ones who now call Holy Cross home. **Barney Oldfield** (1878–1946; section D, lot 290, grave 11), race car driver who set a land-speed record in 1910, is here, as are **Alfred S. Bloomingdale** (1916–1982; section W, tier 37, grave 78), businessman who launched Diners Club, the first credit card company (and whose wife, Betsy, is a close chum of Nancy Reagan); Danish-born **Charles T. Von der Ahe** (1882–1973; St. Ann section), founder of Von's supermarket chain; and **Conrad Hilton Jr.** (1926–1969; section T43, grave 124), son of the founder of the Hilton hotel chain and first husband of Elizabeth Taylor. Real, not reel, royalty here is **Nazli Fouad** (1894–1978; section F, tier 56, grave 77), Queen Mother of Egypt.

A little-known and quickly forgotten name is **Carlotta Monti** (1907–1993; mausoleum, outdoor garden, block 256, niche F3), a minor actress better known as W. C. Fields's mistress. Ironically, W. C.'s wife, **Harriet Fields** (1879–1963; mausoleum, block 153, crypt C3), is also here.

Here too is **Gloria Morgan Vanderbilt** (1904–1965; section D, lot 176, grave 2), mother of *the* Gloria Vanderbilt, fashion designer and socialite. The first Gloria was involved in a lengthy custody battle for "Little Gloria," which she lost. She is here, buried with her twin sister, **Thelma, Viscountess Furness** (1904–1970).

A most intriguing resident is **Russell Birdwell** (1903–1977; section D, lot 215 grave 7), a personality flashy enough to compete for press attention with the movie stars of his day. His first and biggest coup as a Hollywood press agent was to hire an unknown woman in widow's weeds to place flowers at the crypt of Rudolph Valentino on the first anniversary of his death. The image was so compelling that another mysterious "woman in black," unrelated to Birdwell's stunt, repeated the visit every anniversary for decades.

No household name, **Dr. Herbert T. Kalmus** (1881–1963; Grotto of St. Bernadette) had more impact on movies than many a star, as the co-inventor and president of Technicolor. **Chick Hearn** (1916–2002; section F, tier 64, grave 42) is a basketball Hall of Famer for his lengthy career as the on-air voice of the Los Angeles Lakers, doing play-by-play for 3,338 straight games (a record), and making the terms "slam dunk" and "air ball" part of the lexicon.

One of the many pleasures of graveyard hopping is the undercover work, finding now-obscure people who had some significance in bygone eras. That's why the discovery of **Joseph Ignatius Breen** (1890–1965; section P, lot 327) gave us such a kick. Long forgotten now, Breen was director of the Production Code Administration for twenty years (1934–1954). In short, he was the censorship czar for the Motion Picture Association of America and the nemesis of most of Hollywood's creative people.

Actress **Audrey Meadows** (1926–1996; section F, tier 29, grave 58) was best known as Alice Kramden, Jackie Gleason's long-suffering wife in television's still-syndicated hit comedy *The Honeymooners*. **Mack Sennett** (1880–1960; section N, lot 490, grave 1), director and producer of more than 1,000 silent films and at least two dozen talkies, was best known for his Keystone Kops, car chases, bathing beauties, and lowbrow, pie-in-the-face slapstick comedies.

Chris Penn (1965–2006; section CC, tier 54, grave 19), son of director Leo Penn and actress Eileen Ryan and lesser-known brother of Sean Penn, was also an actor, in *Rumble Fish, All the Right Moves, Footloose, Short Cuts, The Funeral,* as a memorable villain in Clint Eastwood's *Pale Rider* (1985), and co-star with his brother, mother, and Christopher Walken in *At Close Range*. Often cast as a heavy (and he *was* heavy), his most visible role was as gangster Nice Guy Eddie in Quentin Tarantino's *Reservoir Dogs*. He rests here with his father, **Leo Penn** (1921–1998; section CC, tier 54,

> ## LUNCH BREAK
>
> We enjoy the bagels, French-dipped brisket of beef, and other sandwiches at the funky, authentic Jewish delicatessen **Roll 'n Rye Deli** (Studio Village Shopping Center, 10990 West Jefferson Boulevard; 310-390-3497). Another standby in the area is old-fashioned, comfy **Petrelli's Steakhouse** (5615 Sepulveda Boulevard; 310-397-1438) for juicy steaks and some Italian dishes.

grave 20), actor, writer, and movie and television director-producer for some forty years. ★*Grounds open 8:00 A.M.–5:00 P.M. daily. Office hours: 8:00 A.M.–4:30 P.M. weekdays, 9:00 A.M.–3:00 P.M. weekends. Mass in the mausoleum chapel 8:30 A.M. daily, except Sunday. Map; list of celebrities; restrooms.*

MARY ASTOR 1906–1987

Most film fans today know Mary Astor for her unforgettable portrayal of Brigid O'Shaughnessy in *The Maltese Falcon* (1941) opposite Humphrey Bogart's Sam Spade, but moviegoers throughout the early twentieth century saw her in many other roles in a career that included more than 120 films.

Born Lucile Vasconcellos Langhanke, she was pushed by her parents into beauty contests, where she was noticed by Hollywood at age fourteen, leading to a bit part in *Scarecrow* (1920). Many roles followed and she worked steadily, starring with John Barrymore in *Beau Brummel* (1924) and again in *Don Juan* (1926).

Her personal life gained more attention than her acting in 1936, when during divorce proceedings against her second husband, Astor's personal diary became public, telling juicy details of her extramarital affair with playwright George S. Kaufmann. But this didn't keep her from being cast in many films as a femme fatale, to whom marriage vows meant little. It also didn't hinder her winning a Best Supporting Actress Oscar for *The Great Lie* (1941).

Astor was as adept at comedy as drama, which she proved in Preston Sturges's *The Palm Beach Story* (1942). Her last performance was in *Hush, Hush, Sweet Charlotte* (1964). Outside her film career she had great success as a writer,

FILM VAULT

Something of a sleeper, **The Palm Beach Story** (1942) is one of our favorite madcap comedies. In it, Astor, Joel McCrea, Claudette Colbert, and Rudy Vallee are all hilarious. Other Preston Sturges works are better known, but this is a gem, for pacing, dialogue, and the goofy all-star supporting cast. And then there's the hilarious Ale and Quail Club . . .

publishing five novels and two best-selling books: an autobiography, *My Story* (1959), which detailed her battle with alcoholism and her failed marriages, and a memoir, *A Life on Film* (1971).

She was married four times and had two children. Suffering from a heart condition, she spent her last few years in the Motion Picture Country Home, dying of a heart attack at age eighty-one. But to film buffs, time stands still and Mary Astor remains forever the two-timing temptress in *The Maltese Falcon*. You will find her at home in section N, lot 523, facing the mausoleum.

CHARLES BOYER *1899–1978*

Fans of French actor Charles Boyer remember him as a matinee idol, with his seductive voice, bedroom eyes, and suave manner, but he was trained as a classical stage

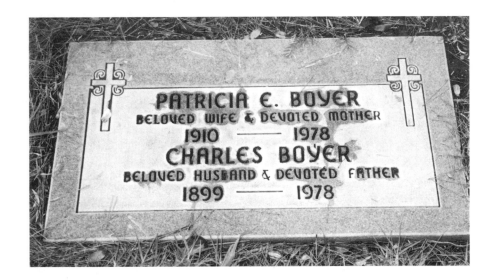

actor in France. Boyer considered himself a character actor and fought against his lover-leading man image. Still, the romantic roles persisted—in *Mayerling, Algiers, Love Affair,* and numerous other films.

When World War II began, Boyer—then age forty—enlisted in the French army. His was a short stay (eleven weeks), but throughout the war he was an enthusiastic supporter of General Charles de Gaulle's Free French government-in-exile.

During a long career, he made twenty-nine European and forty-seven American films. In 1948 he made his Broadway debut in *Red Gloves,* but his major American stage hit was *Don Juan in Hell,* in which his Don Juan was considered by many critics to be his finest performance.

Tragedy stalked his last years. His only child, Michael Charles, committed suicide at age twenty-two. When his wife of forty-five years, **Patricia Boyer** (1910–1978), died, so did he: On the day of her funeral, he committed suicide. It's a poignant story that might have been a Boyer movie. They recline together under the same gray granite stone in the St. Ann section, lot 186, grave 5; next to them is Michael.

JOHN CANDY *1950–1994*

Not all fat men are natural comedians, but John Candy really was, with a sweetness to his humor that made fans love him even as they laughed at and with him. Anyone who watched the Canada-based *Second City TV* will remember fondly his lengthy repertoire of comic characters: clarinetist-polka bandleader Yosh Schmenge, talk-show host Johnny LaRue, Mayor Tommy Shanks, Mr. Mambo, and Gil Hodges, host of the "Fishin' Musician."

Canadian-born Candy scored really big (no pun intended) in Hollywood, making over forty films. Among the keepers are *Splash!; Little Shop of Horrors; National Lampoon's Vacation; Planes, Trains and Automobiles;* and *Canadian Bacon.* Many others were merely broad, though some of these, such as *Uncle Buck,* became hits. His acting skills weren't confined to comedies, as he proved in *JFK,* among other serious dramas.

Candy died in the saddle, so to speak, on location in Durango, Mexico, while filming *Wagons East!,* leaving a wife, two children, and legions of bereft fans. His gilt-edged marker in room 7 of the mausoleum (crypt B1, just above Fred MacMurray and June Haver) has a Sacred Heart in the center and reads "In loving memory * One heart and one soul * We miss you dearly." Amen to that.

BING CROSBY *1903–1977*

"Der Bingle" began life in Spokane, Washington, as Harry Lillis Crosby. His nickname "Bing"—from the *Bingville Bugle,* a comic strip he loved as a kid—fit his easygoing personality. He loved to sing, though he never learned to read music, and in high school formed a small band. One thing led to another, and by the late 1920s he and two partners became the Rhythm Boys. In 1930 CBS offered Crosby his own solo radio show.

Using "Where the Blue of the Night Meets the Gold of the Day" as his theme song, he performed live for twenty straight weeks at New York's Paramount Theatre, a run that ended in contracts with Paramount Pictures and Decca Records. He appeared in over seventy movies, including the popular "Road" series with Bob Hope, but made his fortune—reputed to be more than $150 million at his death—on radio, singing every imaginable type of popular music, from ballads and blues to country-and-western and star-spangled patriotic songs.

His all-time biggest hit was "White Christmas," which he introduced on a 1941 radio program and sang in the 1942 film *Holiday Inn.* All in all, he made an astonishing 1,700 recordings (of which 383 were among the Top 10, while 41 were No. 1). His voice had tremendous range, but he was most comfortable as a bass with baritone quality. Artie Shaw once described him as "the first hip white person born in the United States."

In addition to his natural vocal talent, Crosby was also a smart investor—in real estate, oil, and other commodities—making him one of Hollywood's wealthiest men. Aside from the money, Crosby was much appreciated, winning five Academy Awards in diverse categories (including one for Best Actor in *Going My Way*) and being nominated for an additional three. He also won the first Grammy Lifetime

Achievement Award in 1962, collected twenty-three gold and platinum records, and was among the Top 10 in film box-office draw for fifteen years.

Blessed with a warm, charming public persona, he was Mr. Popularity for five decades. After his death, a book by his eldest son, Gary, attempted to besmirch Bing's image, claiming he was a cold, stern taskmaster who beat the four sons from his first marriage. Another son, Phillip, disputed that, saying the boys were *never* beaten and accusing his brother of writing a sensational book to make money. None of the boys had much success in life, and none lived long enough to claim his inheritance, which Bing had specified would not be awarded until they were old men.

Crosby's first wife, actress **Dixie Lee Crosby** (1911–1952; same site), was an alcoholic who died young from ovarian cancer. Two of their four sons—**Lindsay Crosby** (1938–1989) and **Philip Crosby** (1934–2004), both actors—committed suicide and are buried elsewhere in Holy Cross. Crosby's second marriage in 1957 to a much younger actress, Kathryn Grant, seems to have been a much happier one and produced three children, Harry, Mary, and Nathaniel.

Addicted to golf, Crosby died of a heart attack, coming happily off a golf course in Madrid, Spain, after a good game. His simple granite gravestone, located in the grass in the Grotto section, lot 119, grave 1, bears his etched name—Harry Lillis Bing Crosby—a cross, and the words "Beloved by all." For some reason, the date of birth on the stone is wrong, 1904, a year later than it should be.

JIMMY DURANTE *1893–1980*

James Frances Durante, the son of Italian immigrants, grew up in poverty on New York's Lower East Side, where his large nose made him the butt of neighborhood jokes. Later, as a performer, he poked fun at himself, but never, ever ridiculed others' physical liabilities. In fact, one element of his popularity was his gentle humor and sweet shyness. Comedy didn't come easily to him. He studied classical piano, but when he discovered ragtime, it launched him—at age sixteen—into a series of honky-tonks and dives around New York, sometimes playing songs he had composed himself.

A partnership with Eddie Jackson, a singing waiter, and dancer Lou Clayton, who dubbed him "Snozzola," brought Durante out of his shell, cracking jokes in the raspy, sandpaper voice that fans learned to love. Durante eventually played the Palace—the pride of the vaudeville circuit. Movies followed, then Jimmy's debut on Broadway in *Strike Me Pink,* followed by *Jumbo.*

His career had its ups and downs, but never a dead end. His most "up" period was in the 1940s when he was teamed on a weekly radio show with Garry Moore, in which the syntax-challenged Durante was corrected by the smooth-talking Moore. Durante's line "You teach me to say dem woids right and we're both outa a job" was typical of the show's humor.

Certain songs became classic Durante: "Inka Dinka Doo," "I Ups to Him and He Ups to Me," and "I Know Darn Well I Can Do Without Broadway, but Can

Broadway Do Without Me?" He ended each of his radio shows with the tagline "Goodnight, Mrs. Calabash, wherever you are," leaving listeners guessing who this mysterious woman was. Durante's lips were sealed, even to the grave (which, by the way, is in section F, tier 96, grave 6).

For all his infectious good humor, Jimmy Durante was a reclusive man whose life revolved around his family, a few old friends, and a devotion to charitable causes. In 1972 he had a debilitating stroke, which left him alive—barely—for another eight years. Goodnight, Mr. Durante, wherever you are.

JOHN FORD *1895–1973*

From John Ford's first breath in Cape Elizabeth, Maine, to his last in his home near Palm Desert, California, stretched a continental and cultural divide of great magnitude. Ford, whose given name was Sean Aloysius O'Fienne, was the youngest of thirteen children of Irish immigrants. He went west as a young man and bridged that divide by making movies, becoming in the process one of the best directors of the twentieth century. His films read like a syllabus of great cinema: *The Grapes of Wrath, The Informer, The Quiet Man, Stagecoach, How Green Was My Valley, Drums Along the Mohawk, What Price Glory?, The Searchers, The Man Who Shot Liberty Valance, Mister Roberts*—and that's just for starters.

In a career that spanned sixty years, Ford made 136 feature films and documentaries, for which he collected six Oscars (two were for World War II documentaries). Westerns are still measured against standards he set, using the vast panorama of open space as a backdrop for epic themes of justice, revenge, and chivalry. When it came to moviemaking, Ford was like a man possessed, saying once "If I had my way, every morning of my life I'd be behind that camera at nine o'clock, waiting for the boys to roll 'em, because that's the only thing I really like to do."

FILM VAULT

Considered a landmark western, **Stagecoach** (1939) is a major epic of the Old West, still a joy to watch, with an all-star supporting cast and Ford's strong directing. It was John Wayne's breakthrough movie, and Thomas Mitchell won a Best Supporting Actor Oscar for his memorable role as a drunken doctor.

Between films, he did, however, enjoy booze and binges with his buddies, often on his boat, *Araner*. In a movie culture where spouses are shed as often as underwear, he was married to the same woman from 1920 to the day he died—despite a brief passionate relationship with Katharine Hepburn. In a biography, *Print*

the *Legend* by Scott Eyman, the author warns that Ford often embellished the facts of his life. (In Hollywood, *really?*)

Ford served in the U.S. Navy during World War II and was awarded a Purple Heart for wounds received in the Battle of Midway. Later he lobbied for an admiral's rank, which he finally received and was so proud of, he carried it with him to his final abode here in section M, lot 304, grave 5. Note his gravestone: "Admiral John Ford *1895–1973* Portland, ME—Hollywood." Resting with him is **Mary Ford** (1896–1979), "his beloved wife for 59 years."

RITA HAYWORTH *1918-1987*

In her prime, this beautiful dancer-turned-actress of Spanish-Irish descent (her real name was Margarita Carmen Cansino) had everything she always wanted—or so it seemed: looks, a sizzling screen presence, fame, the adulation of powerful men. She moved quickly from dancing and roles in B movies, typecast as a Latin sexpot named Rita Cansino, to serious drama. In so doing she changed her last name from Cansino to Hayworth, learned how to sing, dyed her hair red, and raised her hairline by electrolysis. Her hemline followed.

Before long Rita Hayworth was a pinup girl for GIs in World War II. Then came *You'll Never Get Rich* with Fred Astaire, *You Were Never Lovelier* (Astaire again), *Gilda* (which established her as a femme fatale and star), *The Lady from Shanghai, Pal*

Joey, and scores of other movies. Late in her career (1955) she won plaudits for *Separate Tables* and *They Came to Cordura* (1959).

Her five marriages were also legendary, all to high-profile men: wealthy Texan Edward Judson, Orson Welles, Prince Aly Khan of Pakistan, pop singer Dick Haynes, producer James Hill. She had two daughters, one with Welles, the other with Khan. For all her fame and on-screen flamboyant sizzle, she was a shy, reclusive, simple person. She once said that all the men she knew fell in love with Gilda but woke up with Rita.

For fifteen years before she died, Hayward was a "dead woman walking," imprisoned by Alzheimer's disease, which makes her polished black granite gravestone—situated below a kneeling angel in the Grotto, lot 196, grave 6, near the path—especially poignant: "Beloved mother . . . to yesterday's companionship and tomorrow's reunion."

BELA LUGOSI *1882–1956*

It wasn't easy being Dracula. Lugosi Bela Ferenc Dezs Blasko, born in Lugos, Hungary, was a classical actor, singer in musical comedies, and, eventually, a handsome heartthrob at the National Theater of Hungary in Budapest and in Hungarian movies. After emigrating to the United States in 1921, he won some romantic roles on Broadway, but in 1927 he was cast as Count Dracula in a play of the same name. It was a huge success, and four years later he reprised the role in *Dracula,* Hollywood's first talking horror film. It too was a hit, and the die was cast.

For the rest of his life, despite good looks and a penchant for romantic and comic roles, he was destined to play creepy villains. Even then, disappointments plagued his career. Unwilling to don the ugly makeup of Frankenstein's monster, he turned down the role, which went to the lesser-known Boris Karloff, who from then on usurped Lugosi as Hollywood's favorite monster-you-love-to-hate. In a career of peaks and valleys, one of Lugosi's peaks was as Igor in the 1939 *Son of Frankenstein.*

Four years later he finally played the monster in *Frankenstein Meets the Wolf Man.* Smaller roles, a series of cheap films, drug addiction, four failed marriages, tours in second-rate shows, a final fifth marriage, hospitalization for drug abuse, insolvency—that pretty well stakes out a sad, lost life. Ironically, at the end—having fought stereotyping for much of his career—the spirit moved him to request burial in his Dracula cape. Only to rise again? After the funeral service, Peter Lorre, so the story goes, looked down at the coffin and said, "Come now, Bela, quit putting us on." Unfortunately, Dracula was grounded at last. His current underworld address is the Grotto, lot 120, grave 1.

FRED MacMURRAY *1908–1991*
JUNE HAVER MacMURRAY *1926–2005*

Fred MacMurray had such a light touch, made acting look easy, and was so versatile, he could be just as convincing as the ethically challenged salesman in *Double Indemnity* (1944), the romantic lead in the sophisticated comedy *Take a Letter, Darling,* the straight lead in the historical romance *Little Old New York,* and as a flier in the exciting *Dive Bomber.* Comedy was undoubtedly his forte, especially the sophisticated screwball type, but he may be best remembered as the ultimate heel in *The Caine Mutiny* and *The Apartment.* He even made the transition to television look easy, as the unflappable father in *My Three Sons,* which ran for twelve years.

MacMurray was born in Kankakee, Illinois, and grew up in Beaver Dam, Wisconsin. Tall, handsome, and athletic, he won twelve varsity letters in high school, and in college (Carroll College, Wisconsin) was considered one of the state's best fullbacks and punters. He also played the saxophone, and left college early to pursue a musical career. In 1930 he appeared on Broadway in *Three's a Crowd,* followed by *Roberta* in 1933. Signed by Paramount Pictures in 1934, he soon became a hot young actor, favored as a co-star by Claudette Colbert, Carole Lombard, Katharine Hepburn (in *Alice Adams*), and later Madeleine Carroll. In a single year he made twelve films, most of them hits.

While MacMurray never achieved the megastar status his early pictures promised, he had steady work for most of four decades (1930s through 1960s). A canny investor, he became one of Holly-wood's wealthiest actors. (He wasn't always so astute in his movie choices: He turned down the William Holden role in *Sunset Boulevard.*)

FILM VAULT

We find ***Murder He Says*** (1945) one of the laugh-out-loud funniest slapstick comedies ever. Fred MacMurray as a pollster of the Gallop variety encounters Marjorie Main's family of hayseed killers, and the results are knee-slapping hilarious. The zany cast and good script make this one of our perennial favorites.

Ohio-born June Stovenour began her career as a child, dancing and singing at local stage events. She was just a teenager when she sang with a dance band, then snared a movie contract with 20th Century Fox and appeared in *The Gang's All Here.* That was in 1943, and for the next ten years she sang, danced, and acted the ingenue in scores of movie musicals the likes of *Three Little Girls, Look for the Silver Lining,* and *Oh, You Beautiful Doll.* Her studio hoped she would be the Next Big Thing, (i.e., the next Betty Grable), and she even co-starred with Grable in *The Dolly Sisters* (1945). But along came Marilyn Monroe, who *was* the next Grable (and then some!).

In 1953 Haver spurned a $3,500 weekly contract and left Hollywood to become a nun in Kansas. As it turned out, her real vocation was not for sisterhood but for marriage. She left the convent after eight months, returned to California, and eventually married widower MacMurray (they had co-starred in the 1945 film *Where Do We Go From Here?*). They had two adopted twin daughters, plus two children from MacMurray's first marriage, and eventually had seven grandchildren and four great-grandchildren. The large MacMurray family lived on a 1,500-acre ranch in Healdsburg, California. By nature, Haver was so buoyant that friends sometimes greeted her by saying "Cheer down, June."

The MacMurray wall crypt (D1) is in room 7 of the mausoleum. Above them is John Candy. On sunny days this side room is flooded with the colors flowing through a vibrant stained-glass window at the end.

WALTER O'MALLEY *1903–1979*

Here in California, Walter O'Malley's grave site (in section P, lot 526, grave 5) is peaceful. This would probably not be the case if he were buried in his native Bronx or in Brooklyn, where older baseball fans still boo O'Malley's name for moving his Brooklyn Dodgers—"dem bums," as locals called their favorite team—from decrepit, cozy Ebbets Field cross-country to Los Angeles.

O'Malley, son of a prosperous merchant who went bankrupt, built a highly successful law practice specializing in—bankruptcies. In 1941 he was asked by the Brooklyn Trust Company to become attorney for the Brooklyn Dodgers team, which was in debt to the bank. In short order, O'Malley acquired major shares in the ball club, which he turned into a highly successful franchise.

By the early 1950s he chafed at Ebbets Field's limitations and coveted a larger facility with more parking. When New York officials disregarded his appeals, O'Malley sold Ebbets Field and moved lock, stock, and ball club to Los Angeles, which ceded 300 acres for a new stadium and agreed to pay almost $5 million for improvements to the area and road construction.

To compound his villainy (as Brooklyn fans perceived it), O'Malley also engineered the New York Giants' move to San Francisco, which enabled the Dodger-Giant rivalry to continue, almost guaranteeing high attendance. His defenders insist that these moves made baseball a truly national game.

Time has probably proved O'Malley right. In 1962, the new Dodger Stadium cost $20 million; in 1979 when he retired—turning the team presidency over to his

son, Peter—the franchise was worth $50 million. (It has since been sold several times.) Today, with nine National League championships and five World Series titles, Los Angeles is one of the most highly regarded teams in baseball. No Dodger-ing that fact.

LOUELLA PARSONS *1880–1972*

Today the name is a mere memory in Hollywood, but in her heyday, from the 1930s to 1950s, Louella Parsons was Hollywood's social arbiter, whose displeasure made movie moguls quake in their designer shoes. She didn't look the part. Small and seriously overweight, La Parsons was a newspaper writer whose beat was Hollywood. But her instinct for gossip, her network of industry "informers" who supplied her with tips, and her eerie ability to scoop competitors made her a presence to be reckoned with.

In her day she was one of the two most powerful women in Hollywood. The other was Hedda Hopper, and the competition for scoops between this tart-tongued twosome was as fierce as machine-gun fire. Ironically, the two were once friends. But in 1937 Hopper became a columnist for a rival paper, and the friendship went kaput.

Though Parsons became famous for her movie columns, she didn't see her first film until she was twenty-four. Illinois-born, she got one of her first jobs in Chicago in 1914, writing the country's first movie gossip column for the *Chicago Record-Herald*. The newspaper was later bought by William Randolph Hearst, who didn't see the need for such a column and fired Parsons. She promptly went to New York and began another gossip column, this time for the *New York Morning Telegraph.*

She later became a syndicated columnist for Hearst and was associated with the Hearst empire for the rest of her career. Her column, originating in the *Los Angeles Examiner,* appeared in over 600 newspapers around the world, with some 20 million readers. In addition to her column, Parsons wrote movie scripts and hosted a weekly radio show in which she interviewed movie stars and, later, another show in which she offered snippets of upcoming films. She also made cameo appearances in movies and wrote two volumes of memoirs, *The Gay Illiterate* in 1944 and *Tell It to Louella* in 1961.

Parsons was married twice, the first time to John Parsons, which produced her only child, Harriet, who as an adult became a Hollywood producer. Her second marriage to Henry W. Martin lasted thirty-eight years, until his death in 1964. At some point in her later life, Parsons—born Louella Rose Oettinger to Jewish parents—became a Catholic. Despite her origins, she was known to express anti-Semitic remarks.

By the time of Parsons's death, there weren't many of her friends or foes left in the movie industry to attend her funeral. The woman who had wielded her gossipy pen as vigorously as a machete died quietly. Her unobtrusive gravestone is in D Section, lot 235, grave 8, under her married name, Martin.

ROSALIND RUSSELL
1912–1976

In more than fifty movies, Rosalind Russell never became typecast. Born in Waterbury, Connecticut, she began her career in summer stock, followed by a few Broadway shows, a Hollywood screen test, and a movie career that stretched from the early 1930s to the late 1960s. While a wisecracking, brainy career woman was her forte, she could play serious roles—*Night Must Fall, Sister Kenny, Picnic, Gypsy,* and *Mourning Becomes Electra* come to mind—with equal aplomb.

Still, she is probably best remembered for her screwball performance as the fast-talking reporter in *The Front Page,* as the bitchy Sylvia in *The Women,* and as the irrepressible Mame in *Auntie Mame,* both the movie and Broadway show. Mame was the role of her life, and at age forty-four she played it with the vigor and energy she brought to all her parts. When her movie career sagged in the late 1940s, she spunkily turned to the stage, touring with great success in *Bell, Book and Candle,* followed by even greater raves in *Wonderful Town,* in which she danced and sang, despite limited skills in both. "I don't sing, I gargle," she said.

One of the few megastars to keep her personal life private, she was the wife of Danish-born, Tony award–winning producer **Frederick Brisson** (1912–1984), and devoted much time to fund-raising for worthy causes. For her efforts, she received the Gene Hersholt Humanitarian Award at the 1973 Oscar ceremonies. Nominated four times for an Oscar, she never won. Her star billing here, with her husband, is in section M, lot 536, grave 2, easily found by the large crucifix two steps above her grave site.

SHARON TATE *1943–1969*

This grave site (St. Ann section, tier 152, grave 6) honors the brief life and tragic death of a young actress, her unborn baby, and three family members. Anyone alive in 1969 remembers the horror of the real-life story that played out on August 9 in the middle of the night in a rented house in Los Angeles.

Sharon Tate was a beauty contest winner from Texas, who had shown promise in her few movies, especially *The Sandpiper* and *Valley of the Dolls.* She married Polish director Roman Polanski in 1968. Polanski was out of town, but Tate (eight

months pregnant) had three friends visiting. Just after midnight, four wild strangers burst in and shot and savagely stabbed all four, plus a teenager who chanced to be there. The strangers belonged to a bizarre cult led by Charles Manson, a maniacal guru addicted to drugs, mayhem, and murder. Manson wasn't with his gang that horrendous night, but he was the instigator of the random murders and is in prison for life, along with two of the actual perpetrators.

By the way, the Polanskis' rental house was at 10050 Cielo Drive—Cielo meaning "heaven" in Italian. Some irony that.

LAWRENCE WELK *1903–1992*

A farm boy from Strasburg, North Dakota, who dropped out of school in fourth grade, Lawrence Welk grew up among Alsatian Germans and didn't learn proper English until he was twenty-one. Yet Welk was no hick when it came to marketing his own music. He parlayed accordion playing into band leading and finally into a role as a television impresario. In the process he made Lawrence Welk a national name and his "Champagne music" famous—smooth, tuneful arrangements of everything from polkas and novelty songs to pop tunes, to dance to and reminisce by.

For more than thirty years *The Lawrence Welk Show* was part of popular music history, never changing its format. The recorded show sounded live and, following Welk's formula, rarely played music that wasn't tried and true. Critics scoffed, but Welk knew his audience wanted sameness and proved it by the continued popularity of the show. His familiar "Ah one, and ah two" count-off before launching each song was echoed in his car license plate, which read "A1ANA2."

Even though the music was considered cornball in some circles, its performers were all highly qualified professional musicians. The New Orleans Dixieland clarinetist Pete Fountain, for instance, was once a staple of the band, and one of Welk's recordings featured jazz great Johnny Hodges on saxophone.

The continuity of Welk's music was only topped by the continuity of his life: He was married for over sixty years, until his death, to the same woman, **Fern Renner** (1903–2002), who is still with him. Welk fans may be reaching their own finales year by year, but those left are a loyal bunch and may still be humming some of his "Champagne" tunes as they pay homage at his grave site in section Y, tier 9, grave 110.

LORETTA YOUNG *1913–2000*

Although she made more than sixty-five movies—sometimes as many as seven or eight a year—Young is probably best known to baby boomers as the star of television's *The Loretta Young Show,* which she hosted and sometimes starred in. This weekly drama in the 1950s won her three Emmys (in 1955, 1956, and 1959).

Gretchen Michaela Young was born in Salt Lake City, Utah, but her family moved to Hollywood when she was three years old. A year later she had her first movie role in *The Primrose Ring.* Throughout childhood, she and her two older sisters were in many silent films. Later, her screen image was usually wholesome, upright, and smart, as in *The Call of the Wild* (1935), *The Story of Alexander Graham Bell* (1939), *The Doctor Takes a Wife* (1940), *The Stranger* (1946), and *The Farmer's Daughter* (1947), for which she won her only Oscar.

Off-screen, Young wasn't always so prim. She eloped with actor Grant Withers when she was seventeen and he was twenty-six. The marriage was annulled the following year (at a time when their movie *Too Young to Marry* was being released—so much of a coincidence that the cynical might think it a publicity stunt). At twenty-one Young evidently had an affair with Clark Gable. She became pregnant, disappeared with her mother to Europe, and returned some months later with an "adopted" baby girl. The baby was later named Judy Lewis, the last name of Young's second husband.

In later years Young was a tireless supporter of Catholic and other charities and active in the Republican Party. On her television programs she aimed for moral, upbeat scripts and messages. Look for Young in section F, tier 65, grave 49, under her mother's name, **Gladys Belzer** (1888–1984). Loretta is not named on the gravestone, one of the few times a star didn't request top billing.

INGLEWOOD, MALIBU, AND SANTA MONICA

Disparate as these three Los Angeles satellites are, each deserves more than a cursory visit. Inglewood alone might keep you scouting for hours, while Santa Monica's Woodlawn Cemetery is a real sleeper.

INGLEWOOD

INGLEWOOD PARK CEMETERY

720 EAST FLORENCE AVENUE; (310) 412-6500

This spacious park of gently rolling hills, shade trees, mausoleums, and obelisks began life, as it were, in 1905. Just south of Los Angeles in the suburb of Inglewood, the cemetery contains many notables: a Civil War–era governor of California, Civil War generals, several U.S. congressmen, pastors of African-American churches, blues musicians, silent-movie actors, and various sports achievers.

Among many worthies is comedian-ventriloquist **Edgar Bergen** (1903–1978; Miramar plot, lot 131, grave 2), whose dummies "Charlie McCarthy" and "Mortimer Snerd" became 1930s–1950s celebrities in their own right. So popular was his act that his radio show ran for more than twenty years, with many listeners believing that Charlie and Mortimer were real. Bergen and Charlie appeared together in eight films, most memorable of which was *You Can't Cheat an Honest Man* (1939) with W. C. Fields (with whom Charlie had a popular radio "feud"). Bergen was awarded an

honorary Oscar in 1938, the only wooden Oscar statuette ever made. Today he is best known as the father of actress Candice Bergen.

The most popular pinup girl of World War II GIs is here: blond, shapely **Betty Grable** (1916–1973; Mausoleum of the Golden West, Sanctuary of Dawn, crypt A-78), star of 1940s musicals and a Top 10 box office draw for nine years.

Charles Brown (1922–1999; Sunset Mission mausoleum, Sanctuary of Bells, crypt 930), performer and composer of "Merry Christmas, Baby" and "Drifting Blues," is here, as are fellow musicians **Ferde Grofé** (1892–1972; Mausoleum of the Golden West, Sanctuary of Faith, crypt E-324), movie composer ("Grand Canyon Suite"), arranger, and conductor, and **Nacio Herb Brown** (1896–1964; Sunny Slope, lot 188), who, collaborating with lyricist Arthur Freed, wrote "Singin' in the Rain," "You Are My Lucky Star," and many other show tunes.

Musicians are here aplenty. They include jazz trumpeter and vocalist **Chet Baker** (1929–1988; Elm 63, division C), the epitome of cool, who played with Charlie Parker, Stan Getz, Gerry Mulligan, and others; **T-Bone Walker** (1910–1975; Capistrano Court, Memorial panel 26), who played banjo and guitar with Cab Calloway; and R & B singer **Kenny Sinclair** (1939–2003; Garden of Peace mausoleum, crypt 138, third row up), member of the doo-wop group called the Six Teens, influenced by Frankie Lymon and the Teen-agers.

Also here is blues composer and singer **Willie Mae "Big Mama" Thornton** (1926–1984; plot M, lot 2486, grave B), who wrote "Ball and Chain" and sang it before Janis Joplin made it famous. Her grave is all the way back to the chain-link fence, twelve graves to the right of the Regent Street sign. **Cornell E. Gunter** (1936–1990; El Sereno section, lot 151), doo-wop singer, R & B musician, and original member of the Robins, is here, too. The **Reverend James Edward Cleveland** (1932–1991; Alta Mesa Gardens, lot 79, mausoleum, crypt 77) did it all musically in gospel—composed, arranged, sang, produced, performed, and founded the Gospel Music Workshop of America—taking it to a new dimension with added elements of jazz, blues, and soul.

Note the presence of actor **Cesar Romero** (1907–1994; Mausoleum of the Golden West, Alcove of Music, Sanctuary of Dreams, niche 408), a Cuban of stellar lineage, grandson of national hero Jose Marti. In Romero's long movie career, he played a gamut of virile heroes, Spanish and Latin lovers, gigolos, and villains, but is best known as the Joker on TV's *Batman*.

Edmond Richard "Hoot" Gibson (1892–1962; Magnolia Plot, lot 92, grave 6) is here, too. Just a funny name today, he was once big stuff, a rodeo champion and western actor with legions of kid fans in action serials of the 1920s and early 1930s. Character actor **Frank Jenks** (1902–1962; Siesta section, lot 257, grave B) was in some 130 films, sometimes playing his trombone. Among them are *His Girl Friday, The Big Broadcast of 1937, Follow the Boys,* and *Christmas in Connecticut.*

Present also are **William Thomas** (1931–1980; Acacia Slope, lot 733, grave D), better known as Buckwheat in almost a hundred "Our Gang" comedies; **William Dellano Byrd** (1966–1993; Manchester mausoleum, Sanctuary of Valor, crypt 901), actor in *Children of a Lesser God* (1986); **Louise Fazenda** (1896–1962; Mignonette section, lot 17, grave 11), silent-screen comedienne and wife of producer Hal Wallis; and even little **Norman Spencer Chaplin** (1919; Del Ivy Plot, lot 496, grave 3), son of Charlie Chaplin and his first wife (sixteen-year-old Mildred Harris), who lived a mere three days and lies beneath a stone inscribed "Little Mouse."

Screenwriter **Robert Riskin** (1897–1955; Mausoleum of the Golden West, Sanctuary of Eternity, crypt L-133), whose script for *It Happened One Night* won an Oscar, is here, as are movie director **Walter Lang** (1896–1972; Sunnyslope, lot 256), who guided *The King and I, Can-Can,* and other films, and director-producer **D'Urville Martin** (1939–1984; Parkview plot, space 886), who also acted in such films as *Guess Who's Coming to Dinner, Rosemary's Baby,* and *Watermelon Man.* His grave is in the northwest corner, five rows from Elm Drive.

Among several major-league baseball players on Inglewood's roster are Hall of Famer **"Wahoo Sam" Crawford** (1880–1968; Resthaven section, lot 475), right fielder for the Detroit Tigers from 1903 to 1917; **Bobby Wallace** (1873–1960; Evergreen section, lot 226, grave A), Hall of Famer and early-twentieth-century infielder; **Jim Gilliam** (1928–1978; Miramar plot, lot 58, grave 10), dynamo of the Negro League and National League Rookie of the Year in his 1953 debut; and **Lyman Bostock** (1950–1978; Parkview section, lot 342, grave D), Minnesota Twins outfield slugger whose promising career—and life—was cut short by a random gunshot.

Other athletes on these fields are professional footballer **Ricky Lynn Bell** (1955–1984; Parkview plot, lot 973, grave D), University of Southern California All-American and Heisman Trophy runner-up (1976), and accomplished volleyball player **Flo Hyman** (1954–1986; Manchester Garden mausoleum, Manchester Court, #224), captain of the 1984 U.S. Olympics team.

Here as well are race car drivers **Louis Meyer** (1904–1995; Acacia Slope, lot 11, grave C), first three-time winner of the Indianapolis 500 (1928, 1933, 1936), who lived to walk away from a horrendous crash and later helped develop the Meyer-Drake racing engine of the 1950s and 1960s, and **John Parsons** (1918–1984; La Ramada section, lot 787), ten-time veteran of the Indianapolis 500, winner in 1950. **Errett Lobban Cord** (1894–1974; Sequoia section, plot 597) didn't race cars but produced them, manufacturing such technically advanced cars of the 1920s as the Cord, Auburn, and Duesenberg; he later became a U.S. senator.

John Gillespie Bullock (1871–1933; Inglewood mausoleum, room D) founded the West Coast's Bullock's Department Store chain. **Paul Revere Williams** (1894–1980; Manchester Garden mausoleum, Sanctuary of Radiance, crypt A-142), known as "architect to the stars," designed homes for A-listers such as Frank Sinatra, Lucille Ball and Desi Arnaz, and Danny Thomas, plus public buildings like the Shrine Auditorium, the Los Angeles County Courthouse, and the Hollywood YMCA. He was the first certified African-American architect west of the Mississippi.

LUNCH BREAK

Jody Maroni's Sausage Kingdom (6081 Center Drive; 310-348-0007) is a chain with a difference: the variety of delicious sausages offered, from Italian to andouille to chicken-apple. In the heart of Culver City, **La Dijonaise Cafe** (Helms Building, 8703 Washington Boulevard; 310-287-2770) is a French bistro serving breakfast, lunch, and dinner. We like its croissants and crepes especially (and also its reasonable prices).

The most prominent politician on these grounds is probably **Tom Bradley** (1917–1998; Sunset Mission mausoleum, vault 1086D), who retired from a twenty-one-year career as a police officer to a seat on the Los Angeles City Council and then a five-term career as mayor of Los Angeles. Earlier, **Fletcher Bowron** (1887–1968; El Portal, grave 214A) was the city's forty-second mayor, elected to restore clean government (which he did) after an era of graft, racketeering, and corruption.

It seems like just yesterday when powerhouse attorneys **Johnnie L. Cochran Jr.** (1937–2005; Manchester Garden mausoleum, Chapel of Honor, crypt 1202) and **Robert Kardashian** (1944–2003; Park Terrace section, lot 628) were dominating television news coverage for their "dream team" defense of O. J. Simpson in the most infamous double-murder trial of the past fifty years. It's ironic that both lawyers should end up so soon afterwards in the same Elysian fields.

A footnote in movie history is **Paul Bern** (1889–1932; Mausoleum of the Golden West, Sanctuary of Faith, section F-96, niche D), first husband of actress Jean Harlow. Writer-director-producer Bern was a big promoter of Harlow's career, which was poised for a huge MGM takeoff when he married her in 1932 amid much Tinseltown hoopla. Then it seemed that Bern was underequipped sexually, a subject of no little consternation to Harlow. It also was revealed that Bern was still married to Dorothy Millette, who had been conveniently tucked away in a sanatorium and forgotten. Oops—not good for Harlow's budding career. Bern died mysteriously, presumably a suicide, and Millette committed suicide. Was it just kindness that prompted Harlow to spring for Millette's funeral and MGM's chief Louis B. Mayer to pay for her gravestone? That's one of Hollywood's most famous unsolved mysteries; we may never know. ★*Grounds open sunrise to sunset daily. Office hours: 8:30 A.M.–5:00 P.M. Monday–Friday, 8:30 A.M.–4:00 P.M. Saturday. Map; restrooms; flower shop.*

RAY CHARLES *1930–2004*

Ray Charles is an upfront and center proof that handicaps can be overcome. This fabulous singer, pianist, saxophonist, and entertainer didn't have it easy. Sometimes he made it even harder on himself, as *Ray,* the movie biography of his tempestuous life, indicates.

Born Ray Charles Robinson in Albany, Georgia, he was five years old when he witnessed his brother George drown in a washtub. That same year young Ray's eyesight began to fail, leaving him completely blind by age seven. He attended the Florida School for the Deaf and Blind in St. Augustine, and it was there he learned to play a variety of musical instruments and read music in braille.

Soaking up many different music styles on the radio, he was heavily influenced by such diverse genres as gospel, country, blues, and jazz. After the death of his mother, fourteen-year-old Ray left school, playing in various bands before moving to Seattle, Washington, in 1945. There he met Quincy Jones, two years his junior. Ray taught Quincy how to read and arrange music, and a friendship formed that would last the rest of Ray's life. Early recordings from this period show the influence of the seminal Nat King Cole. Charles, who dropped his last name to avoid confusion with the famous boxer Sugar Ray Robinson, also began a heroin addiction that would continue for two decades.

Following a move to Los Angeles with his band, the McSon Trio, Charles had his first charted song, 1951's "Baby, Let Me Hold Your Hand." This was just the beginning of his hit parade. He signed with Atlantic Records and in 1953 arranged and played piano on bluesman Guitar Slim's million-seller "The Things That I Used to Do." In 1954 he released "I Got a Woman," which rose to No. 1 on the R & B charts. In this song he incorporated the gospel music that influenced him and helped form what is now termed "soul" music. Charles's band included female backup singers he dubbed the Raelettes, whom he "auditioned" on his own "casting couch."

Charles attracted fans and critical acclaim, as well as criticism, for combining disparate musical influences. He also released some straight jazz albums in the late 1950s that were real standouts, including *Soul Meeting* (1957) and *Soul Brothers* (1958). Then came 1959's double-Grammy-winning album *The Genius of Ray Charles* (featuring arrangements by Quincy Jones) and the release of the smash "What'd I Say?" In this fertile period he released "Georgia On My Mind," "Ruby," and "Hit the Road, Jack," which made it to No. 1 on both the pop and R & B charts and won Charles another Grammy in 1961.

The next year brought yet another direction when he released *Modern Sounds in Country and Western Music,* in which he covered such classic country-western tunes as "Bye Bye Love," "Hey Good Lookin'," and "I Can't Stop Loving You." This surprise hit album climbed to No. 1 on Billboard's pop chart and remained on the chart for two years. Charles followed it up with *Volume Two,* which reached No. 2 on the album charts and produced more hits.

In 1964 Charles struck gold with "Busted," a bluesy, soulful version of a country song. Ironically, that Halloween, Charles himself was "busted" for possession of heroin, his third such arrest. Placed on parole, he kicked his habit in a California sanatorium and shortly afterwards released the pointed "I Don't Need No Doctor" and "Let's Go Get Stoned" in 1966.

In films, Charles recorded theme songs for *The Cincinnati Kid* (1965) and *In the Heat of the Night* (1967). He played himself in comic turns in 1980's *The Blues*

Brothers and in 1996's *Spy Hard,* introducing himself to yet another generation. He also made dozens of television appearances performing songs, and was an honoree at the Kennedy Center Honors in 1986.

While continuing to make records, Charles concentrated on live performances. He also appeared in several commercials through the years, the most successful being his 1991 Diet Pepsi ads. In all, Ray Charles won twelve Grammy Awards (and a lifetime achievement Grammy) and the National Medal of the Arts, and was inducted into the Jazz, Rock and Roll, Blues, and Rhythm & Blues Halls of Fame, as well as being a Lifetime Achievement Award winner in the Songwriter's Hall of Fame.

He was married and divorced twice, and is believed to have fathered twelve children by seven different women. None of his often-turbulent personal life slowed down his extraordinary musical productivity.

This American icon hit the cosmic road at age seventy-three from a liver disease. Peace at last for Ray is in the Mausoleum of the Golden West, Eternal Love corridor, crypt A-32.

ELLA FITZGERALD *1918–1996*

The bronze plaque on Ella Fitzgerald's white marble wall crypt (Sunset Mission Mausoleum, Sanctuary of Bells, crypt 1063, second floor) states "beloved mother and grandmother," but seems inadequate as a memorial to "the First Lady of Song." Anyone who has heard her fabulous voice—with its great clarity, precise diction, and exuberant spirit—carries the memory forever.

Ella was unique as a popular performer. She didn't dance, wiggle, jiggle, or flirt, and she was no great beauty, but her voice could handle anything: jazz, popular songs, blues, calypso, bossa nova, scat (which she practically invented). For almost

sixty years she sang and sang—on records, in concerts, at jazz festivals, on radio and television, even in a few movies—and did so with the best bands, from Chick Webb, who was her mentor and helped shape her style, to Louis Armstrong, Count Basie, Duke Ellington, Earl Hines, Errol Garner, and Oscar Peterson. Her duets with Armstrong were joyous and legendary.

She sang everywhere—on tours to Europe, Asia, and all over the United States. She made almost 150 albums, singing everything from George Gershwin and Cole Porter to Kurt Weill and the Beatles, and won twelve Grammy Awards, an honorary doctorate in music from Yale University, and just about every other honor imaginable. Her nickname, the First Lady of Song, was almost an understatement.

Born in Newport News, Virginia, and brought up in Yonkers, New York, with her last home in Beverly Hills, California (when diabetes complications forced her retirement in the 1990s), Ella sang in a voice that remained strong and true throughout her life. Ira Gershwin once said, "I never knew how good our [his and brother George's] songs were until I heard Ella Fitzgerald sing them."

She sang them all, from the Gershwins' "The Man I Love" and "Let's Call the Whole Thing Off" to Irving Berlin's "Cheek to Cheek." "Sweet Georgia Brown," "How High the Moon," "A Tisket, a Tasket" (which she co-wrote with Van Alexander in 1938), and "Don't Be That Way" are just a few of the songs that bear her imprint. "Oh, Lady Be Good" . . . Ella, you always were—way, way better than good. The best.

CURT FLOOD *1938–1997*

Curt Flood is not in baseball's Hall of Fame in Cooperstown, nor will any ballpark retire his uniform number with a banner on its wall. Yet single-handedly he probably did more to change the game than anyone, other than Jackie Robinson, in the twentieth century. Not by his batting average, though he batted above .300 in six seasons in a fifteen-year career and was an All-Star three times, and not by his defensive skills, though he won seven Gold Gloves for his fielding skills in the outfield. No, what put him in baseball history books was his fight against the "reserve clause," which treated ballplayers as chattel by club owners, who were free to trade or sell their "property" at will.

But let's rewind the reel of his life for a moment. Born in Houston, Texas, Flood played first (1956) for the Cincinnati Reds, then for twelve years as a St. Louis Cardinal. He did well as a Cardinal, but at the end of the 1969 season, St. Louis traded him and three other players to the Philadelphia Phillies. Flood didn't want to play for the Phillies, a poor team, in a stadium known for vociferous, sometimes racially provocative fans.

Flood resisted. He pleaded with Bowie Kuhn, then baseball commissioner, to let him become a free agent and negotiate with other teams, calling the reserve clause similar to slavery. "I do not feel I am a piece of property to be bought and sold irrespective of my wishes," he wrote to Kuhn, who refused his request. Flood sued, claiming baseball had violated the antitrust laws, and his case went as far as the U.S. Supreme Court, which decided in favor of baseball.

Although Flood's battle ended his career, his brave actions eventually led to free agency, which changed the sport forever and made the reserve clause a dead issue. Players with ten years or more of service with the same ball club were now able to negotiate with other teams. This is how players like Alex Rodriquez, Randy Johnson, Pedro Martinez, and dozens of others have wound up as zillionaires who sell their skills and services to the highest bidder. Flood deserves a posthumous medal from the Players Association, but considering how few players know their own sport's history, it is likely that to most twenty-first-century baseball players, the response to his name would be "Curt who?"

After retiring, Flood became a broadcaster for the Oakland Athletics and later a commissioner of a sandlot league in the Oakland Department of Sports and Aquatics. He later wrote a book about the case (*The Way It Is*, his autobiography). In 1997 Flood struck out for the last time with throat cancer. His bronze wall marker is in the Manchester Garden Mausoleum, Sanctuary of Radiance, crypt A-445.

JAMES J. JEFFRIES *1875–1953*

His substantial headstone in the Sequoia plot (lot 122, grave 7) transports us back to the time when Jim Jeffries was the heavyweight boxing champion of the world, a title he held from 1899 to 1905, when he retired undefeated, having beaten James J. Corbett twice.

The son of a successful California farmer, Jeffries was an ungainly 6 feet 2 inches tall, but he developed great upper-body strength and staying power, willing to take on all challengers. The fact that he came from a middle-class family made him immensely popular and helped elevate boxing in the public's eyes.

When the heavyweight title was won by African American Jack Johnson in 1908, there was a clamor from fight fans for a "great white hope" who would challenge what they perceived as an arrogant black man. Fan pressure and a large guaranteed purse lured the retired Jeffries back into the ring July 4, 1910, in Reno, Nevada. The race card was played to a fare-thee-well, but Johnson won handily, the

referee finally stopping the fight in the fifteenth round after Jeffries had been knocked down three times.

That was the end of boxing for good for Jeffries, who couldn't care less, having carried off more than $100,000 from the fight. He later proved to be a smart businessman and real estate investor, his boxing days left far behind. He lived seventy-eight full years until he went down for the final count.

GYPSY ROSE LEE *1914–1970*

Rose Louise Hovick would never have become Gypsy Rose Lee, the best-known striptease artist of all time, if it weren't for an incredibly pushy mother. Mother Rose Hovick's exploits as immortalized in the musical (and later the movie) *Gypsy* probably were not far from the truth. Desperate to get out of life as a Seattle housewife, she was intent on propelling her two young daughters (ages seven and five) into stardom.

Mother Rose promoted her younger, prettier, and more talented daughter, June, onto the vaudeville stage, in an act that kept Rose Louise as part of June's backup group. The act, in various guises, toured the vaudeville circuit of the 1920s. When vaudeville declined and June ran away to marry at age thirteen, the frantic Rose pushed her older daughter onto the burlesque stage, where good looks and a decent body trumped talent.

What Gypsy Rose Lee, as she renamed herself, lacked in natural ability, she made up for in brains. As an ecdysiast, she turned stripping into an art form, and with smart costumes, a touch of comedy, and a lot of style, she soon blossomed into an authentic stage presence. Offstage she cultivated the rich and famous, and became a regular at popular parties and stylish events. She even made a few movies under her real name (Louise Hovick) because Hollywood executives in the era of censorship were too timid to feature a stripper in a proper mainstream film.

Lee later wrote a mystery novel, *The G-String Murders,* which in 1948 became a movie, *Lady of Burlesque,* with Barbara Stanwyck. Lee's autobiography, *Gypsy,* published (intentionally or not) after her mother's death, was a best seller and eventually led to the musical. By way of a footnote, sister June, using the last name Havoc, eventually returned to the stage as a legitimate and very good Broadway actress. We wonder if June chose Havoc, a variation on Hovick, as an ironic comment on the mayhem her aggressive mother wreaked on her daughters' lives.

Gypsy Rose Lee's final act can be caught in the Mausoleum of the Golden West, Sanctuary of Dawn, crypt A-78. A single engraved rose is embossed in her bronze plaque.

SUGAR RAY ROBINSON *1921–1989*

In a sport with few bona fide heroes, Sugar Ray Robinson stood out. Known for his looks, grace, brains, and style, with both quick hands and power, he was a major force in boxing for twenty-five years, from 1940 to 1965. During most of that time he reigned as welterweight champion, then from 1951 until he retired he won five middleweight titles.

Robinson is considered one of the greatest and winningest boxers ever. Various sports experts have called him the best in his weight class in a hundred years and "Fighter of the Century," better even than Muhammed Ali, as Robinson had more wins—175 in 200 appearances. Not that he won all the time: He lost nineteen matches, had six draws, and was briefly suspended for not reporting a bribe attempt.

His first middleweight match was with Jake "Raging Bull" LaMotta, a fight so brutal, it was called the "St. Valentine's Day Massacre." By the thirteenth round LaMotta was so bloodied and so unresponsive, the referee stopped the fight, declaring Robinson the winner and champion.

One reason Sugar Ray fought into three decades was that he couldn't handle money. He blew his fortune—estimated at nearly $4 million—and got in trouble with the IRS for not paying income tax. He had to keep returning to the ring to pay his debts. After his boxing career ended, Robinson supported himself with nightclub acts—singing and dancing—and acting in television.

As an all-round personality, Sugar Ray was a sweetie. He earned his nickname from a sportswriter who called his style in the ring "sweet as sugar." Actually, that wasn't the only part of his name that was made up. His real name, Walker Smith Jr., didn't have the ring needed for the boxing marquee, so the promoter of his very first fight gave him the card of a retired fighter, and from that moment on he was Ray Robinson.

He may be six feet under, but never count Sugar Ray out. His handsome headstone in the Pinecrest section, lot 24, is a reminder of what a presence he was in life.

M A L I B U

J. PAUL GETTY VILLA

17985 PACIFIC COAST HIGHWAY;
(310) 458-2003

This original Getty Museum closed for renovations when the new Getty Center opened a few miles away in the Santa Monica hills as the major repository of the Getty art and antique furniture collection, but is now reopened, more beautiful than ever.

The villa is a pristine gem, set inside a jewel of a classical garden with graceful cypress trees thrusting heavenward, a reflecting pool surrounded by Greek statues, and other antiquities. The villa is now the showcase for Getty classical antiquities.

In the emerald hillside above the villa is Getty's grave, off limits. A magnificent elongated polished granite sarcophagus, it is the final home of one of the richest men in the world in his day. His riches are evident in the idyllic surroundings, though the grave site is not accessible to visitors. ★ *Open 10:00 A.M.–5:00 P.M. Thursday–Monday.*

JEAN PAUL GETTY *1892–1976*

In his day, J. Paul Getty was called the richest man in the world, with a fortune worth over $1 billion. Unlike some other rich men, Getty was willing to admit that he owed his fortune to being staked by his wealthy father, George Franklin Getty. J. Paul was born Jean Paul in Minneapolis, Minnesota, but the family later moved to Los Angeles. The family fortune came from Oklahoma oil, when the state was still Indian Territory, and senior Getty struck it rich on his first oil well.

During J. Paul's college years, he worked at his father's Oklahoma oil fields, learning the business. With his dad's help, young Getty was soon able to buy and sell oil leases. After a year, he made $40,000 and said, "I will stay in Tulsa until I make a million dollars." In 1916, nineteen months after he started and just two years out of college, he met his goal. He was twenty-four years old.

With his first million, J. Paul decided to retire for a while and enjoy California's pleasures, especially the nightlife. His father was shocked, believing that J. Paul would fritter away his new fortune, and ultimately that of the family. Even though J. Paul returned to business a few years later, his father never had full confidence in him again. At his death, the senior Getty left his son $500,000 of a $10 million estate; most of the rest went to his wife, J. Paul's mother.

Years later (1974), J. Paul wrote a book entitled *How to Be Rich* (not *get* rich, but *be* rich) and credited his success to his father. He wrote, "I enjoyed the advantage of being born into an already wealthy family and when I began my business career I was subsidized by my father. While I did make money—and quite a bit of it— I doubt if there would be a 'Getty Empire' today if I had not taken over my father's thriving oil business after his death."

An enthusiastic art collector, J. Paul Getty bought Sutton Place, a sixteenth-century Tudor estate in England, and moved there in the 1950s. Avidly acquiring antiquities and art, he was also good at acquiring spouses (always young ones). He married five times and had five sons by four of his wives. To keep himself in shape he exercised daily, dyed his hair, and had a face lift.

For such a wealthy man, Getty mostly kept himself out of the tabloids. One horrific exception was in 1973 when he refused to pay the ransom for his kidnapped grandson, J. Paul Getty III. His rationale was that he had fifteen grandchildren, and if he paid a ransom for one, it might be an incentive to other would-be kidnappers to go after the

HOUSE CALL

A short drive away, located on a hilltop with views of the mountains and the ocean, **The Getty Center** (1200 Getty Center Drive, Brentwood; 310-440-7300; www.getty.edu) is an absolute "must-see" for anyone visiting the area. A dramatic modern travertine complex, the center (designed by architect Richard Meier) showcases modern and classical art and *objets* in six pavilions. A bookstore, open-air cafes, and a first-rate restaurant (reservations essential) are on the premises.

others. The kidnappers threatened to cut off the ear of the young man. Eventually, they did and sent it to his grandfather. The ransom was quietly paid, and the boy was released. But no publicist could undo the negative impression about Getty that this incident created.

Getty's stinginess, including his reluctance to tip, was legendary. It has been reported that when his body was shipped from England (where he died) to California, the coffin was so cheap and flimsy, the Malibu authorities wouldn't release the remains to his lawyers until he was reinterred in a decent receptacle. It took two years of haggling to get the job done.

Still, his lasting legacy is his enormous art collection, on which he didn't stint. We can all be grateful for that.

S A N T A   M O N I C A

WOODLAWN CEMETERY & MAUSOLEUM

1847 WEST 14TH STREET; (310) 450-0781; FAX (310) 450-0782

Often below the radar of Hollywood-area graveyards, Woodlawn, with its hedge-lined walls, rests unnoticed by the daily barrage of traffic along Pico Boulevard. Small and easily walkable, its twenty-six acres (which extend up to 17th Street) are dotted with several mausoleums and obelisks, statues of angels, and headstones galore, as well as tall palms, pines, and pepper trees. Owned by the city of Santa Monica since 1897, the nonsectarian cemetery is entered through 14th Street, just off Pico.

Drive through the gates, straight ahead on Rose Avenue, then left to Maple Avenue where you'll see a Spanish mission–style building whose outer walls are adorned with espaliered evergreens. Over the entrance door is a round stained-glass panel. The tiny office is on the left as you enter; the rest of the building is a mausoleum and chapel (whose separate entrance facade is gloriously ornate in the Spanish plateresque style). A sunny stained-glass window in colorful oranges, yellows, and reds—like sun rays—is down the hall from the office.

The most noticeable monument on the grounds belongs to the Elks. All-white with a round dome, Ionic Greek columns, and a sign proclaiming "Brotherly Love," it is directly across from the mausoleum.

Woodlawn has its share of buried treasures. For one, there's **Charles Bickford** (1891–1967; next to fence, unmarked grave), a fine character actor. He played in more than ninety movies, including *A Star Is Born* (the 1954 version).

Down the hall from the office in the mausoleum in the second room on the left is the wall crypt of **J. B. Nethercutt** (1913–2004), co-founder of Merle Norman

Cosmetics in 1931. He was a whiz at cosmetic chemistry and created many of the company's products. He also loved vintage autos and collected 250 of them, installing them in the Nethercutt Collection and Museum in Sylmar, California. His wife, **Dorothy Nethercutt** (1914–2004), is next to him. In the mausoleum basement is **J. Kenneth "Red" Norvo** (1908–1999), xylophonist and bandleader.

Among many disparate achievers at Woodlawn is **May Sutton Bundy** (1887–1975; section 17, A-588), professional tennis champion of the early 1900s and first American winner at Wimbledon; her stone has two crossed rackets and says "Always a Champion." German-born **Leon Feuchtwanger** (1884–1958; section 12, lot 187) was the author of popular historical fiction, such as *Jud Suss* and *The Ugly Duchess* is here too. **Fay Webb** (1907–1936; section 12, lot 156), stage and silent-screen actress, was married to Rudy Vallee during the early 1930s.

Two wrestlers are at arm's length at Woodlawn: Italian-born **Baron Michele Leone** (1909–1988; mausoleum, basement), who put wrestling on the television screen, was world champion for two years, and had a huge cult following, especially in the Los Angeles area, and **Joseph Vance Chorre Jr.** (1914–1987; section 17, lot 548, grave D), aka Suni War Cloud, who wrestled from the 1940s to 1960s and was also a part-time actor.

Elzie C. Segar (1894–1938; section 13N½, lot 319, grave B) isn't a household name, but his cartoon creations Popeye the Sailorman, Olive Oyl, and Bluto are embedded in our cultural heritage. **Ted Koehler** (1894–1973; block Cremains, lot 6, grave C) also is better known for his legacy than himself: As a lyricist paired with composer Harold Arlen, he supplied the words to "Stormy Weather," "Let's Fall in Love," "Get Happy," and many other popular songs.

> ## LUNCH BREAK
>
> Santa Monica is so full of good restaurants, it would be hard to pick a dud. A good choice for a delicious repast, with a hundred menu items to choose among, is the **Broadway Deli** (1457 Third Street; 310-451-0616) on the nearby **Third Street Promenade** (which has a number of different ethnic restaurants and cafes). A touch of India is available at the inexpensive and lively **Bombay Cafe** (12021 West Pico Boulevard, West Los Angeles; 310-473-3388), where you can make a light lunch of creative chutneys and naan.

Several sources note that within the confines of Woodlawn is **Christabel Pankhurst** (1880–1958), a member of the famous British women's suffrage family, but the office has no record of her residence here.

Herr and gone is **Heinrich Mann** (1871–1950), author of *Professor Unrat,* a German novel turned into the movie *The Blue Angel,* of which Mann said, "My reputation rests on the legs of Marlene Dietrich." At the time he and his younger brother Thomas fled Nazi Germany, Heinrich was better known internationally, but Thomas's name soon surpassed his. They settled in Los Angeles, where Heinrich later died. The postwar German government wanted to reclaim its heritage, and Mann now resides for eternity in a cemetery in Berlin. Also missing in inaction is songwriter **Vernon Duke** (1903–1969), who was born Vladimir Dukelsky in Russia, left the country at the time of the Bolshevik Revolution in 1917, and eventually ended up first in California and finally in New York.

Sic transit gloria mundi might be appropriate for **Jesse Marvin Unruh's** (1922–1987; section 4S, lot 39, grave D) marker. Once a major player in California Democratic politics, Unruh was speaker of the California Assembly (passing such important bills as the Unruh Civil Rights Act of 1959 and the pro-consumer Unruh Credit Regulation Act), state treasurer, and all-round kingmaker. His power began to fade after losing his campaign for governor in 1970 against Ronald Reagan.

Along with many veterans of different wars is Spanish-American War veteran **Christian F. Steinle** (1878–1986; section A, 17, lot 217) whose modest claim to fame is that at age 107, when he answered the final "Taps," he was the oldest living American veteran of *any* war. ★*Grounds open dawn to dusk daily. Office hours: 8:00 A.M.–4:00 P.M. weekdays, 10:00 A.M.–4:00 P.M. weekends and holidays. Map; restrooms.*

LEO CARILLO *1880–1961*

For those outside Los Angeles, Leo Carillo's name is forever linked with his role as the sidekick Pancho, co-starring in the television series *The Cisco Kid,* with Duncan Renaldo in the title role.

To those in the know, however, Carillo, contrary to his simple on-screen persona, was a college graduate and a descendant of Spanish conquistadores. At one time or another, his ancestors owned huge blocks of real estate throughout southern California. One relative was even the last governor of California before it became a state. Before the Cisco Kid westerns, Carillo appeared in over ninety films as a character actor, usually with a heavy Latino accent. Prior to that, he was a newspaper cartoonist and journalist.

To southern Californians, he will be best remembered as a stalwart conservationist for whom several beautiful parks and beaches are named, the most famous being Leo Carillo State Park, just north of Santa Monica. Additionally, his Carlsbad ranch is now a registered California historical site and a park, the Leo Carillo Ranch Historic Park.

Leo Carillo is buried in section 2, just north of the Fourteenth Street entrance to the cemetery. His gravestone, next to his wife's and daughter's, is beneath a short palm tree in lot 2, next to Rose Avenue.

PAUL HENREID *1908–1992*

What fan of *Casablanca* could forget Paul Henreid as Victor Laszlo, the heroic freedom fighter whom Rick (Humphrey Bogart) saves? That was just one of many roles the suave Henreid played in his five-decade-long movie career. Another fan favorite was in the four-handkerchief film, *Now, Voyager* (1942), opposite Bette Davis.

As the son of a Viennese banker, Henreid's urbane style came naturally. His real name was the top-heavy Paul Georg Julius Henreid Ritter von Wassel-Waldingau. No wonder he shortened it. He studied acting in Vienna, where his stage debut was in a play directed by the famous Max Reinhardt.

A small role in *Goodbye, Mr. Chips* (1939) led him to Hollywood, where he made movies throughout the 1940s and 1950s. In some films he was the hero, as in the swashbuckling *The Spanish Main* (1945), *Song of Love* (1947), and *Siren of Bagdad* (1953). By the late 1950s and 1960s, he was mostly directing, both for the screen and for television's *Alfred Hitchcock Presents, Maverick, Bonanza,* and *The Big Valley.* Only in Hollywood would a debonair Austrian direct American westerns. Coming full circle, in 1964 Henreid directed *Dead Ringer,* in which his former co-star, Bette Davis, starred.

Resting up for eternity, he is in section 3M, off Palm, along with his wife, **Lisl Henreid** (1908–1993).

ORANGE AND SAN DIEGO COUNTIES

California's sunny south has a sizable share of last resorts for the celebrated. And no wonder! The climate is a great one for living, as well as for a rite of passage into the beyond. Both Orange County and San Diego County have been ground zero for some surprisingly disparate people—John Wayne, Richard Nixon, Jonas Salk, and Raymond Chandler among them.

CORONA DEL MAR

PACIFIC VIEW MEMORIAL PARK

3500 PACIFIC VIEW DRIVE; (949) 644-2700

A beautiful final home high above the ocean, Pacific View, which opened in 1958, is partially level land, punctuated throughout with stone benches that are situated beside numerous gravestones, inviting contemplation and nostalgic thoughts. To the left of the main entrance gates is an unusual memorial, awesome in its size and sadness, to victims of drunk drivers, named and with poignant pictures.

Slumbering on these peaceful grounds are persons of various accomplishments, such as U.S. congressman from California **James Roosevelt** (1907–1991; Ocean View section, lot 815, grave B), son of Franklin D. and Eleanor Roosevelt;

George Yardley (1928–2004; Vista Del Mar section, lot 60, grave 1), record-breaking, perennial All-Star basketball player with the Detroit Pistons; and **Dorothy Jones** (1907–1978; Visa Del Mar, lot 632, grave A), writer and wife of famous animator Chuck Jones.

Film editor and producer **Barbara McLean** (1903–1996; mausoleum, Magnolia Court, crypt 691, L5) is also here; her movies included *Viva Zapata, Niagara,* and *All About Eve.* She shares her digs with her husband, director-producer **Robert Webb** (1903–1990), known for *Love Me Tender* and other films.

At least two stuntmen are here, grounded prematurely: aerial stuntman **Paul Mantz** (1903–1965; Mausoleum of the Pacific, Palm Court, Alcove of Devotion, niche 43), who crashed his plane during filming of *Flight of the Phoenix,* and **Frank Tallman** (1919–1978; Bayview Terrace, lot 146-A), whose stunts were seen in *Catch-22, It's a Mad, Mad, Mad, Mad World,* and *The Great Waldo Pepper.*

LUNCH BREAK

On a sunny day (and southern California has no shortage of these) **Chimayo at the Beach** (315 Pacific Coast Highway, Huntington Beach; 714-374-7273) is a casual place for lunch—perhaps a BBQ chicken, bacon, and melted cheddar cheese sandwich—which you might enjoy outdoors facing the water.

Cinematographers are also on these peaceful grounds, notably **Wilfred Cline** (1903–1976; Ocean View, lot 2820, grave A), cinematographer on *Gone With the Wind, Glory* (1956), and many other films for thirty-seven years, and **Harry Perry** (1888–1985; Alcove of Faith, niche 25), whose twenty-three-year stint included *Wings* and *Hell's Angels.*

A brother of James Cagney is here, though James remains in Westchester, New York: actor **William Cagney** (1905–1988; Vista del Mar section, lot 694, grave E). Relatively speaking, **Mary D. Marx** (1916–2002; Magnolia Court, 939, space S), actress and widow of Chico Marx, is also here.

Among musicians, you'll find rock vocalist **Bobby Hatfield** (1940–2003; Lido Terrace section), member of the Righteous Brothers, and **Freddy "Mr. Silvertone" Martin** (1906–1983; mausoleum, Magnolia Court, crypt 884), tenor saxophonist and bandleader, best known for "I've Got a Lovely Bunch of Coconuts." ★ *Grounds open 8:00 A.M. to sundown daily. Office hours: 8:00 A.M.–5:00 P.M. daily. Map; restroom.*

JOHN WAYNE *1907–1979*

It feels like only yesterday: John Wayne's movies are still so widely shown on television, it seems impossible that he's been down under almost thirty years.

Tall (6 feet, 4 inches), handsome, manly, with that familiar swagger, Wayne was a born cowboy—except he wasn't. Born Marion Michael Morrison in Winterset, Iowa, he was never near a real range. He grew up in southern California, and before he made a single movie, he had worked as a truck driver, fruit picker, ice hauler, and soda jerk in his dad's drugstore. An honor student in school, he won a football scholarship to the University of Southern California, but dropped out in his sophomore year when he broke his ankle.

Wayne's movie career began casually as a scenery mover at 20th Century Fox. Working on a John Ford movie about submarines, he volunteered to go into the rough water when the stuntman refused to do so. From then on he was part of the Ford team; with his natural, manly looks, being in a Ford film was almost inevitable. Being a success was no sure thing.

Wayne's first acting attempts were bombs. After a series of more than forty B and C "horse operas," he was hired by Ford for *Stagecoach* and the future looked brighter. But cast as a young Swedish boy in *The Long Voyage Home,* he quickly realized he wasn't a natural actor and his real milieu was the western. He began to work on what he called "this Wayne thing." "I figured I needed a gimmick, so I dreamed up the drawl, the squint and a way of moving meant to suggest that I wasn't looking for trouble but would just as soon throw a bottle at your head as not."

The gimmick worked, making a fortune for Wayne as well as for his films. In movie after movie—*Tall in the Saddle, Rio Grande, The Searchers, Red River, The Alamo, and How the West Was Won*—Marion Morrison played John Wayne. Sure of himself, an uncomplicated fighter for justice, the John Wayne role transferred just as well from westerns to war movies, and he made a bunch of them as well, including *Sands of Iwo Jima, Flying Leathernecks,* and *The Green Berets.* Even late in his career, as the drunken, dissipated Rooster Cogburn in *True Grit* (for which he won an Oscar), Wayne was playing an older Wayne. Rarely in his more than 200 movies did he break the man-of-action mold.

Off-screen Wayne was as unnuanced, likeable, and outspoken as the roles he played. Ultraconservative, he was a big supporter of the Vietnam War and of Republican candidates for president. Yet earlier, according to a recent biography of John Ford (*Print the Legend* by Scott Eyman), Wayne wasn't so anxious to go to war himself. During World War II, he begged Ford to get him a deferment because of the need to make movies. It was not his finest hour.

Nicknamed "Duke" from childhood, Wayne was quick to tell people he was not royalty, as studio press releases implied, but "Hell, the truth is that I was named after a dog!"—his pet Airedale.

This movie icon's final bunk is at the upper end of Bayview Terrace, section 575, nearer Lagunita Court than Ocean View Drive, on a slope to the left of a tree with a "Clark" bench beneath it. His oversize coppery bronze marker, with an engraved lasso border, features bas-reliefs of Spanish mission buildings, an Arizona desert landscape, the great western star on horseback, and his epitaph, which begins "Tomorrow is the most important thing in life" and ends with "It hopes we've learned something from yesterday." His actress daughter, **Toni Wayne** (1936–2000), sometimes called Tony LaCava, is nearby, on a curb in front of her father's grave.

F U L L E R T O N
L A   J O L L A

EL CAMINO MEMORIAL PARK

3953 IMPERIAL AVENUE;
(619) 264-3168

La Jolla is a beautiful place to live, and at El Camino an equally lovely place to spend eternity. Its 210-acre well-tended grounds opened in 1960. Most graves are flat in the grass, but there is a large curve-shaped columbarium facing the road by the man-made pond.

It is no wonder that a few Hollywood types—even having Malibu, Santa Monica, Brentwood, and other pleasure spots at their disposal closer at hand—have chosen to migrate farther south to live and ultimately have their final fade-outs here. Actor **Preston Foster** (1900–1970; Sanctuary of Love 3, crypt 4, tier F) is one. His many films, in which he often played second lead, included *The Informer, The Last Days of Pompeii, The Last Mile,* and *Annie Oakley.*

Other actors here are **William "Billy" Daniels** (1915–1988; Madonna Lawn section, lot 360D), who starred on TV in his own *The Billy Daniels Show* in 1952; **Dorothy Helen Kelly** (1918–1966; Loma Siesta section, lot 132, grave 2), starlet of the early 1940s; and bit player **Jess Kirkpatrick** (1897–1976; Memory Lake Crypts, bay 4, crypt 3, tier C).

El Camino was not **Maurice "Larry" Lawrence's** (1926–1996; Mount Shalom, section 534, space F) first choice as his permanent home away from home. As a U.S. ambassador to Switzerland (appointed by President Clinton) from 1993 to his death in 1996, Lawrence received full military honors in his burial at Arlington National Cemetery. Uh-oh. About a year later it turned out that he had neither been wounded as a merchant marine during World War II as he claimed nor was he ever even in military service. Talk about an audacious padding of the old résumé! Out he went, banished ignominiously, and later checked into this site in El Camino.

Cedric Montgomery Durst (1915–1988; section M, lot 266), whose baseball career lasted seven years with three American League teams (St. Louis Browns, New York Yankees, Boston Red Sox), is on the bench permanently now. **William A. Nierenberg** (1919–2000; Mount Shalom, section 552, space A) played on a different team: A distinguished scientist, he was part of the Manhattan Project, which developed the first atomic bomb.

Still a different type team player was **Milburn Stone** (1904–1980; Vista del Lago, lot 401, space D), an actor who finally made it big—after decades spent struggling in forgettable character parts in equally forgettable movies—as Doctor Adams on *Gunsmoke,* a television series that ran for twenty years. Maybe there's hope after all.

No, the grave marker of **Ray Kroc** (1902–1984; Sunset Couches, bay 2) is *not* in the shape of a Big Mac. The founder of the McDonald's hamburger empire, which made him a multibillionaire, Kroc might have been called *kroc-chety.* He was not universally loved, certainly not by Dick and Maurice "Mac" McDonald, the inventors of the innovative service techniques (such as the food assembly line) that marked the beginnings of the fast-food industry. After Kroc bought the San Diego Padres baseball franchise in the early 1970s, he once vented his spleen for all to hear on the ballpark's public address system, chewing the team out for their dismal performance on the field.

Joan Kroc (1928–2003; same location), his third wife, was another story. A generous philanthropist, she used her huge inheritance from Ray to benefit her San Diego community and was much loved for her good works. One of her largest legacies—more than $90 million—was to the Salvation Army's Ray and Joan Kroc Community Center. ★*Grounds open 7:30 A.M. to dusk. Office hours: 8:00 A.M.–5:00 P.M. weekdays, 8:30 A.M.–5:00 P.M. weekends. Map; restroom.*

LUNCH BREAK

We are partial to **Roppongi** (875 Prospect; 619-551-5252), a handsome fusion restaurant featuring Chinese, Japanese, Thai, Indian, and Indonesian cuisines with a touch of California. You can make a light meal of several of the many starters by themselves. There's an excellent wine list, too.

JOSEPH M. COORS SR. *1917–2003*

This Coors was the grandson of German-born Adolph Coors, who traveled west to Golden, Colorado, to found a brewery. Today, long after the founder's death, Coors is the third-ranking brewery in the United States, producing two-dozen varieties of brew—a huge growth from the 3,500 barrels a year that Adolph produced, proving perhaps that old Adolph had the *coor-age* of his convictions.

Strong convictions evidently run in the Coors family. Joseph Sr. may best be known for two things: his fiery, provocative confrontation with organized labor, which was attempting to unionize Coors plants (resulting in a nationwide ten-year boycott of Coors beer at a time when it was just taking off nationally), and his ultra-conservative, dead-right political views, which led to his co-founding (with $250,000 seed money, plus $300,000 more for the building) of the Heritage Foundation, a right-of-center think tank.

Joseph's business career began with a BS degree in chemistry in 1940, followed by an MA in chemical engineering, both at Cornell University. In 1946 he became a technical director in the family business, became executive vice president in 1975, president two years later, and chief operating officer from 1985 to 1987.

Coors's interest in politics was stimulated by reading *The Conservative Mind* by Russell Kirk and triggered by Paul Weyrich, a conservative whose goal was to establish a policy institute to counteract the influence of the Brookings Institution, a moderate Washington establishment that conservatives believed to be too liberal. Weyrich persuaded Coors to invest, and the Heritage Foundation was born. From 1973 to 1991 Coors was a trustee. He also served one term as a regent at the University of Colorado during the Vietnam War, because he felt the campus tilt at the time was too far left.

Consistent in his beliefs, which his brother Bill described as "as far right as Attila the Hun," Coors certainly put his money where his mouth was, providing funds and support for Ronald Reagan, Barry Goldwater, Orrin Hatch, and Strom Thurmond. He also supported such right-tilted organizations as the John Birch Society, Mountain States Legal Fund, Accuracy in Media, Council for National Policy (where he served as a member of the executive committee), National Strategy Information Center (on the advisory council), and the controversial Nicaraguan Freedom Fund. He now resides in his bier (ahem) in Bell Tower Estates, section 5, lot 1.

PETER ALVIN RAY "PETE" ROZELLE *1926–1996*

Pete Rozelle may have been the greatest football commissioner ever, with a long list of accomplishments, "firsts," and successes in making the National Football League (NFL) the best it had ever been and arguably the best sports league in the world.

On his watch, the NFL grew from ten teams to twenty-eight. He negotiated television contracts that broadcast every single NFL game played during the entire season—a radical change for a league whose teams were rarely seen on TV. Rozelle also persuaded NFL franchise owners to share revenues among teams, thus benefiting all equally.

With the American Football League (AFL) president and all the executives of both the NFL and AFL, he negotiated a merger between the two leagues and persuaded the U.S. Congress to approve it. By the end of his tenure in 1989, the Super Bowl was the most-watched television event of the year, Monday Night Football was ingrained in the American sports consciousness, and the NFL was an American icon (despite two players' strikes and upstart leagues).

Rozelle's choice as commissioner in 1960 wasn't a "given," but more of a surprise. At the time, he was general manager of the Los Angeles Rams, having turned a losing, disorganized franchise into a financial success story. His background was in public relations, beginning while he was still at the University of San Francisco, when he was a student publicist for the USF basketball team in 1949. A Compton, California, homeboy, he joined the U.S. Navy in 1944 and spent eighteen months on an oil tanker in the Pacific before being discharged and attending college.

In retrospect, Rozelle's public relations experience seems almost a prerequisite for the job of commissioner, as it involved public awareness, perceptions, high visibility, and aptitude for negotiation and compromise. He publicly said (many times) that his biggest mistake as commissioner was permitting NFL games to be played two days after John F. Kennedy was assassinated. The AFL postponed *its* games in deference to national mourning. Even so, Rozelle was chosen 1963's "Sportsman of the Year" by *Sports Illustrated,* citing his "aptitude for conciliation." (Perhaps his successor, Paul Tagliabue, learned from Rozelle's mistake; he cancelled all games the weekend after September 11, 2001.)

After retiring, Pete Rozelle had seven years to "smell the daisies" and enjoy the sunshine of Rancho Santa Fe, California, where he retired. His gravestone is in Lake View, bay 2, space 16C.

JONAS SALK *1914–1995*

They don't make 'em like this anymore. When Jonas Salk developed his polio vaccine in 1955, he refused to patent it because he didn't want to profit from something that was intended to benefit mankind. "Who owns my polio vaccine? The people! Could you patent the sun?" he said.

As a child Salk had no interest in science or medicine. The oldest of three sons born in New York City to poor Russian Jewish immigrants, he was brought up to believe in the value of education. He planned to be a lawyer, but in pre-law school he switched to pre-med. So after finishing his BA at the City College of New York in 1936, he attended New York University's College of Medicine and graduated three years later.

The opportunity to work on an influenza vaccine sparked his interest in virology, and he got a research fellowship at the University of Michigan in 1942. A position as head of the virus research lab at the University of Pittsburgh led him there in 1947, where he continued to work on influenza vaccines.

By this time, working with the National Foundation for Infantile Paralysis, Salk set his sights on developing a vaccine for poliomyelitis, or polio. That was an era when polio killed thousands and left infinitely more paralyzed for life. President Franklin Roosevelt had been a victim of polio, so the disease had a high profile in the public mind. Finding a vaccine was a top priority.

It was believed at the time that immunity came only after a person had survived an attack by a live virus, but Salk theorized that a killed or inactivated virus could provide immunity. He first tested his theory on monkeys, then eventually on volunteers (including himself). In 1954 one million children, ages six to nine, were tested nationally. The tests were conclusive, and in 1955 the results were announced and the Salk vaccine began to be administered

> ### HOUSE CALL
> The **Salk Institute** (10010 North Torrey Pines Road; 858-453-4100) is a world-renowned biological research facility on twenty-six beautiful cliff-top acres above the Pacific Ocean. Even nonscientific types can enjoy the free guided tour of the lovely property, which includes a twin complex designed by the late Louis Kahn, a leading modern architect.

nationwide. Two years later cases of polio had dropped by 85 to 90 percent. Today it is a rarity.

In 1962 Salk moved to La Jolla, California, and founded his own institute for biological studies, with genetics and molecular biology the main focus. He was its director and spent much time working on a vaccine for AIDS. He also wrote four books, several of them with one or more of his three sons, who were all medical scientists as well. In 1985 he retired.

Among many awards Salk received for his achievements are the Lasker Award, the Congressional Gold Medal, and the Presidential Medal of Freedom. Salk was married twice, the second time to painter Françoise Gilot, Pablo Picasso's one-time mistress. Their mutual interest in art and architecture was a lasting bond.

Salk's current residency is in the Mount Shalom section, lot 386, space A.

ASCENSION CEMETERY

24754 TRABUCO ROAD;
(949) 837-1331

While this peaceful burial ground on about twenty-five acres is not a frequent stop for celebrity grave hunters, there are two well-known people at rest here. The name of **William Hanna** (1910–2001; section A, row 16, grave 81) may not ring any bells, but if you say Hanna-Barbera, that might be a reminder that the H-B team was responsible for many successes in animation, including *The Flintstones* and *The Jetsons*.

A more sensationalized name here belongs to **Nicole Brown Simpson** (1959–1994). Her murder and that of innocent bystander Ronald Goldman triggered *the* murder trial of the last half of the twentieth century, that of her husband, football icon, commercial pitchman, and movie performer O. J. Simpson. His acquittal raised as many questions as it answered. Her gravestone, etched with a cross and a rose, reads "Always in our hearts." She resides behind the main office, three rows back. ★*Grounds open 8:00 A.M.–5:00 P.M. daily. Office hours: 8:30 A.M.–4:30 P.M. Monday–Saturday.*

LUNCH BREAK

Though noisy, **Peppino's** (23600 Rockfield Boulevard; 949-951-2611), a family-run regional chain, offers fine value for pizzas and pastas. For something a bit different, in the same shopping complex, try **Inka Grill** (23600 Rockfeld Boulevard; 949-587-9008), a small chain specializing in bountiful Peruvian fare.

MOUNT HOPE CEMETERY

3751 MARKET STREET;
(619) 527-3400

A municipal cemetery on 110 acres (only 80 currently occupied), Mount Hope opened in 1871 and has a population of about 76,000 permanent subterrestrial inhabitants. On rambling weathered grounds, the main drive leads past the tiny office (about the size of a rest stop on the highway). The grounds, dotted with head-

stones and a few private mausoleums, are divided by an active railroad track. We watched a train roll by during our visit. Not conducive to letting sleeping bodies lie, but fortunately the trains run infrequently.

Among the grave residents here are many U.S. congressmen and Congressional Medal of Honor winners. Here also are **Elisha A. Babcock** (1848–1922; division 3, section 4, lot 12, grave 7), a Chicago-born civil engineer who made his name and fortune as builder of the landmark Hotel del Coronado in 1888; **John "Jack" Daley** (1883–1967; division 7, section 14, lot 208, grave 3), actor in the 1930s and 1940s; and **Joseph L. Quest** (1852–1924; division 7, section 6, row 4, lot 5, grave 1), who played baseball for six different teams in a nine-year career span.

Nathan Harrison (1823–1920; division 7, section 6, row 9, lot 8) was born a slave in Kentucky, but after a picaresque career with his master, Lysander Utt, and later as a freed man, ended up here as a successful businessman and folk hero. **Alta Hulett** (1854–1877; division 3, section 1, lot 14, grave 3), a pioneer woman lawyer, is also at rest in Mount Hope.

A notable upright gray granite stone on a matching base belongs to **Samuel Brannan** (1819–1889; division 4, section 2, lot 7, grave 2), believed to be California's first millionaire. A convert to the Church of Jesus Christ of Latter Day Saints, he left the eastern branch of the church to sail west to San Francisco, then eventually came by land to San Diego. His gravestone reads "California pioneer of '46 – Dreamer – Leader and Empire Builder." Not a bad résumé for one man.

Thomas Whaley (1823–1890; division 3, section 9, lot 19, grave 6) and his wife, **Anna Whaley** (1832–1913), share a single gray granite stone (with the words "A pioneer family of San Diego" at the top) at the base of a small variegated marble monument. Their home, now the Whaley House Museum in Old Town, is the oldest brick edifice extant in southern California and was once the local courthouse. Believers swear they have seen Anna's ghost—not here, as might be expected, but in their old house. You ghoul, girl. *Grounds open 8:00 A.M.–4:00 P.M. daily (if the road gate is closed, park outside and use the walk-through gate). Office hours: 8:00 A.M.–3:30 P.M. Monday–Friday. Map; restroom.*

> ## LUNCH BREAK
>
> In Old Town, a popular place for traditional Mexican food is **Chuey's Numero Uno** (1894 Main Street; 619-234-6937). Nothing fancy, but reliable and reasonably priced, it's as good for breakfast as for lunch. Fancier and pricier, but worth an occasional splurge, is **Cafe Pacifica** (2414 San Diego Avenue; 619-291-6666), which we like for its fine seafood and creative touches.

RAYMOND CHANDLER *1888–1959*

Crime fiction as we know it wouldn't exist without the hard-boiled similes of Raymond Chandler: "Cops are like a doctor that gives you aspirin for a brain tumor, except that the cop would rather cure it with a blackjack," "The sunshine was as empty as a headwaiter's smile," or "His long fingers made movements like dying butterflies."

Likewise, detective films were never the same after Chandler's Philip Marlowe came on the screen. Private eye Marlowe, perhaps best embodied by Humphrey Bogart's characterization in *The Big Sleep* (1946), was tough, cynical, blunt, and had a soft spot for booze and broads, but held a strict code of ethics. He was a hero made for the movies.

Raymond Thornton Chandler was born in Chicago, Illinois. Surprisingly, he was raised and schooled in England, becoming a naturalized British citizen in 1907. Five years later he was back on this side of the pond, and in 1917 he joined the Canadian army, fighting in France in World War I.

After the war he moved to Los Angeles, the setting for most of his fiction, and began an affair with Cissy Pascal, eighteen years his senior, whom he married after her divorce. Chandler was already having difficulty with alcoholism, which would plague him throughout his life. His day job was as a bookkeeper and auditor for Dabney Oil Syndicate, where he rose to vice president, but his hard drinking cost him the job, so with Cissy's support he turned to writing full-time, publishing his first short story, *Blackmailers Don't Shoot,* in *Black Mask Magazine* in 1932.

Not a fast or prolific writer, Chandler published his first novel, *The Big Sleep,* in 1939, and followed with *Farewell, My Lovely* in 1940. His Marlowe novels, including *The High Window* (1942) and *The Lady in the Lake* (1943), proved successful and got the attention of Hollywood. Chandler's narrative style—owing a debt to Ernest Hemingway's short sentences fraught with tension—was a natural for the film noirs at the time, and he stepped with ease into the role of screenwriter, working with Billy Wilder on *Double Indemnity* (1944), from the novel by James M. Cain.

Chandler and Cissy, who suffered from a chronic lung ailment, moved to La Jolla in 1946, the same year he wrote his only original screenplay, *The Blue Dahlia,* which earned him an Academy Award nomination. He also collaborated on the script for *Strangers on a Train* (1951), based on the Patricia Highsmith novel and directed by Alfred Hitchcock.

Chandler received Edgar Awards from the Mystery Writers of America for screenplay (1946) and for novel (1954). His last outstanding novel (and one with thinly veiled autobiographical elements), *The Long Goodbye* (1953), was published a year before his wife finally succumbed to a longtime illness. Distraught and seeking solace in alcohol, he attempted suicide two months later. He recovered, but continued drinking heavily, only sporadically writing. His final completed novel, *Playback,* was published in 1958.

While president of the Mystery Writers of America, he died of pneumonia in 1959 at age seventy. In all, his legacy was seven novels and about two dozen stories—not much, considering the impact he has had on literature and films.

Chandler's simple gray granite stone, flush with the grass, reads "In loving memory Raymond Thornton Chandler Author" with his birth and death dates. It is hiding in plain sight in division 8, section 3, lot 1577, grave 1. No death trap this.

FAIRHAVEN MEMORIAL PARK

1702 FAIRHAVEN AVENUE; (714) 633-1442 OR (800) 653-2287

Fairhaven began life early in the last century. In 1916 it opened one of the first public mausoleums in California: an ornate edifice with marble brought from Italy, Spain, France, Switzerland, and South America and handcrafted stained-glass windows. The most dramatic plantings on the grounds are the giant redwoods in spacious Lawn M. They shade the grave of **Raymond Cyrus Hoiles** (1878–1970; lot 139, grave 1), libertarian owner and publisher of the *Orange County Register* newspaper.

Few graveyards in southern California are without a roster of Hollywood actors or people connected with the movie business. Fairhaven's thirty-two acres are no exception, but its biggest "star" made history in a different way.

Douglas "Wrong Way" Corrigan (1907–1995; block M, grave 31) was an aviator who in 1938 made headlines all over the world by taking off from New York supposedly for a routine return flight to Long Beach, California, but instead ended up in Ireland. It was no accident, but, like a good actor at heart, the boyish, personable flier pretended it was a navigational mistake. His plane had been deemed unfit for a transatlantic run, but Corrigan was determined to emulate Charles Lindbergh's famous flight. A master mechanic, Corrigan had helped build Lindbergh's *Spirit of St. Louis* and knew what he was about.

> ### LUNCH BREAK
>
> For delicious sandwiches and salads in a coffeehouse setting, try **Gypsy Den** (125 North Broadway; 714-835-8840). Another option is the English pub-like **Olde Ship** (1120 West 17th Street; 714-550-6700), good for bangers and mash, fish and chips, and about twenty really flavorful beers and ales.

Another air enthusiast grounded here is **Glenn Luther Martin** (1886–1955; Old Mausoleum corridor, east tier C, room 2), airplane inventor and barnstorming pilot who formed an aircraft company in 1911 and developed several military planes and bombers. He made a historic flight and was known as "aviator to the stars" (Mary Pickford, for one, flew with him).

Drag racing pioneer **C. J. "Pappy" Hart** (1911–2004; Lawn J, lot 546, space E) organized the first commercial drag car race—in 1950 at the Orange County Airport (now the John Wayne Airport).

Leo Fender (1909–1991; Lawn J, lot 522, space B) changed the nature of rock music with his invention of Fender electric guitars (especially the Stratocaster model) and amplifiers, which were favored by the Beatles and other rock stars. **Francis C. Hall** (1909–1999; Court of Prayer, west tier A, crypt 11-T), distributor of Fender guitars, is also here, resting near Fender.

Also on the grounds are author-evangelist **Corrie Ten Boom** (1892–1983; Lawn A, lot 501, space A, next to a large, beautiful tree in the center of the lawn); artist-photographer **William Mortensen** (1897–1965; Lawn AG, lot 1587, space 1), who pioneered several photographic processes that have subsequently been lost; and actress **Linda Cordova** (1926–1994; main mausoleum, Alcove of Remembrance, N-8), who appeared in *Hombre* and other films. ★*Grounds open 6:00 A.M. to dusk daily. Office hours: 8:00 A.M.–8:00 P.M. Monday–Friday, 8:00 A.M.–6:00 P.M. Saturday, 9:00 A.M.–6:00 P.M. Sunday.*

S A N T A   Y S A B E L

MISSION SANTA YSABEL CEMETERY

STATE ROUTE 79;
(760) 765-0810

From San Diego, take I-8 east to State Route 79 north. About 10 miles north of the town of Julian is Santa Ysabel. The small, white mission is now known as the Saint John the Baptist Church. Tall evergreens are on each side of the church door. Inside the rustic building is a small museum in addition to the church itself. An earlier church on the site dated back to 1818, but had fallen to ruins after the Mexican Revolution. ★*Grounds always open. Church and museum hours: 8:30 A.M.–3:00 P.M. Donations accepted.*

EDMUND LA POINTE *1873–1932*

Known for his work among the Indians of San Diego County, Father Edmund La Pointe spent twenty-nine years visiting reservations at Campo, El Capitan, Inaja, Los Conejos, Los Coyotes, Manzanita, Mesa Grande, Pala, and Rincon, ministering to the residents there as well as to non-Indian parishioners in the area.

Canadian-born, Father La Pointe worked for years at Santa Ysabel before building his mission church in 1924. Widely respected by believers and nonbelievers, he wanted to be buried at the mission. And so he was: His simple grave with a metal cross above it, enclosed by a low, modest metal enclosure, is beside the chapel in the grass, with just three trees nearby.

RICHARD NIXON LIBRARY & BIRTHPLACE

18001 YORBA LINDA BOULEVARD;
(714) 993-3393; WWW.NIXONLIBRARY.ORG

The nine-acre grounds that shelter former U.S. president Richard Nixon's birthplace, library, and archives include a seventy-five-seat amphitheater, museum, and reflecting pool. The setting is a lovely one. The thirty-seventh president's grave is located next to his wife's, **Thelma "Pat" Ryan Nixon** (1912–1993), in the pretty, little rose garden near his transplanted birth house. ★*Open 10:00 A.M.–5:00 P.M. Monday–Saturday, 11:00 A.M.–5:00 P.M. Sunday; closed Thanksgiving and Christmas Day. Admission is charged.*

> ## LUNCH BREAK
> For reasonably priced food with a slight French accent, try **Mimi's Cafe** (18342 Imperial Highway; 714-996-3650), as yummy for breakfast as for other meals.

RICHARD MILHOUS NIXON *1913–1994*

It has been over thirty years since Richard Nixon resigned from the presidency to avoid impeachment and possible conviction and left Washington in disgrace. Yet for us, certain images of him remain crystal bright: his victory sign as he boarded the plane returning him and his family to California; his "I am not a crook" statement; his words after losing the California governor's race in 1964, "You won't have Dick Nixon to kick around any more"; his presidential debate in 1960 against John F. Kennedy.

It isn't every prominent person who comes full circle in life, returning forever to the town where he grew up. In fact, the Nixon Library complex contains his modest, white family home (which had been moved from nearby Whittier). But then, there was nothing ordinary about Dick Nixon. He was a complicated man—shrewd, intellectually well equipped, sensitive, paranoid about enemies real or imagined.

The second of five children of a Quaker mother and a small-businessman father, he was as native to California as oranges. Born in Yorba Linda, he attended

public schools here, graduated from Whittier College, and married a California girl. There was a slight detour to Duke University for law school, then a return to practice law in Whittier.

After a stint as a lieutenant commander in the U.S. Navy in World War II, he answered an ad placed by the state Republican Party seeking a candidate for the U.S. Congress to run against incumbent Democrat Jerry Voorhis. This was the beginning of the cold war, and Nixon ran an aggressive campaign, insinuating that Voorhis's votes in Congress were the same as those of an avowed Marxist. He won and next ran for the U.S. Senate, using similar "scare tactics" to unseat Democrat Helen Gahagan Douglas, whom he constantly referred to as a "pink lady."

From that first political outing to his last, Nixon's campaigns for office were usually marked by controversy involving low tactics, smears, and innuendos, most of which were traceable, directly or not, to the candidate's headquarters, prompting a newspaper editorial early-on to dub him "Tricky Dick," a nickname he bore the rest of his political life.

His questionable tricks against Ed Muskie and George McGovern in the 1972 presidential primaries have been well documented. Ironically, he won reelection that

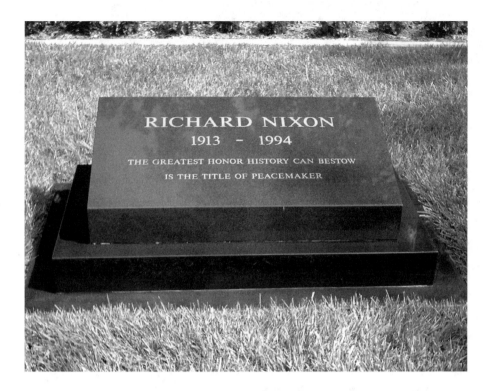

RICHARD NIXON
1913 – 1994
THE GREATEST HONOR HISTORY CAN BESTOW
IS THE TITLE OF PEACEMAKER

year in a 60 percent popular vote landslide, carrying forty-nine states. Dirty tricks needn't have been an option.

Tracing his checkered past, it is easy to see how Watergate evolved. That scandal, which began, so it seemed, as a "third-rate burglary," eventually unveiled a pattern of corruption, break-ins, enemies lists, presidential abuse of power, and other high crimes and misdemeanors that brought down his presidency. He was forced to retire in 1974, just before the threat of impeachment was a fait accompli. His vice president, Spiro Agnew, had to resign *his* office earlier because of bribery, and Nixon had appointed congressman Gerald Ford to replace him. Ford was sworn in as thirty-eighth president, remarking afterwards that "our long national nightmare is over." He then pardoned Nixon.

To his credit, Nixon created the Environmental Protection Agency (EPA), Occupational Safety and Health Administration (OSHA), and the first significant federal affirmative action program. His domestic policies were enlightened by today's standards. He was also applauded for "opening" China and establishing diplomatic relations for the first time in more than twenty years. On the minus side, he ordered the secret bombing of Cambodia, opening the path to genocide in that poor, blighted country.

PATRICIA RYAN NIXON
1912 - 1993
EVEN WHEN PEOPLE CAN'T SPEAK
YOUR LANGUAGE, THEY CAN TELL
IF YOU HAVE LOVE IN YOUR HEART

In later years Nixon attempted to repair his shattered reputation for posterity by writing a number of books, but there was too much evidence for his revisionist view of history to take hold. He died in New York City, where he had a home at the time. He is now permanently at home in the familiar, perhaps comforting soil of California. His epitaph reads "The greatest honor history can bestow is the title of peacemaker," written without irony.

EAST L.A. AND THE DESERT

Horace Greeley had it wrong: Heading east can be just
as rewarding as heading west, especially to grave seekers,
as the following subterranean treasures will reveal.

APPLE VALLEY

SUNSET HILLS MEMORIAL PARK & MORTUARY

24000 WAALEW ROAD;
(760) 247-0155;
WWW.SUNSETHILLS.CC

Located on fifty-two acres, Sunset Hills has only been open since 1996. Its chapel is still a work in progress, but this oasis in the desert has already attracted two substantial permanent guests. ★*Grounds open 8:00 A.M. to dusk daily. Office hours: 8:00 A.M.–5:00 P.M. Monday–Friday.*

DALE EVANS *1912–2001*
ROY ROGERS *1911–1998*

Side by side in the saddle in more than thirty movies, these two western stars are still side by side, sharing the same wide open spaces in their last corral. Their similar-size gravestones, flat in the ground, lie within an elaborate piece of real estate called Rogers' Estate Garden, next to a large pond. Considering the fortune

that this upbeat twosome acquired in decades of hit records and television shows, it is no surprise that their final fade-out would be a grand one.

Neither began life at home on the range. Roy Rogers, born Leonard Franklin Slye to a musical family in Cincinnati, Ohio, grew up on a small farm outside Portsmouth, Ohio, never finished high school, and earned money yodeling at square dances. Dale Evans, born Lucille Wood Smith or Francis Octavia Smith (depending on which source you believe) in Uvalde, a small town in Texas, began work as a stenographer, then rode a beautiful singing voice out of town to Hollywood.

Both began making B movies in the 1940s, mostly together, and their wholesome screen characters began to merge with their real-life personas. Roy was the handsome, upright cowboy who could sing. He epitomized the good guy who took on bad guys and always won. Dale was his pretty girlfriend, who also sang, but onscreen they rarely kissed. Their youthful fans would rather see Roy kiss his horse, Trigger, than a real girl. (When Trigger died, Roy had him stuffed and mounted. Later he joked, "When my time comes, just skin me and put me up there on Trigger.")

On New Year's Eve 1947, Roy, a widower with three children, married Dale, a divorced mom with a son. They later had a daughter with Down's syndrome, who died at age two. In subsequent years they adopted three more children. Roy's oldest son, Dusty, runs the Roy Rogers–Dale Evans Museum in Branson, Missouri.

By the early 1950s Rogers and Evans moved opportunely from films to radio and then television, with *The Roy Rogers Show*. The transition was easy due to their ready-made fan base of some 80 million baby boomers who had loved their movies. Mostly kids, they inhaled all the old-time values of fair play, honesty, integrity, and straight shooting. Most of the TV action took place on the Double R Bar Ranch, with a steady cast of characters that included Trigger, Roy's sidekick Pat Brady (a role Gabby Hayes played in the Roy Rogers films), Dale's horse Buttermilk, and Roy's dog Bullet. The show, which epitomized the romantic myth of the honorable cowboy who kept law and order on the range, ran seven years on NBC and another three years on CBS in reruns.

Evans combined singing with songwriting. She wrote the show's theme, "Happy Trails to You," and some twenty-five other songs. Her "Aha, San Antone" sold 200,000 copies; her "The Bible Tells Me So" was another big seller. Evans became an evangelical Christian and spent many years writing books (seventeen) and lecturing on Christian themes. Her talents were multiple. Billed as "Queen of the West" (Rogers was "King"), she had two comic strips about her adventures on the range and was still doing a television show called *Date With Dale* when she died at age eighty-eight.

Rogers had a talent for making money and keeping his and Evans's wholesome images alive, years after their heyday was over, with merchandising, wise investments, and a national Roy Rogers chain of restaurants. The age of TV innocence is long past, but a glimmer of it is still visible on a spread in Apple Valley.

DESERT MEMORIAL PARK

69920 RAMON ROAD;
(760) 328-3316

In a flatland surrounded by desert, the twenty-six developed acres of Desert Memorial Park came into existence as a cemetery in 1956. It is not unexpected that the burial ground is level land, but the vivid emerald green lawns dotted by swaying palm trees, pines, and oleanders *are* a surprise. The grave markers are mostly flush with the terrain. The office staff is exceptionally friendly and helpful, and the map identifies the graves of many of the ground's notables.

A visitor will find several handfuls of celebrities here, beginning with **Magda Gabor** (1918–1997, section B, row 8, plot 125), one of three glamorous Hungarian Gabor sisters, known more for celebritydom than talent, and her mother **Jolie Gabor** (1900–1997; same location), a trained jeweler who spent less time making jewels than helping her daughters acquire them.

LUNCH BREAK

Just a few blocks away is **Don & Sweet Sue's** (68955 Ramon Road; 760-770-2760), with indoor and outdoor seating, a large sandwich-and-salad menu, tasty soups and sandwiches, and fast service.

This is the last resort of actor **Cameron Mitchell** (1918–1994; section A, row 23, plot 83), whose movie career spanned 165 films, and **Bill Goodwin** (1910–1958; section B, row 1, plot 17), an actor in thirty-three movies, though he was better known as a radio-television announcer with a distinctive voice who introduced *The Burns & Allen Show* on radio for nine years and later was the announcer on *The Bob Hope Show*.

Marjorie Rambeau (1889–1970; section B, row 10, plot 26) turned from being a 1920s siren to a character actress in many films from the 1930s to the 1950s. She was nominated for a Best Supporting Actress Oscar for *Primrose Path* (1940) and again for *Torch Song* (1953). Her last role was in *A Man of a Thousand Faces* (1957), a biography of Lon Chaney.

Baseball fans may want to doff their caps at the grave of "**Pistol Pete" Reiser** (1919–1981; section C, row 12, plot 219), rough-and-tumble outfielder for the Brooklyn Dodgers and the first rookie ever to win the National League batting title. Known for plunging into walls to make a leaping catch, often getting a concussion in the process, he was carried off the field on a stretcher eleven times, thus shortening his career.

Composer **James "Jimmy" Van Heusen's** (1913–1990; section B, row 8, plot 63) many popular songs (written with Sammy Cahn) became huge Frank Sinatra hits— "All the Way," "High Hopes," "Call Me Irresponsible," "My Kind of Town." In all, Van Heusen won four music Oscars and was nominated for ten others. With Johnny Burke, he also wrote "Swinging on a Star," "Going My Way," and "Aren't You Glad You're You?" for Bing Crosby. Urbane composer **Frederick Loewe** (1904–1988; section B, row 8, plot 89) is best remembered as the composer of *Brigadoon, My Fair Lady, Camelot,* and *Gigi.* ★*Grounds open 6:00 A.M.–7:00 P.M. daily. Office hours: 9:00 A.M.–4:30 P.M. daily (closed noon–1:00 P.M.). Map; restrooms.*

SONNY BONO *1935–1998*

When most people think of Sonny Bono, they recall him as the shorter half of the Sonny and Cher singing duo. But he was more than that. Born Salvatore Phillip Bono in Detroit and raised in California, Bono dropped out of high school to become a songwriter. While working as an assistant to wunderkind record producer Phil Spector, Bono co-wrote a song, "Needles and Pins," that was recorded by the Searchers and charted in the Top 20 in 1963.

The next year, Bono married Cher (born Cherilyn Sarkisian), and recording as Sonny and Cher, they released "I Got You Babe," soon followed by "And the Beat Goes On." Both became hits—written, arranged, and produced by Bono. By 1967 the duo had five songs on the charts. Sonny and Cher were wooed by television and starred in the popular *Sonny and Cher Comedy Hour,* which ran from 1971 through

1974. It followed the pattern of other variety shows of that era, in which the male played a buffoon and the female was queen of the wisecracking put-down. Audiences ate it up, though few knew that the material was largely written by Sonny. The show took its toll on the marriage, and Sonny and Cher divorced in 1975.

Bono continued acting, with guest spots and bit parts; for instance, the demented bomber in 1982's *Airplane II: The Sequel*. In the 1980s he opened a restaurant in Palm Springs, California, and, frustrated after running into zoning problems when trying to renovate it, successfully ran for mayor of Palm Springs in 1988. Seemingly a natural politician, with a lifelong laid-back public manner, he went on (after an unsuccessful bid for the U.S. Senate in 1992) to be elected to Congress in 1994 and again in 1996. Quite a surprising professional turn for someone who had never registered or voted until he entered politics at age fifty-two.

As a conservative Republican, Bono was popular in his home district. When he died suddenly from head injuries suffered in a skiing accident, his widow, Mary, served the rest of his term and was subsequently reelected.

Sonny Bono was married four times and fathered three children. His black granite headstone in the grass (section B, row 35, plot 294), with his name carved in the form of his signature, declares "And the beat goes on"—as upbeat as he was in life. To his right is the gravestone of his mother, **Jean Bono** (1914–2005).

WILLIAM "BUSBY" BERKELEY ENOS *1895–1976*

Famed for his musical direction and inspired choreography in early movies, Busby Berkeley (his stage name) had a dirty little secret: He never took a dance lesson.

Actually, William Berkeley Enos got his start in the entertainment world during World War I in the artillery, conducting and directing parades and later staging camp shows for the soldiers. The theatrical bug must have bitten him then, because after the war he tried acting and directing small companies, finally getting a chance to stage dance routines in the musical *Holka-Polka*. His subsequent fame as a Broadway dance director led him to Hollywood.

At the time, dance directors trained the dancers but had little to do with the choreography and directing. Berkeley had loftier ambitions. He talked Samuel Goldwyn into letting him direct and stage the dances himself. Using just one camera—with close-ups of the pretty dancers—he developed synchronized steps and elaborate compositions, photographing the dancers from various angles, especially from above, which produced an awesome kaleidoscope effect.

FILM VAULT

Even though the dialogue is creaky, *42nd Street* (1933) has verve and good humor and is still fun to watch. With the gee-whiz performances of Dick Powell and Ruby Keeler and a wonderful supporting cast, the Berkeley dance numbers, and the song "You're Getting to Be a Habit With Me" are worth the time spent.

What became known as Busby Berkeley compositions showed themselves especially in *42nd Street* (1933), *Dames* (1934), and the *Gold Diggers* series (1933, 1935, 1937), some of which he directed not only the dance sequences, but the entire film. *42nd Street,* with its great production number "Shuffle Off to Buffalo," was such a huge hit, Berkeley received a seven-year contract from Warner Brothers.

His innovative dance sequences eventually became old hat, but he continued to direct musicals in the 1940s. In his last, *Take Me Out to the Ballgame* in 1949,

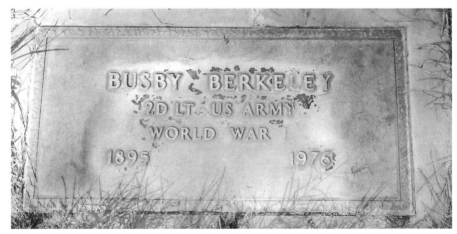

Gene Kelly did the choreography. Berkeley staged a few musical numbers into the 1960s, and as late as 1970 he was asked to stage a revival of *No, No Nanette* on Broadway.

Bubbly and effervescent as Berkeley's work was, his private life was anything but upbeat. He was married three times (unsuccessfully), lived all his life with his mother, and drank too much. Once, presumably while drunk, he hit another car, killing two people. It took three trials, but he was finally acquitted (largely, it is believed, because he was his mother's sole support). He brooded over this until the end of his life. When his mother died, he attempted suicide twice, yet he lived until eighty.

His gravestone lists his wartime service: 2nd Lt. U.S. Army, World War I. He is in section A, row 14, plot 74. To his right is the stone of his third wife, **Etta Dunn Berkeley** (1902–1997).

WILLIAM POWELL *1892–1984*

The word *debonair* was used so often in describing him that it almost seemed like his first name, Debonair William Powell. Yet it took this accomplished actor a long time to achieve that sobriquet. The Pittsburgh-born Powell began his life as an actor in 1912 on Broadway, but it was another twelve years before he went west to Hollywood with a contract from Paramount Pictures.

He made a number of mediocre silent films, often playing a villain, until a breakthrough came as detective Philo Vance in *The Canary Murder Case* in 1929. Other Philo Vance roles followed. It was the talkies, though, that really launched his career as a star. Unlike some silent-screen actors, Powell had a marvelous voice, trained—along with his great comic timing—by his years on the New York stage.

Jumping from Paramount to Warner Brothers, Powell played in several melo-dramas and a tearjerker, *One Way Passage*. But it was at MGM where Powell finally found his métier in *The Thin Man* (1934) with Myrna Loy. It was a low-budget film without much potential, but proved to be such a hit, three sequels were made, the last one in 1947.

Powell soon proved he could handle any role MGM threw at him—comic, dra-matic, melodramatic, romantic—and he was allowed free choice of films, a rarity for stars in the studio era. He could do it all. He played the debonair entrepreneur Flo Ziegfeld in *The Great Ziegfeld* (1936) and, the same year, the educated tramp-turned-butler in *My Man Godfrey,* a screwball comedy with ex-wife Carole Lombard.

As he grew older, he dominated *Life With Father* (1947), for which he earned his third Oscar nomination, and the hilarious *The Senator Was Indiscreet* (1947). Supporting roles in *How to Marry a Millionaire* (1953) and *Mister Roberts* (1955), his last film, were standouts.

An engagement to Jean Harlow ended unexpectedly in her death in 1937. The shock was so severe that Powell didn't make a movie for over a year. When he mar-ried a third time, to a woman twenty-seven years his junior, he retired happily to Palm Springs. Their marriage lasted forty-four years, until his death.

His current residence is in section B, row 10, plot 20. To his right is the grave-stone of his wife, actress **Diana "Mousie" Lewis Powell** (1919–1997; plot 21), with the words "We'll meet again." To his left is the grave of his son, **William David Powell** (1925–1968, plot 19), who was a television writer with credits on *Bonanza, Death Valley, Rawhide,* and *77 Sunset Strip.*

FRANK SINATRA *1915–1998*

Love him or loathe him, Francis Albert Sinatra was difficult to ignore. His vocal style—jaunty, intimate, throaty, as though singing just to you—was the most instantly rec-ognizable of any popular musical artist (along with Bing Crosby's) in the past sixty years. It's difficult to think of "New York, New York," "Fly Me to the Moon," "The Lady Is a Tramp," "My Way," and scores of other popular ballads without inwardly hear-ing Sinatra's version.

"Old Blue Eyes," as he was often called, had a way with a song. He demon-strated that early on with the Tommy Dorsey band, then as a solo act who made teenage bobby-soxers of the 1940s swoon.

In a second career—launched when his singing days had temporarily faded—Sinatra proved he could act, too. For *From Here to Eternity* he won a Best Supporting Actor Oscar, then went on to give first-rate performances in dramas like *The*

Manchurian Candidate, The Man With the Golden Arm, and *The Detective,* plus movie musicals like *Guys and Dolls, On the Town,* and *Pal Joey.* All in all, he made more than sixty films, including those with his Rat Pack pals.

What earned Sinatra disdain was not his talent, but his lifestyle: his friendships with known mobsters and a reckless love-'em-and-leave-'em private life, with so many affairs, even *he* probably lost count (his A-list included Lauren Bacall, Judy Garland, Grace Kelly, Sophia Loren, Shirley MacLaine, Marilyn Monroe, Kim Novak, Lana Turner, Gloria Vanderbilt, and Natalie Wood, but who's counting?). His high-profile marriages and divorces were to childhood sweetheart Nancy Barbato (1939), Ava Gardner (1951), and Mia Farrow (1966). Gardner was reportedly the love of his life.

Then there were the well-publicized bullying threats to and fisticuffs with anyone who got in his way or offended him in public places. In spite of all the negative baggage, Sinatra continued to sing, making records, playing Las Vegas, and touring. Later in life he married Barbara Marx (in 1976), widow of Zeppo of the Marx Brothers, and seemed to have settled down somewhat.

Even in those later years, when his singing voice was a hoarse travesty of what it had been, his upbeat, joshing style continued to endear him to fans. Like it or not, he did it *his* way. His prudent gravestone evokes yet another Sinatra melody with the words "The Best Is Yet to Come."

Sinatra's grave, usually signaled by an American flag and bouquets of fresh flowers, is in section B (the first lawn area straight ahead on the right from the front gate),

row 8, plot 151, at the end of a short row of family members, including from left to right his father, **Anthony Martin Sinatra** (1893–1969; plot 148); mother, **Natalie "Dolly" Sinatra** (1894–1977; plot 149); and uncle **Vincent Mazzola** (1894–1973; plot 150).

FOREST LAWN MEMORIAL PARKS & MORTUARIES

**69855 EAST RAMON ROAD;
(800) 204-3131**

Formerly the Palm Springs Mausoleum, this beautiful, pristinely maintained property is on the block next to Desert Memorial Park. It is totally a mausoleum, not a cemetery. The buildings are beautifully uniform, in the California mission style, with tawny walls and red tile roofs, surrounded by rose bushes and other plantings.

The office staff is, in full Forest Lawn mode, unwilling to provide locations of the residents, but the grounds are sufficiently compact, and with the help of the grounds crew, you should have no trouble finding the notables who are here—and there are a few. Most are located in buildings to the left of the bell tower if you are facing the tower from across the road at the office.

Rumor has it, though we could not confirm this, that some of Rock Hudson's ashes were deposited in the tower, to which there is no access. But there are other notables to look for—and find—among the handsome polished rose marble vaults.

Among those making this mausoleum their final home are **Alice Faye** (1915–1998; Mission San Luis Rey building) and her longtime spouse, **Phil Harris** (1904–1995; same location), who were household names in the 1940s and 1950s. She, the more famous of the two, was a marquee movie star, featured in such musicals as *Alexander's Ragtime Band, Rose of Washington Square,* and *Lillian*

LUNCH BREAK

For tasty sandwiches, soups, and salads, **Don & Sweet Sue's** (68955 Ramon Road; 760-770-2760) is both handy, helpful, and healthy.

Russell and frequently paired with Don Ameche. Singer-bandleader Harris was best known for his comic role on the Jack Benny radio show, in which he played himself as a heavy-drinking bandleader. The couple is together in a glassed-in niche, fourth row from the bottom in the rear center of the niche. His wall vault has a metal dolphin sculpture, hers is a ballerina. Go figure.

Other movie people who have chosen the mausoleum include **Donald Woods** (1906–1998; Mission San Luis Rey), character actor in *A Tale of Two Cities, True Grit,* and many other films from the 1930s through the 1960s.

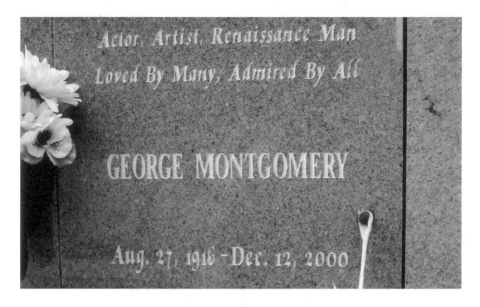

Fourth from the bottom of the building behind Mission San Luis Rey at the right end are some of the ashes of **Dinah Shore** (1916–1994), Southern songbird and television show hostess. The rest of her cremains are at Hillside Memorial Park and Mortuary in Culver City, California. Coincidentally, her first husband, actor **George Montgomery** (1916–2000), is just a few steps diagonally across the walkway, in the rear of the building, next to Mission San Luis Rey, at the end row right. Part of his ashes are here, the rest in Great Falls, Montana.

Just around the corner is actor **Buddy Rogers** (1904–1999; second from bottom left), onetime husband of Mary Pickford. *Grounds and office open 8:00 A.M.–5:00 P.M. daily. Map; restrooms.*

JOHN PHILLIPS *1935–2001*

John Edmund Andrew Phillips, "Papa John," was born on Parris Island, South Carolina, and was focused on music from an early age. In the late 1950s Phillips was a member of the Journeymen, a folk trio that didn't distinguish itself from the myriad other folk bands trying to make a name in New York's Greenwich Village at the time.

Phillips decided to try a new direction in the early 1960s. He and his second wife, Michelle (née Gilliam), nine years his junior, were putting together a band with friend Denny Doherty when Cass Elliot (a friend of Denny's) joined as the fourth member. The newly formed group, the Mamas and the Papas, hit big with their first album, *If You Can Believe Your Eyes and Ears* (1966), which featured "California Dreamin'" (No. 4 on *Billboard's* chart) and "Monday, Monday" (No. 1). Phillips was

PHILLIPS

JOHN EDMOND ANDREW

Papa John Phillips
"California Dreamin"
Beloved Husband, Father & Friend
Aug. 30, 1935 – Mar. 18, 2001

FARNAZ

Loving Wife & Mother

Jan. 27, 1950

the leader, main writer, and arranger, and they went on to release four more albums before disintegrating as a band.

In 1967 "Papa John" produced the Woodstock forerunner, the Monterey Pop Festival, featuring The Who, Otis Redding, Janis Joplin, and Jimi Hendrix. Phillips also co-wrote the hippie anthem "San Francisco" (be sure to wear some flowers in your hair), which was a big hit for his friend Scott MacKenzie. For the next decade and a half, drugs and addiction consumed much of his time, as he revealed in his autobiography, *Papa John* (1986). Despite several attempts, he never managed to get his musical career on track again.

In 1998 the Mamas and the Papas were inducted into the Rock and Roll Hall of Fame. Three years later Papa John Phillips expired of heart failure at age sixty-five. He was married four times and left three daughters (actress Mackenzie and singers Chynna and Bijou) and two sons. His large wall crypt, with room for his widow to his right in the same vault, is located around the corner from Dinah Shore.

C O A C H E L L A

COACHELLA VALLEY CEMETERY

82925 AVENUE 52;
(760) 398-3221; FAX (760) 398-1032

This public burial ground, comprising sixty acres, dates back to 1927. Its office is to the right of the entrance. There are no gates to keep anyone in or out.

Two celebrity graves are of special note in this quiet place. **John Van Druten** (1901–1957; unit 4, lot 16, block 1) was both an actor and a playwright. It was the latter for which he is best known, having written *The Voice of the Turtle* (1943) and *I Remember Mama* (1944), both of which were big hits on Broadway and on the silver screen. Van Druten adapted *Voice* for the film version himself.

Frank Capra (1897–1991; unit 8, lot 289, block 77) is on the right, just beyond the administration building. His family emigrated from Sicily in 1903. With a chemical engineering degree from Throop Institute (later the California Institute of Technology), he joined the U.S. Army twenty-four days before the 1918 armistice was signed. Two years later he became a naturalized American citizen. In the early 1920s he got into silent movies, writing and directing "Our Gang" comedies and other shorts, and cutting his comic teeth with Mack Sennett.

It has been said that Capra's inspirational, sentimental movies were the result of his pride as a naturalized American. Whatever the reason, he made almost thirty films, some of them blockbusters. They usually combined lively humor with strong strains of patriotism and wholesome values. Among them: *Mr. Deeds Goes to Town, You Can't Take It With You, Mr. Smith Goes to Washington, Meet John Doe, It's a Wonderful Life, State of the Union, Pocketful of Miracles.* His comic flair was perhaps most visible in *It Happened One Night* (which won five major Academy Awards). A documentary he made during wartime, *Why We Fight,* is considered one of the propaganda masterpieces of all time. ★*Grounds open 5:00 A.M.–8:00 P.M. daily. Office hours: 7:00 A.M.–4:00 P.M. Monday–Friday. Map; restrooms.*

LUNCH BREAK

Light and attractive, California style, is **Polo Grill** (81900 Avenue 51, Indio; 760-347-9985), a good choice for an agreeable lunch.

E A S T   L O S   A N G E L E S

CALVARY CEMETERY & MAUSOLEUM

4201 WHITTIER BOULEVARD; (323) 261-3106

The flat grassy grounds, dotted with an occasional palm or pine tree, of this popular 137-acre Catholic burial site are spacious but unexceptional. This site is really *New* Calvary, though it is *old* (by California standards), dating back to 1896. *Old* Calvary, where Cathedral High School now stands, is long closed. This Calvary's grounds are divided into twenty-three sections, with religious names like St.

Christopher, Gethsemane, Christ the King, Our Lady of Guadalupe, and so on. There are lawn crypts, three mausoleums, more than fifteen private family mausoleums, and a section (O) for cremated remains.

The grounds contain Christian statuary and religious shrines, like Our Lady of Grace (section R), Stations of the Cross (section F), and All Souls chapel (section F). Note the topiary cross at the cemetery entrance and topiary shrubbery throughout. The Jewish Home of Peace Memorial Park is just across the street, making for an easy two-in-one trip.

Calvary's main mausoleum, on the first road to the left beyond the office, is something else. Cream and tan, with rounded domes and stained-glass windows, the 1929 building has an entrance right out of a Cecil B. DeMille spectacular. Near the top of the steep steps leading up to the main door, on both sides, hosts of 10-foot-high art deco stone angels, like sculptural versions of Rockwell Kent's illustrations, seem to trumpet each arrival.

Inside, the walls and archways are two colors of marble. Another set of stairs leads to a serene chapel, with soothing taped music. Side passages off the chapel have marble walls lined with crypts. Here, up front on the right side of the chapel, can be found **Lou Costello** (1906–1959; crypt 354), half of the Abbott-Costello comedy team of "Who's on first?" fame. He is buried under his family name, Louis Francis Cristillo, along with his wife, **Anne Costello** (1912–1959), and one-year-old son, **Lou Costello Jr.** (1942–1943), who drowned.

Edward L. Doheny Sr. (1856–1935; on the right across from the altar), oil magnate and candidate for vice president in 1920, is here. **Henry Tifft Gage** (1852–1924; block 107, crypt C-5) was the twentieth governor of California (1899–1903).

Harry Sinclair (1876–1956; main mausoleum, private room with a half-gate marked "Sinclair") is in the chapel of the mausoleum as well. A failed pharmacist, he became a millionaire oilman and founder of Sinclair Oil Company. His reputation was tarnished by involvement in the Teapot Dome scandal of the Warren Harding administration.

Awaiting the final trumpet call elsewhere at Calvary are many bishops and at least one cardinal–**Timothy Manning** (1909–1989), resting near All Souls Chapel in section F. There are also nuns, early Spanish and Mexican settlers of Los Angeles, city mayors, and a number of Congressional Medal of Honor recipients. **John E. Reagan** (1883–1941) and **Nelle C. Reagan** (1883–1962), parents of U.S. president Ronald Reagan, are within these sacred confines in section R, lot 306, graves 11 and 12.

Oh yes, and many movie people are on the premises, such as Polish-born **Pola Negri** (1899–1987; main mausoleum, block 56, crypt E19), sultry stage and silent-screen actress and lover of Rudolph Valentino. Also here is **Mabel Normand** (1894–1930; main mausoleum, block 303, second row from bottom, second crypt from the left), gifted comic actress of the silent screen and lover of Mack Sennett (and supposedly Charlie Chaplin as well). She was featured in many Sennett comedies and in *Tillie's Punctured Romance* (1914) with Chaplin. Drugs, alcohol, and tuberculosis did her in at age thirty-six.

Mexican-born **Ramon Novarro** (1899–1968; section C, lot 586, grave 5) is here as well. Singer, silent-movie actor, and star of *Ben-Hur: A Tale of the Christ* and *The Prisoner of Zenda,* he was a matinee idol in his day, and was brutally murdered by two street hustler brothers.

Actor **Frank Fay** (1891–1961; section F, lot 1583, grave 12) is perhaps best known as Barbara Stanwyck's first husband (from 1928 to 1935). Movie actor **John Hodiak** (1914–1955; main mausoleum, block 303, crypt D-1, same row as Mabel Normand) starred in Alfred Hitchcock's atypical film *Lifeboat* (1944), opposite Tallulah Bankhead.

Cedric Gibbons (1893–1960; section H, lot 117) was ubiquitous from the 1910s through the 1950s, as art director and designer on more than 1,500 MGM movies. He even designed the Motion Picture Academy's Oscar—and *won it* eleven times. Another distinction: His name is on more film credits than any other Hollywood personage.

Jimmy McHugh (1894–1969; main mausoleum, block 33, crypt E-9), popular composer of cheery songs (like "The Sunny Side of the Street"), nominated five times for the Oscar for Best Song, is also present at Calvary. There are at least two poets on the premises: **Edwin Markham** (1852–1940; section E, lot 2005, grave 9) and poet laureate **John Steven McGroarty** (1862–1944; section F, lot 1693, grave 9). A major-league baseball player, **John Charles Lush** (1885–1946; main mausoleum, room A, crypt E5), is here as well. He pitched for the St. Louis Cardinals and Philadelphia Phillies.

In the bad old days of racial stereotyping, **Stepin Fetchit** (1902–1985; section K, tier 13, grave 116), whose real name was Lincoln Theodore Monroe Andrew Perry, epitomized in his stage and movie roles the once-prevalent cruel comic caricature

LUNCH BREAK

As the run-down neighborhood surrounding Calvary and Home of Peace offers little except fast-food spots, we suggest you head for downtown Los Angeles and the solid comfort and conviviality of **Ciudad** (Union Bank Plaza, 445 South Figueroa Street; 213-486-5171; www.ciudad-la.com), an upscale place with Nuevo Latino specialties. The food is great, and so are the surroundings.

of African Americans. Performing such roles was the only way he could find steady work. ★*Grounds open 8:00 A.M.–5:00 P.M. daily. Office hours: 8:00 A.M.–5:00 P.M. Monday–Friday, 8:00 A.M.–4:00 P.M. Saturday, 10:00 A.M.–3:00 P.M. Sunday. Main mausoleum hours: 8:00 A.M.–4:00 P.M. weekdays and holy days, 9:00 A.M.–4:00 P.M. Sunday. Map; restrooms.*

ETHEL BARRYMORE *1879–1959*

While Ethel, the middle child in the theatrical Barrymore family, acted most of her life (for fifty years), she is best remembered for her later movies, made when she had become matronly in appearance. *None But the Lonely Heart* (for which she received an Oscar for Best Supporting Actress in 1945) comes especially to mind.

Yet young Ethel was a beauty, besieged by beaux, one of whom was Winston Churchill. Her marital choice was a bad one, to an abusive businessman. Perhaps because she protected her private life from public attention, Ethel seemed the most stable of the three talented Barrymore siblings. There probably wasn't a theatrical family in the twentieth century as gifted—in looks and talent. She is in a crypt near her brother Lionel in the main mausoleum, block 60, crypt 3F.

JOHN BARRYMORE *1882–1942*

Of the three Barrymores, John, the youngest, was the golden one, blessed with "matinee idol" good looks, charisma, and enormous ability. He could act comedy with a light touch, but his strong suit was tragedy, especially Shakespearean. In his

day he "owned" the roles of Hamlet and Richard III. Alcohol, the Barrymore "curse," eventually did him in, as it had his father, Maurice, a star of *his* generation.

Four failed marriages and numerous flings didn't help; eventually John's acting became a flamboyant caricature of his glory years, and his personal life was the stuff of tabloids. Even so, his few film performances when he was way beyond his prime—in *A Bill of Divorcement, Dinner at Eight, Grand Hotel,* and *Twentieth Century*—were riveting.

Alcohol *per se* didn't kill him, but it helped. This apocryphal story is told of his funeral wake: Afterwards, his chum Errol Flynn went on a binge, went home, and found Barrymore seated on a chair in his living room—mutual friends had "borrowed" the body and propped it up at Flynn's as a joke.

Barrymore's ivory-colored wall crypt 352 in the main mausoleum now lies empty but bears the words "Good night sweet prince." This epitaph harks back to *Hamlet* and is the title of a famous Barrymore biography by Gene Fowler. *This* prince's remains were belatedly returned to Philadelphia's Mount Vernon Cemetery to reside with his parents in perpetuity.

LIONEL BARRYMORE *1878–1954*

The oldest of the family acting trio, Lionel was the least dedicated. Yet he had a long, fruitful career in films, beginning in 1924. His movie credits—which number more than seventy—include *Sadie Thompson, Grand Hotel, Dinner at Eight, Treasure Island, David Copperfield, Captains Courageous,* and *You Can't Take It With You.*

He was confined to a wheelchair for the last seventeen years of his life. Curiously, in that chair he made the movies he is probably best remembered for—playing crotchety Dr. Gillespie in the Dr. Kildare series and Potter in *It's a Wonderful Life.*

Like his siblings, Lionel succumbed to alcoholism, as well as morphine and cocaine. There are no dates on his crypt, which lies just above his brother John's (main mausoleum, block 352), nor on that of his wife, actress **Irene Fenwick Barrymore** (1887-1936), which is to his left.

IRENE DUNNE GRIFFIN *1898–1990*

Her elegant, ladylike demeanor and quiet family life didn't make headlines, but Irene Dunne was one of the most versatile movie actresses of the 1930s and 1940s. Not only was she a gifted comedienne with a light touch (*Theodora Goes Wild, The Awful Truth, My Favorite Wife*), but she could emote with the best of them (*Love Affair, Anna and the King of Siam, I Remember Mama, Cimarron*). And she could sing! From childhood in Louisville, Kentucky, until she tackled Broadway, she was trained as an

opera singer. Her light, crystal-clear soprano was better suited to musical comedy, and her star debut was as Magnolia in *Showboat*.

Dunne's delicate beauty made her a natural leading lady and serious actress. Yet she loved playing comedy, once saying, "Big emotional scenes are much easier to play than comedy. An onion can bring tears to your eyes, but what vegetable can make you laugh?"

After her movie career tapered to an end, she still had a life—and a busy one: as a wife and mother, Republican activist, alternate delegate to the United Nations (appointed by President Eisenhower), supporter of many charities and Catholic causes, and recipient of a Kennedy Center Honor awarded by President Reagan. Her medals as a Dame of Malta and Knight of the Order of the Holy Sepulcher are glued to the front of her marble crypt in the main mausoleum (though we noticed on our most recent visit that one medal had been pried off). Similar medals adorn the crypt of her husband of thirty-seven years, **Francis D. Griffin** (1883–1965). Theodora may have gone wild, but Irene never did (so far as we know). (Note that on Dunne's marker her birthdate reads 1901, but she was actually born in 1898.)

FERDINAND JOSEPH LA MENTHE "JELLY ROLL" MORTON *1890–1941*

"Jelly Roll" Morton—whose nickname had a sexual connotation best not mentioned here—was born into a Creole neighborhood in New Orleans, to parents in a common-law marriage. His father's name was La Menthe, Lamothe, or Lemott, depending on who was spelling it. Later, Jelly Roll took the name of his stepfather, anglicizing it from Mouton into Morton.

If anyone's life epitomized the early raucous days of jazz, Jelly Roll's did. He pimped, worked in brothels, got into knife fights, and all the while played one of the best pianos in Storyville, the red-light district of New Orleans. Eventually leaving the Big Easy, he ended up in Chicago in 1923. Three years later he made his first records for Victor, the major recording company of the time, under the label "Jelly Roll Morton & His Red Hot Peppers," which featured Kid Ory, Barney Bigard, and other New Orleanians.

In 1931 Victor dropped his contract, the market for Dixieland jazz having declined, and Morton found himself touring with a burlesque act. He ended up in Washington, D.C., as a bartender, manager, and pianist at a lowdown dive in a black neighborhood. Fortunately for him, he was heard by musicologist Alan Lomax, whose career was spent recording and preserving music.

In 1938 Morton began recording interviews with Lomax for the Library of Congress, alternating playing, singing, and talking, in order to preserve the jazz heritage for posterity. Lomax loved the off-color songs of Storyville, and Morton was happy to oblige. A great talker, Morton was also something of a braggart, taking credit as the originator of jazz. To do so, he fudged his birth date, saying it was five years earlier than it actually was. He even had a business card with the words "Creator of Jazz and Swing." To this day, Morton is often credited as being the father of jazz.

Not that his accomplishments weren't real and his songs and tales weren't mostly true. He wrote dozens of songs and played piano like an angel. Among his best-known songs are "Wolverine Blues," "Black Bottom Stomp," "Sidewalk Blues," "Shreveport Stomp," "Red Hot Pepper," "Mint Julep," "The Finger Buster," "Jungle Blues," "Pontchartrain," "The Original Jelly-Roll Blues," and "King Porter Stomp," which became a big Fletcher Henderson and Benny Goodman hit.

Planning a new life in Los Angeles, with new music and arrangements, he died shortly after he arrived. His grave is number 4, lot 347, in section M.

HOME OF PEACE MEMORIAL PARK AND MAUSOLEUM

4334 WHITTIER BOULEVARD;
(323) 261-6135

The grounds of this old Jewish cemetery, which dates back to 1855, are lovely, if crowded. Palms, pines, and cypress trees shade the grounds, which are dotted with bougainvillea and other shrubs. Around the office is the fragrant scent of jasmine.

There are substantial private mausoleums and scores of upright headstones in rough-cut gray granite lined in tight rows. The main mausoleum resembles a mosque, with modified keystone Arabic arches and gray granite columns with creamy white capitals and minarets. There is a chapel inside, as well as stained glass throughout. Dark corridors are lined with rows of wall vaults. Unfortunately, the lighting is so dim that the names on the bronze markers are difficult to read. (We suggest you carry a flashlight.) Behind the mausoleum in the Garden of Maimonides is the Sephardic community section.

On the grounds, one of our all-time-favorite cemetery monuments belongs to William and Ethelle Rubin. It consists of a granite fireplace, with "flames" licking at the hearth; alongside the fire are two life-size armchairs made of stone, one for William and one for his wife.

Home of Peace seems to have been the cemetery of choice for several of Hollywood's most influential early moguls. **Carl Laemmle** (1867–1939; mausoleum, Laemmle Family Room), founder of Universal Pictures in 1915, was responsible for scores of successful films but was just as well known among movie cognoscenti for his nepotistic policy of employing relatives—at one time as many as seventy were on the studio payroll.

There are three imposing Warner Brothers sites here: Jack's, Sam's, and Harry's. **Samuel Warner** (1885–1927; section D, in front of the mausoleum) is in the family mausoleum with his parents. **Harry Warner** (1881–1918; section D, private mausoleum behind the family one) shares his private space with his wife Rea, son Lewis, daughter Doris, and her husband, **Charles Vidor** (1900–1959), who directed such films as *Gilda* (1946) and *Love Me or Leave Me* (1955). **Jack Warner,** most famous of the brothers, is on his own. ★*Grounds open 8:00 A.M.–4:00 P.M. daily, except Saturday. Office hours: 9:00 A.M.–4:00 P.M. daily, except Saturday. Map; restroom.*

"CURLY" HOWARD *1903–1952*

One of the most visited graves here is that of everyone's favorite member of the Three Stooges slapstick comedy act, Curly (born Jerome Lester Horwitz in Brooklyn, New York). In front of his upright headstone (located behind the mausoleum in the Western Jewish Institute section, row 5, grave 1) can be found numerous tokens of affection left by fans.

Curly was the fifth and youngest Horwitz brother, but certainly the most colorful and popular among fans, in large part because his persona was the innocent and most cartoonlike of the three. It is no accident that almost all American males born between 1950 and 1970 can do a spot-on imitation of Curly's vocal and physical signatures—whether it's his "nyuck nyuck nyuck," or his "whoop whoop whoop" (the latter accompanied by the alternating palms slapping down the length of his face), or his lying on his side on the ground and propelling himself in a circle with his legs, as though riding a bicycle in a dimension known only to him. In this way he was a relative of Harpo Marx's movie persona, in which the laws of physics didn't apply.

Countless times in the Stooges' short films, Moe attacks Curly's head with a variety of steel tools, over which Curly's head triumphs. Oh, the detoothed saws, the blunted axes, picks, chisels, knives, gun barrels, car bumpers, and other weapons foiled by Curly's shaved pate, which triumphed repeatedly against the deadly real world and, more pointedly, against Moe's avarice. Young boys had to cheer the round head with the screwed-up face. To this, one of us also pleads guilty.

Jerome was not part of the original Stooges act when it began. He became "Curly" when he replaced his brother Shemp as the third of Ted Healy's Stooges in 1934. When they signed with MGM, he appeared with his brother Moe and Larry Fine in what are considered the *real* Three Stooges' films. Jerome/Curly, typically attired on-screen in a too-tight suit and a bowler hat, had to step out of the Stooges' lineup in 1946 after suffering a massive stroke on the set of *Half Wit's Holiday,* the

Stooges' ninety-seventh short. Married four times, he was never again able to be Curly, passing on at age forty-eight after years of declining health.

"SHEMP" HOWARD *1895–1955*

Samuel Horwitz was pegged "Shemp" because his European mother's strong accent when she called him Sam came out "Shemp," and it stuck. Shemp was in the first Three Stooges lineup with his younger brother Moe and Larry Fine (all of whom took the stage name "Howard") when they performed in vaudeville as part of an act billed as Ted Healy and his Stooges.

LUNCH BREAK

See nearby lunch sites recommended on page 250 or page 262.

Shemp's first and only early performance on film as a Stooge is in 1930's *Soup to Nuts*. He departed the act to pursue character roles in films such as *The Bank Dick,* starring W. C. Fields, and *Buck Privates* with Abbot and Costello, to name just two of scores of film roles, more than seventy in all. He was replaced in the Stooges' lineup by his baby brother, Jerome (Curly).

Despite a successful career as a character actor, Shemp returned to the Stooges, replacing Curly as the third Stooge after Curly's stroke. Thus he was reunited with his brother Moe and Stooge middle-man Larry. (The "musical chairs" cast changes are almost a Stooges routine in themselves.) Next to Curly, Shemp is still the fan favorite, bringing to the mix some unforgettable characteristics, such as his "yip yip yip," delivered on the inhalation of breath. In addition, Shemp had a head of slicked-back long hair that would become unleashed whenever he was doing his third-Stooge shtick. He appeared in over sixty Stooges shorts, many being remakes.

At age sixty Shemp died of a heart attack in a cab on his way home from a boxing match. His crypt is in the mausoleum, Corridor of Eternal Life East, 215-E (right side, fifth column in, second row from the bottom).

LOUIS B. MAYER *1885–1957*

Of all the studio heads and tycoons of Hollywood's Golden Age, probably none was more successful than Louis B. Mayer, paterfamilias of Metro-Goldwyn-Mayer (MGM). During the Depression, he became the first business executive to make $1 million a year and MGM was the only studio to pay dividends.

A surprise here is the modesty of Mayer's memorial. A man who made millions and controlled the lives of scores of high-profile stars, directors, and others has a minimalist bronze plaque in the rear of the mausoleum's Corridor of Immortality (crypt S-405). It reads, simply, "Beloved Husband and Father."

Like all the other early businessmen turned studio heads, Ukranian-born Eliezer Meir began his working life in a field unrelated to movies. Like his father, Meir-turned-Mayer was a scrap-metal dealer in St. John, New Brunswick, Canada, but quickly (in 1907) realized the potential of movies and opened his first movie theater in Haverhill, Massachusetts. Before long he had the largest movie theater chain in New England.

Soon the ambitious young man headed west, co-started a movie production company, sold it, and was kept on as studio head. As such, he was dedicated to making "only pictures that I won't be ashamed to have my children see." It was a highly successful concept, and during Mayer's twenty-seven-year regime, MGM rolled out an average of one movie a week, such amazing films as *Anna Christie* (1930), *Grand Hotel* (1932), *Mutiny on the Bounty* (1935), *A Night at the Opera* (1935), *Romeo and Juliet* (1936), *The Good Earth* (1937), *The Wizard of Oz* , *Ninotchka, Gone With the Wind* (all three in 1939), *Gaslight* (1944), and *Father of the Bride* (1950). The list goes on and on.

The MGM repertoire of stars filled a galaxy, a veritable who-was-who of Hollywood's Golden Age: Clark Gable, Joan Crawford, Laurel and Hardy, Spencer Tracy, Elizabeth Taylor, Katharine Hepburn, Lana Turner, Judy Garland—and that's just for starters. One of Mayer's personal discoveries was Greta Garbo.

As studio head, the short, nervy, cigar-chomping Mayer worked hard to keep his independent, temperamental stars on a short leash. To protect MGM's investment in talent, he did everything he could to keep his stars' names out of the paper—unless the publicity was positive, like the opening of a new movie. His turf battles with producer Irving Thalberg and later producer-scriptwriter Dore Schary are legion in Tinseltown lore. Although Mayer was tough as nails and feisty as yeast, his relationship with his stars was rarely as tempestuous and acrimonious as other studio heads' (notably Harry Cohn and Jack Warner) were.

After such a full, sometimes frenetic life, Mayer's last words, "Nothing matters," seem strangely accepting. Although his crypt marker reads 1885 as his birth date, the actual year was 1882, proving that movie vanity wasn't limited to the stars.

JACK L. WARNER *1892–1978*

As the youngest of twelve children of Polish immigrants in London, Ontario, Jack Warner was always fascinated by show business. After the family moved to Youngstown, Ohio, he and three brothers—Harry, Albert, and Sam—started a modest movie theater business, with Jack singing and dancing before the film began. Moves to Newcastle, Pennsylvania; New York City; and then Hollywood followed.

In 1923 three of the brothers incorporated as Warner Brothers Pictures, Inc., (Harry had died in 1918) and built a large studio on Sunset Boulevard. Their first film was released in 1926: *Don Juan,* which starred John Barrymore and employed a completely synchronized musical score. The following year brought *The Jazz Singer,* and the year after that, the full-length feature *Lights of New York,* the first all-talking movie ever made.

Warner Brothers, with Jack as studio head (and Sam as president), led the way into Hollywood's Golden Age, with many top-notch films. But Jack's penny-pinching ways and refusal to let Warner's contract players work for other studios enraged stars like Bette Davis, who fought court battles over this "peonage." There were pluses and minuses to the old studio system in Hollywood, and Jack Warner embodied both.

Sam Warner was estranged from Jack after they agreed to sell their stock, but Jack pulled a fast one and kept his, realizing a huge profit. Sam never spoke to his brother again, which explains the separate but equal burial sites.

Jack Warner's large private grave site, in the A section near a four-way cross-road, is pure serenity, with its own garden; roses, bird-of-paradises, and other flowers in planters along the sides; a polished reddish brown granite border; trees; a walkway and tiled fountain; and the sarcophagus of Jack and his wife, **Ann Warner** (1909–1990), with the word "Together" at the bottom.

ROSE HILLS MEMORIAL PARK & MORTUARY

3888 WORKMAN MILL ROAD;
(562) 699-0921;
WWW.ROSEHILLS.COM

A beautiful property, all 3,500 acres of it, this is as much a park as a burial ground, with more than 7,000 rose bushes in 600 varieties staggering their blossoms over most of the year. There are Japanese gardens, a lake and arched Japanese-style bridge, and a meditation house. What could be more compatible with a peaceful memorial park?

Most gravestones here lie flush to the ground, creating the effect from afar of unadorned grassy hillsides (a la Forest Lawn) edged in the distance by mountains. Lovely old trees—evergreens, palms, and olives—have a harmonious effect. Sections reflect the rising, hilly nature of the park, beginning with names like Garden of Prayer, Marigold Lawn, and Garden of Eternity, leading up to Gateway Terrace, Alpine Terrace, and Oceanview.

Upon entering the grounds, an extensive rose garden is on the left. There are two gates, and the office is in a large building on the right. It looks like a huge, bustling hotel lobby, furnished with clusters of couches and comfortable chairs. There are restrooms on three floors and an elevator to take you there.

At the desk a cheerful, businesslike staffer will provide you with a map and instructions on how to find those for whom you are searching (in our case it was Alvin Ailey). We had the feeling we were consulting a hotel concierge.

Rose Hills has its share of notable professionals—actors, musicians, singers, authors, military leaders, and politicians. Illustrious residents include dominant athletes like footballers **Robert Chandler** (1949–1995; The Gardens, lot 7, private garden), wide receiver with the Buffalo Bills and Oakland Raiders and later a television host, and Hall of Famer **William Roy Lyman** (1898–1972; Suncrest, lot 1563, grave 1), who played tackle for the Chicago Bears.

Among baseball players here are **Robert Meusel** (1896–1977; Garden of Prayer, lot 5310, grave 1), who played for the New York Yankees; **Wally Hood** (1895–1965; Whispering Pines, lot 5167, grave 4), outfielder with the Brooklyn Dodgers and Pittsburgh Pirates; and **Alan Anthony Wiggins** (1958–1991; Garden of Benevolence, lot 1629, grave 4), player with the San Diego Padres and Baltimore Orioles, whose seven-year career was curtailed by drug abuse.

Alexander Chavez (1929–2003; Aspen Lawn, lot 4207, grave 1) is here, a 1940s–1950s boxer nicknamed "Fabulous Fabela," later inducted into boxing's Hall of Fame. Also present in spirit are professional golfer **Jerry Barber** (1916–1994; Garden of Reflection, winner of seven PGA Majors and later golf club and equipment designer and manufacturer; race car driver **Mickey Thompson** (1928–1988; Garden of Reflection, lot 1576, grave 1-2), who died not on the fast track but was murdered; and driver **Dave MacDonald** (1936–1964; Garden of Rest, lot 8034, grave 1), champion Indy 500 racer.

Anyone who remembers the old Charlie Chan movies will recall the detective's "number one son," played by **Keye Luke** (1904–1991; Memorial Chapel Garden, lot 434, grave 2). **Haing S. Ngor** (1940–1996; Alpine Terrace, lot 2274, grave 2) is also at rest on these grounds. The Cambodian-born actor, who won a Best Supporting Actor Oscar for his role in *The Killing Fields,* was murdered—not in war-ravaged Cambodia, but in a Los Angeles parking lot.

Other actors of note are **William Hopper** (1915–1970; Memorial Urn Garden, space 201), son of gossip columnist Hedda Hopper, who played detective Paul Drake on the *Perry Mason* television series, and Western actor **Curley Bradley** (1910–1985; Cherry Blossom Garden, lot 62, grave B), who played with Gene Autry.

Actor **Timothy Carey** (1929–1994; Sunshine Terrace, lot 2482, grave 1), whose movie and television career spanned some forty years, appeared in *East of Eden* with James Dean. He also played South Dakota Slim in *Beach Blanket Bingo* and other "beach party" films. ★*Grounds open sunrise to sunset daily. Office hours: 8:00 A.M.–5:00 P.M. daily. Map; restrooms; flower shop.*

ALVIN AILEY JR. *1931–1989*

Alvin Ailey was born in Rogers, Texas, but it was his family's move to Los Angeles when he was twelve that shaped his life. While in junior high school, his class attended a performance of the Ballet Russe de Monte Carlo, and young Alvin was mesmerized. Further exposure to dance, this time the modern Katherine Dunham Dance Company, and he knew what he wanted to do with his life.

BELOVED SON
ALVIN AILEY, JR.
1931 † 1989
FOREVER IN OUR HEARTS
THE COOPER FAMILY

He began formal lessons with Lester Horton, founder of the first integrated dance company in the United States, which launched him on his professional career. When Horton died in 1953, Ailey became director of the company at the ripe old age of twenty-two and soon began to choreograph his own works.

Word of his ability traveled fast, and in 1954 he was invited, along with his friend Carmen de Lavallade, to perform in a new musical, *House of Flowers,* a colorful tale of Haiti, with a book by Truman Capote. The show was a critical, but not commercial, success. Even so, it brought Ailey to New York, where he began to visit and study with many dancers, including Martha Graham, Doris Humphrey, and Charles Weidman. Wanting to expand his theatrical repertoire, he even studied acting with Stella Adler. This led to acting roles, but his primary interest continued to be dance.

As his dance style evolved, Ailey organized in 1958 the Alvin Ailey American Dance Theater, which continues to this day. His goal was to create a dance company that would combine modern dance traditions with African-American cultural heritage. To achieve this, he created ballet after ballet, almost eighty in all. His masterpiece, in the view of many critics, is *Revelations,* created in 1960.

Although Ailey died at fifty-eight of AIDS, his works are his legacy, many of them still performed at the Joffrey Ballet, American Ballet Theatre, the Dance Theatre of Harlem, and abroad at the Paris Opera Ballet and La Scala Ballet in Milan. Dance critic Anna Kisselgoff of the *New York Times* wrote, after his death, "You didn't have to know Ailey personally to have been touched by his humanity." He would no doubt have approved of that.

Alvin Ailey's black tombstone bears a photographic image of his face in the stone and the words "Beloved son." He resides in the Garden of Affection, near curb 185, down seventeen rows, the thirteenth grave to the right.

NORTHERN CALIFORNIA

While so many of the state's most celebrated dead reside in southern California, the northern part, especially the San Francisco axis, has its share of famous, infamous, and influential, too. Authors, naturalists, educators, pioneers, statesmen, and entrepreneurs—they all contributed to the greatness of this large state, which is hosting them for eternity.

CARMEL

MISSION SAN CARLOS BORROMEO DE CARMELO

3080 RIO ROAD (HIGHWAY 1); (831) 624-1271

Often called the jewel of the twenty-one Spanish missions strung along the coast from San Diego north to San Francisco, the Carmel Mission is the second in California founded by Fray Junipero Serra. He is buried at the altar in the sanctuary. The mission began in 1770 and became the headquarters of the entire mission chain, though the church itself wasn't finished until 1797, thirteen years after his death. It is notable for the richness of its eighteenth-century Renaissance reredos, unique among all the California missions. The entire mission complex is an oasis of peace and beauty. ★Grounds open 9:30 A.M.–4:30 P.M. Monday–Saturday, 10:30 A.M.–4:30 P.M. Sunday. Modest donation requested.

FRAY JUNIPERO SERRA *1713–1784*

This resolute Spanish Franciscan priest was humbly born in a small whitewashed house on the Balearic island of Mallorca, off the east coast of Spain. He first arrived in the Americas in 1749. Over the course of a long life (for that time), he walked thousands of miles up and down the California coast establishing missions. His goal was to bring Christianity to the local Indians while shoring up the coast for Spain with farming settlements.

LUNCH BREAK

Delicious French fare is available at **Patisserie Boissiere** (Mission Street at Carmel Plaza; 831-624-5008); Sunday brunch is special. A pleasing Italian option is **Il Fornaio Cucina Italiano** (Ocean at Ponte Verde; 831-622-5100), open straight through the day. Clint Eastwood's **Hog's Breath Inn** (San Carlos at Fifth; 831-625-1044) offers a casual publike atmosphere for its burgers and steaks.

Though only 5 feet 2 inches tall, he was indomitable. Despite an ulcerous leg infection (the result of a poisonous insect bite) that plagued him throughout his years in the New World, he limped all along the coast and through Mexico, baptizing almost 1,000 Indians, confirming more than 600, and delivering sermons that observers called spellbinding.

Considering the state of the country, which was then part of New Spain—with few roads, limited supplies, and unfriendly local inhabitants—his accomplishments were all the more remarkable. His iron constitution finally gave in to a tubercular infection. He died at his favorite mission and lies buried in its sanctuary. Three of his fellow Franciscans are resting nearby.

HOUSE CALL

Take time to enjoy the entire **Carmel Mission** property, not just the church. The museum—with several relics of Father Serra, his bronze statue in the garden, and the living quarters, with his sparse little cell (where he died)—are all worth seeing. In the cell are his few possessions: a chair, desk, wooden bed, and candlestick. Period. In the graveyard to the right of the church are graves of other eighteenth-century priests and missionaries.

CYPRESS LAWN CEMETERY

1370 EL CAMINO REAL;
(650) 755-0580

If ever there were a City of the Dead, it is Colma, just 5 miles south of San Francisco in San Mateo County. Colma's seventeen cemeteries exist for one reason: In 1900 San Francisco decreed, "Enough!" Because of epidemics and neglected, overgrown cemeteries, there would be no more burial grounds within the city or county limits. Thenceforth the remains of many graveyards, such as Laurel Hill, were evicted like delinquent tenants in the dead of night and reburied elsewhere. Colma is the beneficiary with at least five notable final retreats.

By far, Colma's major repository of the rich, famous, and interesting is this beautiful hilly burial ground where so many distinguished people have found a final refuge. Beyond the massive, castlelike gray stone entrance portal of Cypress Lawn, with its rounded Norman arch and crenellated roofline, are rolling hills, monumental trees, and an impressive number of stately mausoleums belonging to California's pioneer and blue-chip families, resting among diplomats, governors, U.S. senators and congressmen, and military heroes.

The rarefied company includes **Elias J. Baldwin** (1828–1909; section K, lot 259, private mausoleum), who made a fortune in the Comstock Lode, built the Baldwin Hotel (San Francisco's finest at one time), and owned Rancho Santa Anita in the south, which later was the site of the Santa Anita racetrack.

Also in residence are **James C. Flood** (1826–1889; triangle B, private mausoleum), one of the Comstock Lode silver kings, and German-born **Adolph Claus J. Spreckels** (1815–1908; section L, lot 177, private mausoleum), who expanded a grocery and small brewery business into large land holdings in California and Hawaii, where he grew rich on sugar cane and sugar beets, earning the soubriquet "Sugar King."

William Henry Crocker (1861–1937; East section, lot 23), president of Crocker Bank, which helped finance San Francisco's reconstruction after the 1906 earthquake, was also a University of California regent for almost thirty years. Also present for the final roll call are Finnish-born **Gustave Niebaum** (1842–1908; section L, lot 4), a much respected pioneer vintner and founder of Inglenook Winery, and **Lloyd Tevis** (1824–1899; East section, lot 15), a successful San Francisco lawyer,

partner (with George Hearst) in highly lucrative western mining ventures, and head of Wells Fargo Bank for years.

Henry Mayo Newhall (1825–1882; section I, lot 347) is here. He was the owner of six California ranches with some 143,000 acres, and his descendants founded Valencia and Newhall, California. Also on the premises is **Paul Kalmanovitz** (1905–1987; East section, lot 9), founder of the S&P Corporation of California and numerous breweries. His $1.2 billion legacy funded many charities, including hospitals and universities.

Writers residing here are **Hubert Howe Bancroft** (1832–1918; section L, lot 27), author of thirty-nine books on the history of the West; **Isabella Alden** (1841–1930; Rose Mound, plot 327), nineteenth-century children's book author; and **Gertrude Franklin Horn Atherton** (1857–1948; section N, columbarium, niche 111, tier 5), author of sixty books and scores of magazine and newspaper stories on the Old West, especially pre-Anglo California.

Samuel Marsden Brookes (1816–1892; section L, grave 169), portraitist, miniaturist, landscape painter, and leading still-life artist of the nineteenth century, is now part of the landscape. Others bedded down here for eternity include movie actress **Laura Hope Crews** (1879–1942; Rose Mound, lot 65), who played in *Gone With the Wind;* stage actress **Blanche Bates** (1873–1941; mausoleum, section E, niche 60, tier 4), original star of David Belasco's *The Girl of the Golden West* and other early-twentieth-century plays; and stage and movie actor-screenwriter **Hale Hamilton** (1883–1942; Cedar section, lot 13, division 1), who appeared in seventy-eight films, including *The Greater Glory, Love Affair, I Am a Fugitive from a Chain Gang,* and *The Woman in Red.*

Here making night music perhaps are **Melvin "Turk" Murphy** (1915–1987; Acacia section, lot 35, grave 83), jazz trombonist in 1930s dance bands, who also played with Lu Watters' Yerba Buena Jazz Band, and **Calvin E. Simmons** (1950–1982; West section, lot 24), musician, conductor of the San Francisco Boys' Chorus at age eleven, and the first African American to become conductor of a major U.S. symphony orchestra (Oakland Symphony).

Athletes also have made their final homes at Cypress Lawn, such as **Monte Attell** (1885–1960; Maple Mound North, grave 400), bantamweight boxing champion of the world 1909–1910, and **Francis "Lefty" O'Doul** (1897–1969; section I, lot 108), major-league pitcher and outfielder with the New York Yankees and four other teams.

A-list residents include **Hiram W. Johnson** (1866–1945; Cedar Mound, lot 127), widely respected progressive Republican governor and U.S. senator from 1917 to 1945; **Reverend William Ingraham Kip** (1811–1893; East section, lot 22), mis-

sionary, first Episcopal bishop of California, and founder of many parishes; and social reformer **Thomas Mooney** (1882–1942; Palm Mound, lot 301).

Here you will find aviation pioneer **Lincoln Beachey** (1887–1915; section D, lot 23), daredevil stunt pilot in the early days of flying, who is believed to have influenced Charles Lindbergh and "Hap" Arnold, and inventor-engineer **Andrew Smith Hallidie** (1836–1900; West section, lot 10), who came west to make a fortune in the mines, but made it inventing and patenting equipment, cable ropeway systems, and devices that made mining easier.

Scottish-born horticulturist **John McLaren** (1846–1943; West section, lot 8) was so devoted to his adopted country, he planted trees for fifteen years in San Francisco, turned its sand dunes into Golden Gate Park, and served as parks superintendent for more than fifty-three years, planting some two millions trees in the process.

Then there is **Charles Stewart Howard** (1877–1950; section B, above chapel, private mausoleum), who might recline here in dust-to-dust obscurity except for a 2001 book, *Seàbiscuit: An American Legend* by Laura Hillenbrand, and the subsequent movie, *Seabiscuit,* which brought Howard's name back into the limelight. He made a mint selling Buicks in the western United States, but after the death of his son in a freak truck accident, he turned his attention to race horses. In 1936 he bought a plucky, undersized thoroughbred named Seabiscuit, and the rest, as depicted in the splendid 2003 film, is racing history. **Frank "Frankie" Howard** (1911–1926) resides permanently here with his father.

LUNCH BREAK

Just a short distance away is the reasonably priced **Basque Cultural Center** (599 Railroad Avenue, South San Francisco; 650-583-8091), with agreeable French and Spanish cooking and an old-fashioned, friendly atmosphere.

Another young man, **Nick Traina** (1978–1997; West side, Elm Park), who OD'd on drugs, is here shrouded by giant shrubbery. He was the son of popular novelist Danielle Steele, who wrote about him in her book *His Bright Light.* Still with a following is **Steve Silver** (1944–1995; section F, lot 277), theatrical impresario who created San Francisco's popular campy musical revue *Beach Blanket Babylon.*

The Laurel Hill Monument honors the 35,000 souls, San Francisco's early pioneers, whose remains were brought to Cypress Lawn when Laurel Hill Cemetery, dating from 1854, was closed in 1940. ★*Grounds open 8:00 A.M.–4:30 P.M. daily. Office hours: 8:00 A.M.–5:00 P.M. weekdays, 8:30 A.M.–5:00 P.M. weekends. Map; restrooms.*

CHARLES DEYOUNG *1845–1880*

DeYoung is a prominent name in San Francisco cultural circles, but it was not always so. When Charles was about five years old, he emigrated to the area with his family from France. At age twenty, he started, with his younger brother Michael, an eight-page theatrical handbill. Its first scoop was breaking the news of Abraham Lincoln's assassination. This led them to launch a full-fledged newspaper, the *San Francisco Chronicle,* which is still going. Charles became editor in chief, Michael the treasurer.

Early on, they decided that to survive, the *Chronicle* had to parlay gossip, scandal (real or invented), and all the "news" unfit to print. Before long, the paper had the largest circulation west of the Mississippi River and featured bylines by Mark Twain and Bret Hart.

DeYoung's scandal-mongering about the city's prominent society members led to daily death threats, libel suits, and whippings by cane or pistol by outraged citizens who felt wronged. In 1879 deYoung presumably went too far. He printed a story about the hidden illegitimate affair of a Baptist minister, Isaac Kallich, who was running for mayor at the time. Kallich denounced him from the pulpit as a "hyena of society." DeYoung in turn was outraged and shot the minister outside his church. Fortunately, Kallich survived and actually won the election (as a backlash against deYoung's tactics).

Money and influence kept deYoung from being indicted for the shooting, but the matter wasn't over. The *Chronicle* continued attacking Kallich until his son, Milton, finally had had enough. He rushed into deYoung's office and shot him to death. As an indication of public sentiment, Milton Kallich was acquitted of the murder. One juror even commented, "I would have done the same thing myself."

You can't miss the deYoung grave in section O, a 15-foot-tall statue of a stern, frock-coated Charles, holding a clutch of papers in his right hand, with his name writ large beneath his feet, astride a tall pedestal surrounded by shrubbery.

WILLIAM RANDOLPH HEARST *1863–1951*

Citizen Kane is one of Hollywood's all-time great movies, but it muddies the waters if you are attempting to sort out the real life of newspaper magnate William Randolph Hearst, on which much of the *reel* life was ostensibly based. Hearst's father, George, was a success in his own right, making his fortune in gold mining in the West. He bought a flimsy newspaper, the *San Francisco Examiner,* to settle a gambling debt and later became a U.S. senator. His wife, Phoebe, started their son, William, on the road to a lifelong interest in art and collecting by taking him on an extensive tour of Europe when he was just ten years old. Her cultural interest sparked his.

Phoebe had ambitions for her only child. She sent him to an eastern preparatory school (St. Paul's) and then to Harvard in 1882. While much of his college time was spent goofing around, he became business manager for the *Harvard Lampoon,* and learned a bit about newspapering as an apprentice to Joseph Pulitzer, who later took him on at the *New York World.*

While still in college, William begged his father, who had recently acquired the *Examiner,* to let him run it. Surprisingly, the senior Hearst agreed, and in 1887 William took over the newspaper. Modeling the upstart daily on Pulitzer's tabloid success, he upgraded the paper's equipment, hired a talented staff,

HOUSE CALL

San Simeon (San Simeon State Park, 750 Hearst Castle Road; 805-927-2020 or 800-444-444; www.hearstcastle.org), Hearst's palatial Spanish Renaissance-style castle, commands the top of a hill overlooking 127 acres that extend down to the Pacific. Eclectic in its authentic Spanish, French, Italian, and Moorish architectural elements, the castle features lavish baronial furnishings, antiquities, paintings, and sculptures. The castle, its landscaped grounds, swimming pools, and accoutrements convey the lordly lifestyle of Hearst at his apogee. Five tour choices (reservations must be made weeks ahead) offer insights into various aspects of his life and personality.

and began a ferocious rivalry with Pulitzer, swallowing up paper after paper. In the process, he transformed himself into the major press baron of the age. The name William Randolph Hearst was admired, feared, and detested for generations.

Hearst called his style the "new journalism"—with shorter, snappier, cutting-edge stories and sensational (not always factual) reporting. Critics called it "yellow journalism" for many of the same reasons and blamed the Hearst papers' inflammatory rhetoric for pushing the United States into the Spanish-American War.

Like his father, Hearst gravitated to politics, but the only office he ever won was as a U.S. congressman from New York's eleventh district—not the power platform such an ambitious man craved. From youthful Democratic leanings, Hearst became steadily more conservative as he grew older, and his papers became a bastion for conservative thought and opinion.

In his personal life, Hearst was always attracted to the theater, marrying one showgirl, Millicent Wilson, and taking another, Marion Davies, as a mistress. From 1917 onward, he spent the rest of his life with Davies, mostly at his spectacular estate, San Simeon, where he lavishly entertained Hollywood and other royalty and dignitaries of every stripe. Although he inherited one fortune and made another,

Hearst's imperial lifestyle brought him serious financial problems late in life (he was never able to finish San Simeon), forcing him to relinquish control of numerous business properties.

The Hearst family mausoleum at the corner of sections E and H, a magnificent Grecian temple with Ionic columns on all sides, reflects the exuberance he had for living—and dying. Here he resides in manorial style, along with his mother, **Phoebe Apperson Hearst** (1840–1919), and father, **George Hearst** (1820–1891). Also in the spacious premises are two of his five sons: **William Randolph Hearst Jr.** (1907–1992), who earned his stripes as a reporter, foreign correspondent (co-sharing a Pulitzer Prize in 1956), and forty-year-long editor in chief of the entire Hearst chain, and last surviving son **Randolph Apperson Hearst** (1915–2000), chairman of the Hearst Corporation for twenty-three years (1973–1996). Randolph was the father of Patty Hearst, who made tabloid headlines in the 1970s by being kidnapped and eventually escaping.

JOSEPH LINCOLN STEFFENS *1866–1936*

Lincoln Steffens, as he was known professionally, was a rarity for California in his time: He was native-born, not an émigré from the East. His father was a successful San Francisco businessman who provided a privileged childhood for his son and sent him to study in France and Germany. He finished college at the University of California, Berkeley. It was at Berkeley that young Steffens was radicalized in his political and social views.

His entire career as a writer, which began at *McClure's* magazine, a highly respected journal at the time, was spent investigating and exposing government corruption. This type of factual, honest reporting was such a novelty in that era, it was called muckraking (raking up the muck), and it made him and two other *McClure's* writers, Ida Tarball and Ray Stannard Baker, famous.

Steffens's articles were collected in two books, *Shame of the Cities,* published in 1904, and *The Struggle for Self-Government,* 1906. Both caused a sensation. He later wrote *The Traitor State,* a diatribe against New Jersey's use of incorporation (a system still used today in Delaware). In 1906 all three of *McClure's* muckrakers

(Steffens, Tarbell, and Baker) left the magazine to form their own publication, *American Magazine*.

Steffens became increasingly radicalized by the failures he saw in his own government and began covering foreign revolutions, first the Mexican revolution in 1910, later the Russian one in 1919. His most famous line, often quoted and occasionally attributed to others, was the result of a 1921 visit to Russia, after which he wrote glowingly, "I have seen the future, and it works." At the time, he felt revolution was the only way to secure governmental reform. However, he later became disillusioned by Stalin's brand of communism; by 1931, when Steffens wrote his memoirs, he had turned on it completely.

Today Lincoln Steffens is mostly a literary footnote, but in his day he was considered as iconoclastic as Michael Moore. His grave is in section F, lot 6.

HILLS OF ETERNITY MEMORIAL PARK

1301 EL CAMINO REAL;
(650) 756-3633

This Jewish cemetery, which dates back to 1892, is down the road from Cypress Lawn, offering the opportunity to combine visits. Actually, it is possible to have a three-in-one, for attached to Hills of Eternity like a Siamese twin is Home of Peace Cemetery, which shares the office and provides maps.

> ## LUNCH BREAK
> **Gunther's Restaurant and Cafe** (1601 Meridian Avenue; 408-266-9022) is down the road from the cemetery and good for a casual sandwich-type lunch. **Gordon Biersch** (33 East San Fernando Street, San Jose; 408-294-6785) is handy, too. Don't pass up its delicious garlic fries, with burgers, salads, and other California fare.

While Wyatt Earp is Hills of Eternity's most famous permanent boarder, a recent arrival, **Phillip York Goldman** (1964–2003; Gardens of Eternity mausoleum, Carmel unit), also has a distinguished résumé, especially for a man who died at age thirty-nine. A scientist and businessman, Goldman graduated from Princeton with a computer science degree, acquired nineteen patents, worked for Apple Computers and General Magic, co-founded WebTV Inc. (which was later sold to Microsoft), and then founded Malblocks. *Grounds and office open 8:30 A.M.–4:00 P.M. daily, except Saturday. Map; restroom.*

WYATT EARP *1848–1929*

As has been said, death is full of surprises. It is also an equal opportunity employer. Who would expect to find Wyatt Barry Stepp Earp—the famous gun-toting marshal of the Wild West—resting peaceably in a Jewish cemetery in northern California? The explanation is simple: Lying with him is his wife, or common-law wife (depending on which source you believe), **Josephine Sarah Marcus** (1861–1944), daughter of a Jewish San Francisco merchant. Earp's first wife died and his second marriage failed, but the union with Josephine, legal or not, survived until his death.

Like many old western yarns, the Earp legend is as shifty as the many desperadoes he faced. This much seems true: He was born in Illinois, grew up in Iowa, and the family kept tilting westward, finally settling in San Bernardino, California, in 1864. As a young man, Wyatt crisscrossed the West, hunting buffalo, driving stagecoaches, and working for the railroad.

As a U.S. marshal—in Wichita and Dodge City, Kansas, and finally Tombstone, Arizona—Earp was reportedly a fast thinker with a fast gun. In his entire career as a lawman he was never even hit accidentally by a bullet. His celebrated battle at the OK Corral in Tombstone in 1881—in which he, his brothers, and Doc Holliday shot it out with Billy Clanton and the McLowery brothers—has been so mythologized, it is almost impossible from this distance to separate hard fact from serial exaggerations.

For two years (1885–1887) Earp and Josephine lived in San Diego, where he—ever the gambler and speculator—bought land and saloons in what is now the revived Gaslight Quarter. In 1897 Earp (with Josephine) headed to Alaska during the gold rush and ran a saloon, then followed the gold mania to Tonopah, Nevada, where he again gambled, mined, and ran a saloon, alternating living high and low.

His final years were reportedly marked by poverty, scratching out a living by mining in the Mojave Desert in winter and summering in Los Angeles, where he died peacefully before his legend could be firmly cemented in Hollywood westerns. W. J. Hunsacker, Wilson Mizner, Tom Mix, and William S. Hart were pallbearers at his funeral, which Josephine, usually always at his side, was too grief-stricken to attend.

Cremated, Earp's ashes were taken north to Hills of Eternity for burial. Josephine joined him fifteen years later, as their joint grave marker indicates. The polished granite gravestone—located in plot D, section 2, lot 12, grave 2—says "nothing's so sacred as honor and nothing's so loyal as love." Perhaps nothing's so apt as this description of a long life.

HOLY CROSS CATHOLIC CEMETERY

1500 OLD MISSION ROAD;
(650) 756-2060

A 280-acre Catholic burying ground, Holy Cross opened in 1887 and is the oldest and largest cemetery in town. Some of its acreage has not yet been developed. Fieldstone pillars at the entrance lead into the spacious grounds, which contain a chapel with frescoes by Thomas Lawless; Holy Cross mausoleum, where all of San Francisco's archbishops recline; All Saints mausoleum, with an imposing bronze sculpture on the front (by local artist Rosa Estebañez); and a Priests Circle, where

many archdiocesan priests are at peace, facing a central marble carving of the Last Supper.

Private mausoleums and religious statuary are scattered throughout the rolling hills and greenswards dotted with eucalyptus, palm, pine, and oak trees; shrubs; and flowers. In this restful landscape can be found many notable civic leaders, bankers, politicians (mayors, governors, U.S. senators and congressmen), educators, and military people.

The foremost politico in his last hurrah is **Edmund G. "Pat" Brown Sr.** (1905–1996; section D, on the left of the main road, near the office), San Francisco native, straight-shooting district attorney and state attorney general, and two-time governor of California (beating Richard Nixon once). He was the patriarch of one of the state's leading Democratic families, and was defeated for a third gubernatorial term by a novice politician named Ronald Reagan.

George Moscone (1929–1978; St. Michael section) was the thirty-fourth mayor of San Francisco, whose term was tragically interrupted by a disgruntled supervisor, Dan White. Aggrieved by the mayor's gay rights policies and his appointment of gay rights activist Harvey Milk to the Board of Permit Appeals, White rushed into Moscone's office and murdered him and Milk, later using the famous "Twinkie" defense.

Here as well are such movers and shakers as **James G. Fair** (1831–1894; section H, mausoleum to the right of the chapel), a senator, founder of the Fairmount Hotel, and one of the four "silver kings," partners in the Comstock Lode; **Amadeo P. Giannini** (1870–1949; section H, next to Fair's grave), founder of the Bank of Italy, which later became Bank of America; **Cyril R. Tobin** (1880–1977; section D, behind office), founder of Hibernia Bank; and **Georges de Latour** (1856–1940; section I), founder of Beaulieu Vineyards.

On the grounds also are **Abigail Anne Folger** (1943–1969; main mausoleum, hallway N), Folger coffee heiress and victim (with Sharon Tate) in the Manson murders; **Vince Guaraldi** (1928–1976;

LUNCH BREAK

The best place to eat around here, too, is the **Basque Cultural Center** (599 Railroad Avenue, South San Francisco; 650-583-8091).

Star of the Sea, row 40, grave 8), jazz pianist and composer of the "Peanuts" theme song and other songs for the Charles Schultz cartoons; and sculptor **Benamino Bufano** (1890–1970; section W, northeast of the main community mausoleum), who made the statue of St. Francis that marks his grave.

Once world-renowned soprano **Maud J. Symington** (1878–1964; section D) is here. Famed for her Wagnerian roles, she studied in Dresden, Germany; sang at Covent Garden, London, and New York's Metropolitan Opera; and was a member of the Munich Opera for eight years. It wasn't over until she sang.

Among several major-league baseball players here are **Frank "The Crow" Crosetti** (1910–2002; All Saints mausoleum, Corridor of St. Agnes), who played shortstop for the New York Yankees for seventeen years (1932–1948), eight of them on World Series championship teams, and was their third-base coach for twenty years, and **Henry "Hank" Sauer** (1917–2001; section G2, row 19, grave 18), a fifteen-year major leaguer with four different National League teams (Reds, Cardinals, Cubs, and Giants), twice an All-Star outfielder, MVP in 1952, and a coach for thirty-four years. ★*Grounds open 8:00 A.M. to dusk daily. Office hours: 8:30 A.M.–5:00 P.M. daily, except Sunday. Map and self-walking tour; restrooms.*

MICHAEL HENRY DEYOUNG *1849–1925*

Michael deYoung co-founded the *San Francisco Chronicle* with his brother Charles, four years his senior. After Charles was murdered by an irate reader-victim, Michael took over the editor's job and continued the paper's libelous, attack-dog editorial policies. The paper was so despised by San Francisco society that writer Ambrose Bierce commented, "Hatred of deYoung is the best test of a gentleman."

Like his brother, Michael was also shot (by the son of sugar mogul Claus Spreckles, whose business practices the *Chronicle* had criticized), but unlike Charles, he survived and lived another forty-one years. During that time he built the M. H. deYoung Museum in Golden Gate Park, proving that something good (art) could come of something bad (calumny).

His imposing family mausoleum is in section I.

HOUSE CALL

The **M. H. deYoung Memorial Museum** (Golden Gate Park, San Francisco; 415-838-3330), Michael's legacy, is a local treasure—a vast repository of four centuries of American art, plus art from all over the world. Its west wing houses the **Asian Art Museum,** an additional treasure trove. A cafe on the premises is a helpful addition.

JOSEPH PAUL DIMAGGIO *1914–1999*

"Joltin' Joe" DiMaggio, the "Yankee Clipper," was a baseball Olympian. As an out-fielder for the New York Yankees, he won three MVP awards, had a career batting average of .325, was easily elected to the Hall of Fame in 1955, and for his modest, hardworking, no-hijinks playing style was one of the most popular Yankees of all time. During his years with the Bronx Bombers, 1936–1951, the team won ten American League championships and nine World Series. Today, as baseball records are being demolished right and left, his 1941 streak of hitting in fifty-six straight games still stands.

In 1969 sportswriters named him the "Greatest Living Player"–though Ted Williams fans might disagree. DiMaggio was so proud of this accolade that in his innumerable public appearances at Yankee Stadium and elsewhere, he insisted that this title be included in his introduction (Joe wasn't quite as modest as he liked to appear).

Number eight of nine children of Sicilian immigrants, he was born in the seaside village of Martinez, California, but the family soon moved to the Italian neighborhood of North Beach in San Francisco. Three DiMaggio brothers—Joe, the older Vince, and younger Dominic—all turned to baseball for fun and eventually their livelihoods.

Joe never finished high school and was habitually shy and socially inept. His

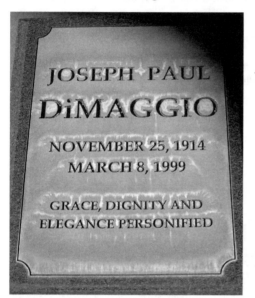

first marriage failed during the World War II years, when he served as a physical education teacher. Years later, his second marriage to Marilyn Monroe, over his family's objections, lasted nine months and caused his excommunication from the Catholic Church. The crush he supposedly had on her even after her death became legendary. In one version of the legend, he had red roses placed on her crypt at Westwood Village Memorial Park three days a week for twenty years. Another version says it was a bouquet once a year on the anniversary of her death. Considering his widely known penuriousness, we'll go with the once-a-year version.

Joe DiMaggio died at his home in Hollywood, Florida, but his funeral was held in the North Beach church that he attended as a youth and where he married the first time. A memorial mass at St. Patrick's Cathedral in New York was as well attended as a rock concert by Yankees fans and celebrities of all stripes, not just pinstripes. While he is at rest here, to Yankees fans he will be perpetually enshrined at Yankee Stadium, along with his retired uniform number (#5) and his center field marker.

His large monument banked with plantings, just southwest of the Clergy circle in section I, row 11, area 6/7, is hard to miss. It is set into a cross-shaped base and has the name DIMAGGIO at the top and a crucifix on the front. On DiMaggio's headstone at the foot of the monument are the words "Grace, Dignity, and Elegance Personified." A good recap of his life, but it omits some crucial innings.

HOME OF PEACE CEMETERY AND EMANU-EL AND GARDEN OF PEACE MAUSOLEUMS

1299 EL CAMINO REAL; (650) 755-4700

As we were saying, Home of Peace abuts Hills of Eternity and they share the same office. Home of Peace's twenty-five acres at the foot of the San Bruno Mountains form a palm-dotted backdrop for the notables residing here in perpetuity. This is the third burial ground formed by the Emanu-el congregation.

Resting here, along with several U.S. congressmen, is **Alfred Hertz** (1872–1942; mausoleum, columbarium, tier 6, niche 5039), conductor of the San Francisco Symphony Orchestra, known for his interpretations of Richard Wagner's music.

Prussian-born **Adolph Sutro** (1830–1898) built an underground vault here for his wife and young daughter, but he is buried in an undisclosed place in Sutro Heights. A mining engineer, Sutro was also a silver baron, creator of the Sutro Tunnel to the Comstock Lode, mayor of San Francisco (1894–1896), and builder of the most ambitious of the cliff houses (The Castle) and the Sutro Baths.

Also here is film producer **Walter Wanger** (1894–1968; indoor mausoleum). He was famous during Hollywood's silent era and Golden Age for producing *The Sheik, Stagecoach, Joan of Arc, Algiers,* and *Foreign Correspondent* but was even better known for his role in shaping the careers of Rudolph Valentino, Claudette Colbert, Henry Fonda, Joan Bennett (whom he married), Elizabeth Taylor, and Richard Burton, among others.

By far the best-known "name" at Home of Peace is **Levi Strauss** (1830–1902; private mausoleum, section 2, plot C, end of Middle Road), the itinerant dry-goods salesman whose creation of sturdy denim trousers with copper rivets at the strain points gave him immortality—almost two centuries' worth and counting. His ubiquitous blue jeans—or Levi's—are more of a living memorial to him than his large, columned granite mausoleum, imposing as it is. ★*Grounds and office open 8:30 A.M.–4:00 P.M. daily, except Saturday. Map; restrooms.*

JACK LONDON STATE HISTORIC PARK

2400 LONDON RANCH ROAD;
(707) 938-5216

The knoll in the Valley of the Moon seems a perfect backdrop for the grave of writer Jack London, who loved this Sonoma Valley land and began acquiring pieces of it in 1911. It is now an 800-acre park with hiking trails; a man-made lake created by the author himself; canopies of oak, madrone, and redwood trees; and views of Sonoma and the Mayacamas Mountains. Also in the park and open to view are the Jack London cottage; a museum called House of Happy Walls, which contains London artifacts and memorabilia; and the ruins of Wolf House, a home he built that burned down just before he moved in. ★*Grounds open 9:30 A.M.–5:00 P.M. in winter, 9:30 A.M.–7:00 P.M. in summer. Museum hours: 10:00 A.M.–5:00 P.M. daily. Parking fee ($3.00 per vehicle); brochure ($1.00); restrooms.*

LUNCH BREAK

Sonoma Valley is full of choice places to eat. Just 3 miles north of town is the modest, informal **Cafe Citti** (9049 Sonoma Highway, Kenwood; 707-833-2690), offering homemade pasta and other northern Italian dishes and good desserts at moderate prices, along with outdoor dining.

JACK LONDON *1876–1916*

Some authors just *write* about adventure, but Jack London *lived* it—and then wrote about it. His parents both came from pioneer stock. London was born in San Francisco, where his father eked out a living as a scout, trapper, and frontiersman before moving to Oakland. The family's impoverished life on the Oakland waterfront forced young Jack to quit school early. He delivered newspapers and worked in a cannery and then on an ice wagon. All the while he spent his spare time in the public library, feeding his imagination with books on travel and adventure.

No mere Walter Mitty, he put in time as an oysterman and as a seaman and sealer, hunting seals off the Siberian coast. Tramping all over the country, he was arrested and spent time in jail. By then he had written and sold a few stories, and he decided to change his life. He finished a year of high school and, through heavy cramming, was admitted to the University of California, Berkeley. He lasted half a year, ran out of money, then joined the gold rush mania and headed for the Klondike to earn money so he could write again. Beset by scurvy, he had to return home after a year.

Between 1899 and 1903 he was a writing dervish, producing stories, essays, poetry, serials, and newspaper work, as well as eight books. One of these, *The Call of the Wild* (1903), is considered his finest work and holds up beautifully even today.

By then he was becoming famous and in great demand on the lecture circuit. In 1904 the *San Francisco Examiner* sent him to cover the Russo-Japanese War. The next year he and his second wife, Charmion Kittredge, took off on a voyage around the world in a 45-foot yacht. By the time they reached Australia, London was so ill, they had to return to California. From then on, London the wanderer became London the landlubbing rancher—though he did take time out to sail round the Horn and go to Vera Cruz, Mexico, as a war correspondent. In a sixteen-year period he published forty-three books, with seven more published posthumously.

When he died of uremic poisoning—having lived a lifetime and a half—London was just forty years old. His grave is marked by a red lava boulder, which covers the sealed copper urn with his ashes. A wood-slatted fence surrounds the massive rock. Within the fence's confines are the wooden headboards of two pioneer children, **David** and **Lilly Greenlaw,** who died in 1876 and 1877; their graves were here when London bought the land.

HOUSE CALL

South in Oakland is the waterfront area with Heinold's First and Last Chance Saloon (56 Jack London Square; 510-839-6761), where London worked on his most famous novels. Also in the square is a reconstruction of his Klondike cabin in which he spent the freezing winter of 1898.

M A R T I N E Z

JOHN MUIR NATIONAL HISTORIC SITE

4202 ALHAMBRA AVENUE;
(925) 228-8860; WWW.NPS.GOV/JOMU

The 1882 home and grave site of the famous naturalist John Muir are now administered by the National Park Service. A visitor center shows films about Muir and his life. The grave is about 1 mile south of the Muir homestead, near the banks of

Alhambra Creek. It is part of a family site, carefully planned by John Strentzel, Muir's father-in-law. Buried there are Strentzel and his wife; Muir and his wife, Louie Strentzel Muir; their daughter, Wanda Muir Hanna, and her husband, Thomas Rae Hanna; plus Louie's uncle and two of her siblings who died young. All the gravestones are cut from the same granite, as is the curbing that marks the perimeters. When John Strentzel chose the site, he planted a pear orchard, along with a manna gum tree and cedar, thus shading the graves. ★*Grounds, house, and visitor center open 10:00 A.M.–5:00 P.M. Wednesday–Sunday; closed major holidays. Map; $3.00 admission.*

JOHN MUIR *1838–1914*

Known as the "Guardian of Yosemite" and "Naturalist of the Sierras," John Muir preserved as much wilderness as was possible for one man to do. What he would think today of the commercial encroachments on our national parks we don't even want to contemplate.

Muir was born in Scotland and emigrated with his family to the United States in 1849, where his parents started a farm in Wisconsin. As a young man, he abandoned the University of Wisconsin for a job as an industrial engineer in Indianapolis. There a factory accident temporarily blinded him.

Before long he embarked on what he called the "university of the wilderness," a 1,000-mile trek from Indiana to Florida. He planned to continue walking to South America, but a bout of malaria intervened. He then turned his sights to California. All nature lovers should be thankful he did, for it was largely his efforts that helped save and protect the state's magnificent wilderness.

HOUSE CALLS

Muir's seventeen-room home, in the National Historic Site, is in the Italianate Gothic style, typical of a late-nineteenth-century upper-middle-class home. Muir called the library his "scribble room," and it best evokes the man. Another memento: **Muir Woods National Monument and Beach** (Mill Valley; 415-388-2595), the last redwood stand in the Bay Area, leading to a sandy ocean beach, good for swimming and picnicking.

Muir was something of a Renaissance man, with self-taught skills as an inventor, engineer, geologist, explorer, writer, and environmentalist before the word was in common usage. Probably Muir's greatest accomplishment in a seventy-six-year-long life was preserving Yosemite and turning it into a national park. He took on loggers and sheep farmers and usually won. He battled hard to prevent Yosemite's Hetch Hetchy Valley from being dammed, but lost that one.

Muir's gifts of persuasion, in person and in his writings, were considerable: He took President Theodore Roosevelt camping to convince him the best way to protect Yosemite was through federal control and management; he used his friendship with E. H. Harriman and other influential people to lobby Congress to pass conservation laws; he helped found the Sierra Club in 1890 and was its first president for twenty-two years (until his death). He was influential in the creation of several national parks, and his work on conservation laid the groundwork for the creation of a federal park overseer, which finally happened in 1916 with the formation of the National Park Service.

He wrote poetically and lovingly of nature in hundreds of magazine and newspaper articles and several books. In *Our National Parks* he described an avalanche in which he was caught: "This flight in a Milky Way of snow flowers was the most spiritual of all my travels; after many years, the mere thought of it is still an exhilaration." In the same book he wrote of the bear: "In my first interview with a Sierra bear we were frightened and embarrassed, both of us, but the bear's behaviour was better than mine."

In photographs Muir, with his big bushy beard, resembles a mountain man, but his gentleness and respect for nature overflow in all his printed works. He and his wife's black granite headstones, side by side, have identical gracefully curved shapes at the top. They are carved with matching floral designs, which resemble thistles, the national flower of Scotland, Muir's homeland.

O A K L A N D

MOUNTAIN VIEW CEMETERY

5000 PIEDMONT AVENUE;
(510) 658-2588

Designed by Frederick Law Olmsted and established in 1863, Mountain View Cemetery in the Oakland hills opened two years later on 220 beautiful acres, with massive double main entrance gates and three chapels. Following Olmsted's philosophy, Mountain View emphasizes harmony between nature and man, and is in the garden tradition of the parklike cemeteries of New York state and New England.

Its sweeping vistas of the bay, broad avenues encompassing the slopes of six hills, and sheltering shade trees—California live oak, Italian cypress, Lebanese cedar, and Italian stone pine—all make Mountain View a visual delight. There are grassy knolls; an impressive "Millionaires' Row" of substantial private mausoleums shaped like Egyptian pyramids, Gothic churches, and Greek temples; and obelisks topped by melancholy angels and funereal urns. A section of Civil War burials is bordered with antique cannon balls.

The crème de la crème of the settlers and powers of the Bay Area reside here—doctors, lawyers, businessmen, mayors, and governors. Among them are industrialist and engineer **Warren A. Bechtel** (1872–1933; main mausoleum, ground floor), founder of the firm that bears his name, and his son **Stephen D. Bechtel** (1900–1989; same location), who expanded the company into the international giant that Bechtel Corporation is today.

From beginnings as a dry goods salesman, **Charles Crocker** (1822–1888; section 35, Millionaires' Row mausoleum) became a successful businessman and partner in the Central Pacific Railroad. Other local magnates include **Domingo Ghirardelli** (1815–1894; section 27), founder of the chocolate company that bears his name. His mausoleum is topped by a doleful statue resting on her laurels—literally.

James A. Folger (1835–1889; section 37), founder of Folgers Coffee Company, is here, as are **Francis Marion "Borax" Smith** (1846–1931; section 35), miner, hotel developer, and founder of U.S. Borax, and **Walter Blair** (1830–1888; plot 28, grave 11), entrepreneur and dairy farmer with some 600 acres in Piedmont, California.

LUNCH BREAK

Just three blocks away on the same street is the retro **Fenton's Creamery** (4226 Piedmont Avenue; 510-658-7000), famous since 1894 for its ice cream, humongous sundaes, and tasty sandwiches. For a California-French menu and relaxed ambience, **Citron** (5484 College Avenue; 510-653-5484) is a real delight. In warm weather, head for the back patio.

Several governors and sheriffs have made this their final home, as has powerhouse **William E. Knowland** (1908–1974; niche M8J), U.S. senator for fourteen years and senate majority leader, also editor of the *Oakland Tribune*.

Artists are here as well, notably **Thomas Hill** (1828–1908; plot 36, grave 261), a landscape painter of the Yosemite Valley and early member of the Bohemian Club. **Bernard Maybeck** (1862–1957; mausoleum, Urn Garden, plot 359), architect and designer of homes in the arts and crafts style, was responsible for the design of the 1915 Panama-Pacific Exposition's Palace of Fine Arts in San Francisco. He was also architect Julia Morgan's teacher and mentor.

Racing no more, aggressive, high-wired race car driver **Edward "Smokey" Elisian** (1926–1959; plot 52D, lot 466) is in dead silence, his Indianapolis 500 days long past. Professional baseball catcher **Ernie Lombardi** (1908–1977; Outside Garden mausoleums, building 2, crypt 343, tier 1) won two batting titles. His greatest years were with the Cincinnati Reds, but he also played for three other major-league teams. His failure to make the Hall of Fame embittered him, but he was inducted eight years after his death. Some consolation!

It seems odd to find among all the distinguished residents of Mountain View a victim of a horrendous murder, whose killer was never caught. **Elizabeth Short** (1924–1947; section 66, marker 798), a wannabe movie actress, is known in the annals of unsolved crimes as the "Black Dahlia." Her brutal death (in which the body was beaten, sodomized, and cut in half) in Los Angeles read like fiction and indeed has been the subject of movies, a play, a novel by James Elroy (1987), and numerous fictionalized accounts for almost sixty years. ★*Grounds open 7:30 A.M.–5:00 P.M. weekdays, 9:00 A.M.–5:00 P.M. weekends and holidays. Office hours: 8:00 A.M.–4:30 P.M. weekdays, 10:00 A.M.–4:00 P.M. weekends and holidays. Map; restrooms.*

HENRY J. KAISER *1882–1967*

One might never have guessed, back in 1895 in Sprout Brook, New York, that a thirteen-year-old school dropout would parlay a small construction business into a major industrial giant with assets of more than $2.7 billion in mid-twentieth-century dollars. Henry John Kaiser—with a surplus of brains, energy, and creativity, along with boundless optimism—found an outlet for all four, but moved west to do it.

At age twenty-five he began work in the construction business and started a road-paving company, making it a model of efficiency, speed, and economy. This led to lucrative road-building contracts, such as a $2 million contract to pave 300 miles of highway in Cuba. Then, beginning in 1931, in conjunction with other contractors, he obtained contracts to build the Hoover, Bonneville, Parker, and Grand Coulee dams, as well as to construct the piers for the Oakland–San Francisco Bay Bridge.

Famed for his I-can-do-it spirit, Kaiser had his share of upbeat aphorisms, such as "When your work speaks for itself, don't interrupt." By the start of World War II, Kaiser's restless imagination led him into shipbuilding, and by 1945 his company's Liberty ship project had built 1,490 vessels, earning him a record for speed and the unofficial title "father of modern American ship building." His innovative techniques to meet production goals are still in use today in military and commercial shipbuilding.

Always thinking ahead, in 1944 Kaiser anticipated the postwar need for housing, transportation, and health care and began developing enterprises in all these fields. His venture into home building was a continuing success. Manufacturing house products (aluminum, gypsum, and the like) led him to produce 10,000 homes.

His automobile business, Kaiser Motors, was another story: too little, too undercapitalized, too late to compete with the big boys of Detroit. At first, the Kaiser operation in the old Ford Motor plant in Willow Run, Michigan, did well, producing airplanes as well as cars. But cancelled contracts and limp sales forced the plant to relocate and finally shut down.

HOUSE CALL

The **Kaiser Center** (300 Lakeside Drive; 510-271-6146), a complex with cafeterias, restaurants, and a gorgeous three-and-a-half-acre roof garden full of trees, flowers, fountains, and a pool, also features free changing art exhibits on the mezzanine floor.

It was in health care that Kaiser really polished his legacy. The medical plan that he started for his workers in 1942 was opened to the public in 1945 and became the largest privately sponsored health-care plan in the world. It subsequently evolved into Kaiser Permanente, a major innovative player in the field of managed health care.

In later years, Kaiser left management of his many enterprises to his son and retired to Hawaii. He had discovered its charms on a building project there in the early 1950s, the first of many Hawaiian projects he would undertake—hospitals, a world-famous hotel, housing developments, medical schools and centers, even a dream city called Hawaii Kai. Although he died in Honolulu, his free spirit is back in Oakland. His own final housing project is in the main mausoleum, second floor.

JULIA MORGAN *1872–1957*

Don't tell Julia Morgan that women's lib began in the 1960s. This pioneering San Francisco architect was one of the first women to enroll in the University of California's School of Engineering and receive a BS. She was also the first woman to be admitted to the École des Beaux-Arts in Paris and one of the earliest—and perhaps the first *woman*—architect to be licensed by examination in California. Later, in 1921, she was one of the first women admitted to the American Institute of Architects.

One of her early jobs was to work on the new Greek Theatre and Hearst Memorial Mining Building at the University of California, Berkeley. This led to a life-long association with Phoebe Hearst (mother of William Randolph) and the Hearst family. Morgan's work included a building program at Mills College (a Phoebe Hearst project), the Hearst Gymnasium for Women at Berkeley, and a refurbishing of Hearst's Examiner Building after the great earthquake and fire.

Over a long professional life, which included some 700 projects, she is best known for San Simeon, William Randolph Hearst's castle south of Monterey, the most famous of many Hearst family estates she worked on. Her efforts on the castle

1841	CHARLES BILL MORGAN	1924
1845	ELIZA WOODLAND MORGAN	1930
1880	GARDNER B. MORGAN	1913
1870	PARMELEE MORGAN	1918
1876	AVERY MORGAN	1944
1872	JULIA MORGAN	1957
1874	EMMA MORGAN NORTH	1965
1871	HART HYATT NORTH	1950
1914	MORGAN NORTH	1978
1917	FLORA D'ILLE NORTH	1986

included traveling extensively in Europe to purchase ornate furnishings and art-works to integrate into the architectural design. Hearst trusted her aesthetic eye. With all the details, it is no wonder it took twenty-eight years to finish the job. Even then, with Hearst's death in 1951, it was never totally done. Considering his penchant and hers for adding flourishes and acquiring new objets, it probably never would be.

Her rough-hewn granite headstone, in which various family members are included, rests on a quiet slope in section 33.

FRANK NORRIS *1870–1902*

Benjamin Frank Norris may be seldom read today, but he was a trailblazer in his brief heyday (he died at the shockingly young age of thirty-two of a ruptured appendix). Born in Chicago, he came to California at age fourteen to live with his father. He later studied art in Paris, where he fell under the influence of the naturalistic writings of Émile Zola and Guy de Maupassant. He was later often dubbed the "American Zola."

Norris went from the University of California, Berkeley, to Harvard, and then to work on a magazine called *The Wave.* He introduced his novels *Blix* and *McTeague* (considered by critics to be his finest work) in 1899, as part of a trilogy (*Vandover and the Brute* was published posthumously in 1914) about San Francisco. With a saloon for every ninety-six residents, the crime, vice, and lowlife of the city after the gold rush struck Norris as the perfect setting for a novel about moral decay.

Norris's most famous epic novel was *The Octopus* (1901), which, with *The Pit*

(1903), was intended to be part of a trilogy about the real-life conflict between California wheat farmers and the railroads. To research the subject, he spent two months in the countryside near Hollister.

While Norris's prose may seem overly dramatic today, he was reacting against the staid Victorianism of his time. And while he wrote about real injustices, his characters were not just cardboard figures to make political points, but were complex and three-dimensional. The "good guys" had their flaws just as the bad guys did.

Who knows how many other books might have come from his pen, if it weren't for his untimely death? This came right after he and his beautiful young wife had bought a ranch from Robert Louis Stevenson's widow just west of Gilroy. His gravestone, engraved with three blades of wheat—to commemorate *The Octopus*—lies in section 12, lot 105, shaded by four Irish yew trees.

P A L O   A L T O

ALTA MESA MEMORIAL PARK

695 ARASTRADERO ROAD;
(650) 493-1041

Begun in 1904 as a nonsectarian cemetery, this woodsy, well-groomed 72-acre landscape is dotted with classical and ulta-modern memorials, as well as a surfeit of flowers and plantings.

Resting peacefully (one assumes) on these grounds are a number of achievers. Singer, television host, and radio announcer **Ernest "Tennessee Ernie" Ford** (1919–1991; lot 242, sub 1, urn garden) is one, as is fellow musician **Ronald "Pigpen" McKernan** (1945–1973; Hillview section, Bb16, lot 374), who played percussion with the Grateful Dead and was a onetime lover of rock star Janis Joplin.

Husband-and-wife novelists **Charles Gilman Smith Norris** (1881–1945; block 2D) and **Kath-**

> ### LUNCH BREAK
> If you have a yen for superbly fresh sushi, there's **Fuki Sushi** (4119 El Camino Real, between Arastradero and Page Mill Roads; 650-494-9383), which is visually pleasing as well.

leen Thompson Norris (1880–1966; same location) are together still. He was an author, dramatist, and editor for several magazines; she was probably the bigger name as a novelist (sort of a tamer Danielle Steel of her era), author of such best-selling works as *The Foolish Virgin, Bread Into Roses, The Venables,* and *Family Gatherings.* ★*Grounds open 8:00 A.M.–6:00 P.M. daily. Office hours: 8:00 A.M.–4:30 P.M. weekdays, 10:00 A.M.–4:00 P.M. weekends. Map; restrooms.*

DAVID PACKARD 1912–1996

It is fitting that David Packard's final address is near that of his mentor, Frederick Terman. Packard's earliest home was Pueblo, Colorado, where he grew up, the son of a lawyer and high school teacher. It was during the Great Depression when young Packard entered college, working his way through Stanford as an engineering student. In engineering school, both Packard and fellow student William Hewlett attracted the attention of professor Frederick Terman, who encouraged them to experiment with electronic device production.

Packard graduated; married his Stanford sweetheart, Lucile; took a job at General Electric in Schenectady, New York; and was lured by Terman back to Stanford, along with Hewlett, with a fellowship to earn his MA. The Depression was rough on graduate students. The Packards worked and rented half a house, offering a portion to bachelor Hewlett; the garage was used as a workshop for fledgling experiments.

HOUSE CALL

Preserved as "the birthplace of Silicon Valley," Packard's little two-family Depression-era house (367 Addison Avenue, Palo Alto), where all the Hewlett-Packard experiments began, is on the California Registry of Historic Places. It is not yet open to the public, but can be seen as a drive-by.

With their MA degrees, the two men, with Terman's financial and moral support, set up their business in 1938 with a $538 start-up kitty, flipping a coin to see whose name would be first on the company letterhead. Hewlett won, but Packard became management leader. He named the first product, a sound oscillator called HP200B, and won the first order—eight oscillators at $72 each, sold to Walt Disney Studios for use on the soundtrack for *Fantasia.*

Hewlett's role as inventor and device developer was briefly curtailed by World War II, but the new company continued to grow. By 1948 Hewlett-Packard (HP) was a $1.5 million corporation with some 1,000 employees. The two men played to their expertise—Hewlett in the laboratories and workshops, Packard in management—and created a system widely copied by other industries. This included a profit-sharing plan based on production, maternity leave, day-care programs, an open work environment, job protection, continuing education, and other benefits.

HP's enormous success made Packard (and Hewlett, too) a wealthy man, money that he and his wife used to found the David and Lucile Packard Foundation, a major private philanthropy that continues to fund projects in many fields. Packard was also a director of the Wolf Trap Foundation for Performing Arts, vice chairman of the California Nature Conservancy, and a trustee of the Herbert Hoover Foundation, Hoover Institution, and the American Enterprise Institute. His solid conservative Republican credentials led him to a post as deputy secretary of defense in the Nixon administration and later as a consultant on many government panels and commissions.

Of all the awards, honors, honorary degrees, and appointments David Packard received in his eighty-three years, none probably pleased him more than the Presidential Medal of Freedom, the highest civilian honor, for a lifetime of philanthropic works. It doesn't get much better than that.

His present address is Oak Grove, subdivision 9, lot 249.

FREDERICK EMMONS TERMAN *1900–1982*

In his lifetime, Frederick Terman achieved a full measure of acclaim—as professor, then dean, provost, and finally acting president of Stanford University, a career extending over forty years. That doesn't include the years he spent at Stanford getting a bachelor's in chemistry and an master's in electrical engineering. (He broke the Stanford cord by getting his doctorate at the Massachusetts Institute of Technology.)

One aspect of his fame overrides all others in the public eye: the richly deserved title of co-founder, or co-father, of Silicon Valley. It was Terman who far-sightedly decided to convert some unused land at Stanford into an industrial park. This was before World War II, and the concept was a new one—the first university-owned industrial park ever. It went on to become the biggest and best-known such place in the world—and still is.

That alone wouldn't earn him that extra bit of recognition. What did was Terman's influence on two of his star graduate students, David Packard and William Hewlitt. He persuaded them to form a company and to move it from their garage to the Stanford campus. They were the first, others followed, and by the war's end the Stanford Industrial Park was booming.

A decade later, when William Shockley was planning a business in the new field of semiconductors, Terman persuaded him to do so in Palo Alto and helped him find the best and brightest in the field. Many of Terman's graduate students went on to great careers in what became known as Silicon Valley. Hewlitt and Packard's phenomenal success eventually led them to found the Frederick Terman Memorial Fellowship with a $300 million donation to Stanford.

In the meantime, Terman, while provost of the university, hugely expanded the science, engineering, and statistics departments, which won them major research grants from the U.S. Department of Defense, no small thing. The grants, along with the research they generated, greatly enhanced Stanford's reputation as a major educational institution and, not incidentally, added to the rapid growth of Silicon Valley. Though Terman might never have thought of himself as Mr. Chips, his title as co-father of Silicon Valley is well deserved.

Terman acquired his zest for learning and scholarship at the foot of a master: his father. **Lewis Madison Terman** (1877–1956), here with him in the postlife, was an educator, psychologist, philosopher, developer (with H. G. Childs) of the revised Stanford-Binet IQ test, and, oh yes, also a professor at Stanford.

Look for Frederick Terman in Oak Room A, niche 281-A.

STANFORD UNIVERSITY

1201 WELCH ROAD, STANFORD;
(650) 723-2300

This world-renowned center of higher education was founded in 1891 by two easterners, Leland and Jane Stanford, in memory of their only son. Both Leland and Jane have chosen the sprawling, bucolic university grounds, which they loved, as their final earthly address. The Stanford mausoleum is open to the public only one day a year, Community Day, the last Friday in April.

LUNCH BREAK

While there are cafes and lunch stops right on campus, consider **La Strada** (335 University Avenue; 650-324-8300), a delightful trattoria with wood-fired thin-crust pizzas and imaginative Italian fare.

LELAND STANFORD 1824–1893
JANE ELIZABETH STANFORD 1828–1905

One of northern California's macrobusiness, social, and political leaders in the late nineteenth century, Leland Stanford was neither California born nor bred. Born into a hard-working, relatively prosperous farm family of eight children just outside Albany, New York, he clerked in an Albany law firm and was admitted to the bar in

1848. Having married Jane Lathrop, daughter of a wealthy local merchant, Stanford went west to make his fortune, leaving her safely behind in Albany.

At first, he traveled only as far as Wisconsin to open his own law firm. In 1852, when his offices and library went up in flames, he did what half of America seemed to be doing: He joined the rush for gold in California. But Stanford did not go to dig for gold, but to earn it in business and the law.

His five brothers had gone before him to Sacramento, making good fortunes as merchants, selling equipment to gold miners. Stanford joined them, eventually bought them out, and returned home to bring Jane back to California with him. From then on, life for the Stanfords assumed the fast track. Leland, a genial personality, discovered an affinity for politics and ran for governor twice, winning on the second try in 1861.

As Republican governor during the Civil War, he managed the tricky task of keeping California in the Union. He also used his political clout to get land grants and bonded loans from Congress to help him and three partners build the eastbound section of the planned transcontinental railroad. Stanford's governorship was a brief two years, but he went on to become president (for life) of the Central Pacific Railroad in 1863 and a U.S. senator in 1885 (until his death).

Railroads were a growth stock at the time, and Stanford's investments in other rail lines made him an enormously rich man. He and Jane built a magnificent mansion in what became known as San Francisco's Nob Hill section and bought 650 acres in Palo Alto to build a country home and raise horses. When on a European trip in 1884 with their only son, Leland Jr., the boy died of typhoid fever at age fifteen. Just after his death, Stanford reportedly said to his wife, "The children of California shall be our children."

An apocryphal story is that they wanted to endow Harvard, but were greeted so coolly by the president as Western hicks, they decided to take their money back home to California. The truth is, the Stanfords always intended to use their vast wealth in California, but weren't sure whether to start a university, a museum, or a technical school. They asked Charles W. Eliot, president of Harvard, for his advice; he recommended a university.

The story of how Stanford University grew on the Stanfords' Palo Alto farmland shows how much the couple really did make California's children their own. They were involved in everything: consultations with Frederick Law Olmsted on the landscaping, finding the proper architect to design the buildings, choosing the right president and faculty. Finally, after six years of planning, the university opened in 1891 with 559 students enrolled.

Everything was coming up roses, but two years later Leland Stanford died, his estate was tied up in probate court, and the new university was in financial crisis. But Jane Stanford rallied. She reduced her personal staff, trimmed her personal expenses, and turned everything else over to the university. In 1898 the estate was settled, and Jane was able to give $11 million to the university trustees. A lovely legacy. No wonder the stately Stanford mausoleum holds a special place of honor on the university's appealing campus.

SACRAMENTO

SACRAMENTO CITY CEMETERY

1000 BROADWAY;
(916) 448-0811;
WWW.OLDCITYCEMETERY.COM

A mammoth, sculptural boulder signals the entrance to this peaceful city cemetery, with the office on the left. On twenty-eight acres, it is shaded by a multitude of palm, pine, oak, and American elm trees and is dotted with flowering bushes, roses and wildflowers, obelisks, and mausoleums. There are even a few of the old wooden headboards left.

The grounds are as impressive as the résumés of many of the full-time residents, yet not too long ago the cemetery was weedy, overgrown, and neglected, and many graves were vandalized. Formation of the Old City Cemetery Committee in 1987 gradually turned this revered old place around, making it an Eden of flowering beauty.

A large bronze marker at the front of the entrance boulder reads "Resting place of California pioneers, this cemetery was established in 1850. Many of the victims of the cholera epidemic of that year are buried here (600). Included among the graves of illustrious Californians are those of Governors Bigler, Newton Booth and William Irwin, General George Wright, hero of the Mexican War, and Mark Hopkins, co-builder of the Central Pacific Railroad, General Albert M. Winn, founder of the Native Sons of the Golden West, Hardin Bigelow, first mayor of Sacramento, William S. Hamilton, son of Alexander Hamilton, E. B. Crocker, founder of the Crocker Art Gallery and Reverend G. C. Wheeler, organizer in 1850 of the First Baptist Church."

That's just for starters. Also here are U.S. congressmen, Civil War Congressional Medal of Honor recipients, veterans of foreign wars, Masons, Odd

Fellows, and western pioneers. The Bigler mentioned on the verbose marker was **John Bigler** (1806–1871; section B, Odd Fellows, grave BB 37H, to the right of the entrance), who was California's third governor, the one who signed the bill making Sacramento the state capital in 1854. **Newton Booth** (1825–1892; section A, grave 50-02) was both governor and later a U.S. senator.

A name symbolic of Sacramento is **John A. Sutter Jr.** (1826–1897; section A55, on the left side of Cypress Avenue, just beyond Chapel Square to the right), son of a Swiss immigrant. A discovery on his land instigated the 1849 gold rush. Sutter Jr., on land deeded him by his father, laid out the makings of a town and called it Sacramento City. It soon became the entry point to gold rush country and prospered, growing to a population of 10,000 in seven short months. Sutter's monument reads "Founder and planner of the City of Sacramento 1848. Died in Acapulco, Mexico. American Consul for 24 years. Reinterred in Sacramento with his only surviving daughter, Anna Sutter Young. Born Acapulco September 18, 1888. Died San Francisco January 24, 1970." Sutter also gave the first ten acres to jump-start this cemetery, which in 1849 was called the "public graveyard."

> ## LUNCH BREAK
>
> As a change of pace, the Thai-Vietnamese food at **Lemon Grass** (601 Munroe Street; 916-486-4891) is a delight and moderately priced as well. **Ristorante Piatti** (571 Pavilions Lane; 916-649-8885) has delicious wood-fired pizzas and other Italian dishes, plus outdoor dining.

Western pioneer **Amos P. Catlin** (1823–1900; section B 59, grave 188) was responsible for spearheading the effort to make Sacramento the state capital. **Brigadier General George Wright** (1801–1865; section 50, grave 42) was not just a "hero of the Mexican War" as the entrance boulder states, he was also a gallant soldier in many other military engagements: the Seminole War in Florida, the Indian Campaign in the Pacific Northwest, and the Civil War, during which he was given command of the Pacific Coast by President Lincoln.

Grave markers dated earlier than 1850 suggest the bodies were brought here from older graveyards. One such—the earliest marker on the grounds—belongs to **Franklin B. Davis,** who died in 1846. **William Stephen Hamilton** (1797– 1850; Hamilton Square), Alexander Hamilton's youngest son, came west for the gold rush and died the next year. He may be the cemetery's most restless spirit: He was exhumed twice and buried three times in three different locations. Now in the square named for him, he is surrounded by flowering shrubs and trees, with enough natural beauty for him to stay put.

Prominent residents **Judge Edwin Bryant Crocker** (1818–1875), brother of rail-road baron Charles Crocker, and his wife, **Margaret Rhodes Crocker** (1822–1901), reside here off Maple Avenue. In 1885 Judge Crocker's widow donated his massive European art collection to the city, along with the exuberant Victorian mansion in which it was installed. The Crocker Art Museum (216 O Street; 916-264-5423), the oldest public art museum west of the Mississippi River, has been much expanded since then and is considered the finest art museum in the Sacramento Valley.

The most colorful character in these confines is probably **James L. Butler** (1855–1923; just off the parking lot). While chasing a mule one day near Tonopah, Nevada, he stumbled over a rock with silver ore in it, thus uncovering what turned out to be one of the richest silver mines and mining districts in the West. It made him a rich man; what happened to his mule is not known. Butler was in the vault here for years, but when his family stopped paying for his space, he was buried in an unknown grave in the indigents' section. Later, the Old City Cemetery Committee erected a 3-foot-high memorial stone for him, easily spotted off the parking lot. ★*Grounds open 7:00 A.M.–7:00 P.M. daily in summer, 7:00 A.M.–5:00 P.M. daily in winter. Archives office hours: 10:00 A.M.–3:00 P.M. Monday–Friday. Map; self-guided tour brochure; restrooms. Numerous free themed tours are offered throughout the year, led by docents of the Old City Cemetery Committee.*

MARK HOPKINS *1815–1878*

The highly visible, magnificent burnished red sarcophagus with MARK HOPKINS etched into the top has two tall granite urns set on posts on both sides of its base. A bronze plaque reads "Some 350 tons of Rocky Mountain red granite form the sarcophagus that entombs the remains of this forty-niner who ultimately became one of the legendary 'big four' in railroad history and the treasurer of the Central Pacific Railroad Company. This monstrous vault took a year and a half in construction and was completed in 1880 at a cost in excess of $80,000." Located in the Pioneer section, B124-0, the grave is easily reached; turn right at the cemetery entrance and follow the road to the right.

HOUSE CALL

Though located in San Francisco, not Sacramento, the "Top of the Mark," meaning the **Mark Hopkins Intercontinental San Francisco Hotel** (1 Nob Hill; 415-392-3434), has long been a city attraction for its spectacular, nonpareil views. The connection to Hopkins is tenuous: merely the name and the fact that Hopkins built his mansion on Nob Hill. Having a pre-dusk drink there is a requisite for many city visitors.

While the plaque hits the highlights of Hopkins's remarkable life, there is more to the story of this Hendersonville, New York, man of Puritan stock. Prospering as a local merchant and studying law, he was struck with gold rush fever and followed the masses to California. With merchandising smarts, he opened a general store in Placerville, smack in the middle of all the mining activity, hauling the goods from Sacramento by ox cart.

Before long, Hopkins expanded into the wholesale grocery business with Collis Huntington, and soon the two men joined Charles Crocker and Leland Stanford in even grander schemes. Most productive were their railroading ventures, first the Central Pacific, then Southern Pacific, which covered the whole state and added a second transcontinental route. The "Big Four" had it made, but such roaring success never went to Hopkins's head. In a time of fast money made and lost, of deals pledged and broken, Hopkins as the company treasurer was like a lodestar, a model of honesty and integrity, trusted by all. He was a regular churchgoer (in a raucous, debauched environment), and he and his wife, Mary Sherwood, lived well but unpretentiously.

SALINAS

GARDEN OF MEMORIES MEMORIAL PARK

760 ABBOTT STREET;
(831) 422-6417

LUNCH BREAK

What could be more appropriate when visiting Steinbeck's grave than to have lunch at the house where he was born? The handsome, substantial, turreted, **Victorian Steinbeck House** (132 Central Avenue; 831-424-2735) is now a lunch-only place, serving a set menu of soup or salad, main course, vegetable, and nonalcoholic drink. Also zesty: **Tu Casa Taquena** (875 Hamilton Avenue, Menlo Park; 650-321-5188), upscale Mexican with reasonable prices.

At first glance, this garden of final repose on twenty-seven-plus acres in the middle of town seems modern and rather conventional. But it was founded in 1860, and some of the really old tombstones and monuments of pioneers, early settlers, and military heroes are embellished in stone with considerable sculptural (and sepulchral) charm. There are statues of horsemen, a Woodman of the World, angels, rifles, clasped hands, tender children, and other creative touches—a pleasure to muse and meander through leisurely. No wonder a writer would find it appealing for his final draft. ★*Grounds open 8:00 A.M. to dusk daily. Office hours: 8:00 A.M.–5:00 P.M. (closed noon to 1:00 P.M.) Monday-Friday. Map; restroom.*

JOHN STEINBECK *1902–1968*

Abraham Lincoln once said, "God must be a lover of the common people, or He would not have made so many of them." One could accurately say the same in describing John Steinbeck's literary characters.

John Ernst Steinbeck III was born in Salinas to a middle-class family. His mother was a schoolteacher who encouraged her son's interest in literature and writing. As a youth, he worked on area farms and ranches in the summers, giving him empathy for field hands and itinerant laborers, and also cementing his love and knowledge of the Salinas and San Joaquin Valleys and of Monterey, where most of his stories would be set.

Steinbeck attended Stanford University as an English major, but dropped out

and moved to New York City to try to make it as a writer. Failing to get published, he returned to California and worked odd jobs to support his habit—writing. Three unacclaimed novels were published before he gained critical recognition with *Tortilla Flat* (1935), about a group of colorful Mexicans living in Monterey during the Great Depression. With success came financial security as Hollywood bought the rights and turned it into a film starring Spencer Tracy in 1942.

Steinbeck found more fame with the dramatic novel *Of Mice and Men* (1937), which was turned into a stage play and filmed at least three times. Arguably the best screen version was the first in 1939 with Lon Chaney Jr. as the mentally challenged Lenny and Burgess Meredith as George his migrant worker buddy. It's a story tailor-made for good acting. In general, his stories translated well to the screen. *The Red Pony,* published in 1937, became a film in 1949 with Steinbeck writing the screenplay. *Cannery Row* (1945) was filmed with Nick Nolte and Debra Winger in 1982; *The Pearl* (1947), for which Steinbeck also wrote the script, was a Mexican-produced film in 1949; and *East of Eden* (1952) was a 1955 blockbuster, with James Dean in his first starring role. (Steinbeck proved himself a talented screenwriter. He later scripted the 1952 *Viva Zapata,* which starred Marlon Brando.)

In 1939 came *The Grapes of Wrath,* Steinbeck's greatest work,

HOUSE CALL

For exhibits about Steinbeck and many aspects of his life, you might visit the **National Steinbeck Center** (1 Main Street; 831-796-3833; www.steinbeck.org). The center's archives, open only by appointment, contain the author's notebooks, photos, and first editions.

for which he won the Pulitzer Prize in 1940. That same year, the novel was released as a film, directed by John Ford and starring Henry Fonda and Jane Darwell as Tom and Ma Joad. Both Ford and Darwell deservedly won Oscars.

If Steinbeck had written no other book than *The Grapes of Wrath,* he would have earned his niche in American literature. The story, about poor Oklahoma dust bowl farmers migrating to California to find work, showed Steinbeck's empathy for the plight of the migrants. Along with the literary praise, Steinbeck earned the enmity of many landowners in the West, who branded him a Communist. At the same time, the Left thought he wasn't radical enough. In fact, he described himself as an FDR Democrat.

In *The Winter of Our Discontent* (1961), a subtle, nuanced, often overlooked novel, Steinbeck set the story on Long Island. In *Travels with Charley* (1962), his final book, he relates his trip across the United States in a camper with his poodle, Charley, meeting a cross-section of the populace.

The New York literati tended to scorn Steinbeck's gifts, branding him a "popular" author, but he earned his recognition elsewhere. In 1962 he won the Nobel Prize for Literature, and in 1964 Lyndon Johnson awarded him the Presidential Medal of Freedom. Best news of all for any author, alive or not, is that *he is still read!*

Steinbeck was married three times, with two sons from his second marriage. His last wife of eighteen years (here with him) was **Elaine Anderson Scott Steinbeck** (1914–2003). At block N-5 a metal sign says Steinbeck, but the upright headstone is marked Hamilton, the name of Steinbeck's mother's family. In front of it are five flat gray stones for family members. John Steinbeck's is in the middle of three on the right.

SANTA ROSA

LUTHER BURBANK HOME & GARDENS

SANTA ROSA AND SONOMA AVENUES;
(707) 524-5445;
WWW.LUTHERBURBANK.ORG

This historic property in downtown Santa Rosa (across from City Hall and Juilliard Park) perpetuates the memory of one of America's best-known pioneering horticulturists, Luther Burbank. In addition to his house, there are gardens, a greenhouse, a carriage house with exhibits, and a gift shop. He is buried in the lawn, but there is no marker. ★*Grounds and gardens open 8:00 A.M. to dusk daily. Tours available 10:00 A.M.–4:00 P.M. Tuesday-Sunday, April–October. Modest admission fee to house and greenhouse.*

LUNCH BREAK

At the edge of town is **zazu** (3535 Guerneville Road; 707-523-4814), popular with locals for its delicious, creative New American–northern Italian dishes and its funky roadhouse spirit. Another good option is **Cafe Citti** (9049 Sonoma Highway, Kenwood; 707-833-2690) for its northern Italian dishes and good desserts at moderate prices, plus outdoor dining.

LUTHER BURBANK *1849–1926*

Like so many nineteenth-century California entrepreneurs, Luther Burbank came from somewhere else. He was born on a farm near Lancaster, Massachusetts, and though he had just a high school education, he had a keen interest in nature and

science and loved tinkering with inventions. Two mentors took an interest in the young man—his uncle, a Boston museum department head, and the uncle's friend, naturalist Louis Agassiz—both of whom encouraged his enthusiasm for nature.

When his father died, Burbank and his family moved to a smaller farm. At age twenty-one he bought seventeen acres of land near Lunenberg, Massachusetts, and began experimenting with crossbreeding and hybridizing plants. In 1871 his success with a potato seed ball resulted in a small potato crop, which led him to sell the rights to the potato for $150. With the money, the young man went west to a better climate for seed experimentation, joining three of his brothers in Santa Rosa. He later wrote his mother that "this is the chosen spot of all this earth as far as Nature is concerned."

In Santa Rosa Burbank established a nursery garden, built a greenhouse, and began experiments that improved and added beauty and nutritional value to the world. On his fifteen-acre Gold Ridge Farm in nearby Sebastopol, which he bought in 1885, he introduced, over a fifty-year career, some 800 new varieties of fruits (especially berries, apples, cherries, peaches, quinces, and nectarines), flowers (notably many new forms of lilies), vegetables (sweet and field corn, tomatoes, squash, asparagus, peas), and grains. These included 242 different fruits and nuts, 26 different vegetables, 91 different ornamentals, and 9 different grains, grasses, and other forage. His work developing so-called spineless cacti as forage proved invaluable for cattle in arid areas.

HOUSE CALL

Burbank's 1885 experimental farm, **Gold Ridge Farm** (7781 Bodega Avenue, Sebastopol; 707-829-6711), which had fallen into decline after his wife's death, has undergone restoration. The cottage is on the National Register of Historic Places. You may take a self-guided trail tour with a free map year-round, or a docent-guided tour by appointment April through October.

Carrying on his plant hybridizations, Burbank often had up to 3,000 experiments in the works at any one time, involving millions of plants. It is widely acknowledged that his experiments sped up the science of plant breeding by at least twenty years. Yet his ultimate goal was not fame or wealth, rather, as he said, "I shall be contented if, because of me, there shall be better fruits and fairer flowers." Could anyone be more deserving of admission to the Inventors Hall of Fame? In 1986 Burbank was inducted posthumously.

LAST WRITES

Ubiquitous as California cemeteries are, they are not the only choice many permanent Californians have made. Many have been cremated, with their ashes scattered to the four winds or spread over the great Pacific Ocean. Certain others have chosen the lasting privacy of family grounds, with no accessibility to strangers. You may be wondering, so here are a few whose graves you cannot chart.

ASHES TO ASHES

Bud Abbott (1895–1974), the straight man of the famous comedy team Abbott and Costello. Ashes scattered in Pacific Ocean.

Ansel Adams (1902–1984), world-famous photographer, mostly working in California. Ashes placed on Mount Ansel Adams summit in the Ansel Adams Wilderness, California.

Desi Arnaz (1917–1986), Cuban-born entertainer, bandleader, and co-star of television's *I Love Lucy* with his then-wife, Lucille Ball. Ashes scattered.

Cliff Arquette (1918–1974), comic actor and grandfather of Rosanna, David, and Patricia. Ashes scattered by the Telophase Society.

Jean Arthur (1900–1991), beguiling actress with a distinctive voice who starred in many classic comedies and dramas of the 1930s and 1940s, such as *Mr. Deeds Goes* to Town, Mr. Smith Goes to Washington, The Plainsman, You Can't Take It With You, The Talk of the Town, The More the Merrier, and, of course, Shane. Ashes scattered off Point Lobos, California.

George Axelrod (1922–2003), playwright and screenwriter who wrote scripts for such films as The Manchurian Candidate, The Seven Year Itch, Will Success Spoil Rock Hunter? and Breakfast at Tiffany's. Ashes scattered at sea.

Richard Boone (1917–1981), actor and star of television's Have Gun, Will Travel. Ashes scattered in the Hawaiian islands.

Eddie Bracken (1915–2002), stage, screen, and television actor for more than seventy years, who could sing and play comedy and drama; his biggest hits were The Miracle of Morgan's Creek, Hail the Conquering Hero, and National Lampoon's Vacation. Ashes given to family or friend.

Marlon Brando (1924–2004), considered America's greatest actor of the mid-twentieth century, on stage and in such films as On the Waterfront, A Streetcar Named Desire, Viva Zapata!, The Wild One, Last Tango in Paris, Apocalypse Now, and The Godfather. Some of his ashes spread on his South Pacific island and others scattered at an undisclosed spot in Death Valley, California, along with those of Wally Cox, his longtime friend.

Red Buttons (1919–2006), carrot-topped comic and character actor, Oscar winner for Best Supporting Actor in Sayonara (1957). Best known as a participant in countless celebratory "roasts" who "never got a dinner." Ashes given to family or friend.

Johnny Carson (1925–2005), comedian turned host of NBC's long-running late-night television program, The Tonight Show, for thirty years. Ashes given to family or friend.

Wilt Chamberlain (1936–1999), one of the best basketball players ever, who was criticized for claiming in his autobiography that he had slept with 20,000 women. Location of ashes unknown.

Kurt Cobain (1967–1994), musician, composer, and leader of the grunge band Nirvana; committed suicide. Ashes scattered in several places, including the Wishkah River in Washington.

Wally Cox (1924–1973), comedian best known for his television roles on Mr. Peepers and Hollywood Squares. Ashes given to his friend Marlon Brando; after Brando's death, Cox's and some of Brando's ashes scattered in Death Valley, California.

Quentin Crisp (1908–1999), English actor, author, and gay icon. Ashes given to executor of his estate.

Dennis Crosby (1935–1991), actor and son of Bing Crosby and his first wife, Dixie Lee. Ashes scattered in northern California.

John Denver (1943–1997), folk and country singer, musician, and composer of "Rocky Mountain High" and other hits. Ashes scattered over the Rocky Mountains high in Colorado.

Andy Devine (1896–1977), cowboy singer and comic actor. Ashes scattered at sea.

I. A. L. Diamond (1920–1988), screenwriter and associate producer who worked with Billy Wilder on *Some Like It Hot, The Fortune Cookie, The Apartment,* and *Irma La Douche.* Ashes scattered at sea.

Brian Donleavy (1901–1972), character actor in *Beau Geste, Destry Rides Again,* and scores of other movies. Ashes scattered at sea.

Melvyn Douglas (1901–1981), actor who starred in some of the best films of the 1930s and 1940s, both comedies and dramas; one of only three actors to receive these three major awards: Oscar (for *Hud*), Emmy (*Inherit the Wind*), and Tony (*The Best Man*); married to politician-actress Helen Gahagan Douglas. Ashes retained by family in Vermont.

Ann Dvorak (1924–1979), movie actress who appeared in *Scarface* (1922). Ashes scattered.

Frederick S. Eaton (1855–1934), native-born Californian, onetime Los Angeles mayor, and engineer; called the father of the Los Angeles water system (fictionalized in *Chinatown*). Ashes buried in Long Valley, California.

Edna Ferber (1885–1968), novelist who wrote *Show Boat, Giant,* and *Cimarron,* all of which were turned into acclaimed films. Location of ashes unknown.

Henry Fonda (1905–1982), major movie and stage star, whose credits include *The Lady Eve, The Grapes of Wrath, Mister Roberts, 12 Angry Men, On Golden Pond,* and many other first-rate comedies and dramas. Ashes scattered.

John Frankenheimer (1930–2002), television and movie director, whose best films were probably *Birdman of Alcatraz, The Manchurian Candidate* (1962 version), *Seven Days in May,* and *Ronin.* Ashes given to family or friend.

Greta Garbo (1905–1990), beautiful movie star of the 1930s, famous for *Grand Hotel, Queen Christina, Camille, Ninotchka,* and for her reclusiveness. Ashes given to her niece, Gray Reisfield.

Jerry Garcia (1942–1995), much-revered musician of baby boomer era, leader of the Grateful Dead rock band. Half his ashes scattered in the Ganges River, India, half beneath the Golden Gate Bridge, San Francisco.

Earle Stanley Gardner (1889–1970), crime novelist who created Perry Mason. Ashes scattered.

Marvin Gaye (1939–1984), R & B and soul singer ("I Heard It Through the Grapevine"); shot by his father. Ashes scattered in Pacific Ocean.

Will Geer (1902–1978), movie and television actor who played Grandpa Walton on *The Waltons.* Ashes in Shakespeare Garden at Will Geer estate, Topanga Canyon, California.

Theodor Geisel (1904–1991), better known as Dr. Seuss, author and illustrator of some of the funniest and most popular children's books ever written, many translated to television. Location of ashes unknown.

Cary Grant (1904–1986), handsome, urbane Hollywood icon whose movie career spanned three decades, as talented at sophisticated comedy as in serious roles; among his gems are *The Philadelphia Story, Arsenic and Old Lace, To Catch a Thief, Notorious, Charade,* and, of course, *North by Northwest.* Ashes scattered in California.

Woody Guthrie (1912–1967), folk singer and composer whose best-known song is "This Land Is Your Land." Ashes scattered in Atlantic Ocean.

Buddy Hackett (1924–2003), rubber-faced stand-up comic and comic actor whose movies included *It's a Mad, Mad, Mad, Mad World* and *The Love Bug;* appeared on television talk shows and the game shows *What's My Line?* and *Hollywood Squares.* Ashes given to family or friend.

Alan Hale Jr. (1918–1990), actor best remembered as the Skipper in the television comedy *Gilligan's Island.* Ashes scattered at sea.

Margaret Hamilton (1902–1985), character actress who is especially remembered as the Wicked Witch in *The Wizard of Oz.* Ashes scattered over her property in Amenia, New York.

George Harrison (1943–2001), composer, rock musician, and member of the Beatles. Ashes scattered over several rivers in India.

Phil Hartman (1948–1998), masterly mimic (known for his Bill Clinton impression) and comic actor on *Saturday Night Live,* whose movie career was just taking off when he was killed by his deranged wife. Ashes scattered over Emerald Bay, Catalina Island, California.

Howard Hawks (1896–1977), producer and versatile director whose films included *The Dawn Patrol, Twentieth Century, His Girl Friday, Ball of Fire, To Have and Have Not, The Big Sleep,* and *Gentlemen Prefer Blondes.* Ashes scattered.

Dick Haymes (1918–1980), popular crooner who sang in the style and era of the early Sinatra. Ashes given to family.

Van Heflin (1910–1971), character actor in movies (*Shane, Johnny Eager*) and second lead on Broadway (in the Jimmy Stewart role in *The Philadelphia Story,* for one). Ashes scattered over Pacific Ocean.

Alfred Hitchcock (1899–1980), famous English-born film director of mysteries and thrillers, whose best work included *Psycho, Rear Window, North by Northwest, Notorious, The Lady Vanishes,* and *Vertigo;* known for innovative camera techniques, using a McGuffin to get the story moving, and for appearing as a walk-on in all his films. Ashes scattered.

FILM CLIP

North by Northwest (1959) is considered one of Hitchcock's very best films, and it's our favorite of his as well. Starring Cary Grant, Eva Marie Saint, and James Mason, it has everything: mystery, thrills, romance, humor, witty dialogue, terrific photography, good musical score, and a fine supporting cast.

William Holden (1918–1981), often-underrated movie actor whose best work was in *Bridge on the River Kwai, Sunset Boulevard, Stalag 17,* and *Network.* Ashes scattered in Pacific Ocean.

L. Ron Hubbard (1911–1986), author and founder of Scientology. Ashes scattered over Pacific Ocean.

Rock Hudson (1925–1985), handsome matinee idol of the 1960s, frequently paired with Doris Day in romantic comedies. His public image as a macho "hunk" was belied by his private homosexual lifestyle; he was one of the first celebrity victims of AIDS. Ashes scattered at sea.

Robinson Jeffers (1887–1962), free-verse poet who used Greek and Roman themes in many of his poems, like *Medea,* one of his best; lived in Carmel and wrote *Californians* about this coast. Ashes scattered at his Carmel home.

Chuck Jones (1912–2002), much-acclaimed animation pioneer who was the creator of Wile E. Coyote and Road Runner and the witty perfector of Bugs Bunny, Elmer Fudd, Daffy Duck, and other famous cartoon characters. Ashes scattered at sea.

Janis Joplin (1943–1970), hard-drinking, hard-living rock star singer who died too young of a drug overdose. Ashes scattered in Pacific Ocean along northern California coast.

FILM CLIP

Singin' in the Rain (1952), which some consider the greatest movie musical ever, has a lively, funny story by Betty Comden and Adolph Green, musical gems like Donald O'Connor's "Make 'Em Laugh," Gene Kelly's and Cyd Charisse's dancing, and Kelly's winning title number.

Gene Kelly (1912–1996), dancer, actor, and director whose best movie roles were in *Singin' in the Rain, The Pirate, The Three Musket-eers,* and *An American in Paris.* Ashes given to family or friend.

Dennis King (1897–1971), actor-singer on stage and screen who was featured in many musicals like *Vagabond King* and *Rose Marie.* Ashes given to family or friend.

Andre Kostelanetz (1901–1980), composer and symphony orchestra conductor. Ashes scattered in Pacific Ocean off Kauai, Hawaii.

Veronica Lake (1919–1973), movie actress best known for her long blond hair, which covered half her face; starred in *This Gun for Hire, Sullivan's Travels,* and *The Blue Dahlia.* Ashes scattered in the waters off Miami, Florida.

Elsa Lanchester (1902–1986), British character actress known for her role as the bride in *Bride of Frankenstein* (1935), among many other films. Ashes scattered at sea.

Peter Lawford (1923–1984), handsome actor who was married at one time to Patricia Kennedy, JFK's sister, and was a member of Frank Sinatra's Rat Pack. Ashes scattered, but there is a memorial at Pierce Brothers Westwood Village Memorial Park, Los Angeles.

Ross MacDonald (1915–1983), author of hard-boiled detective fiction in the Raymond Chandler–Dashiell Hammett mode, with private eye Lew Archer as hero. Ashes scattered in Santa Barbara Channel, California.

Harpo Marx (1885–1964), curly-wigged harpist and beloved member of the Marx Brothers comedy team for his zany pantomime rascality. Ashes reputedly scattered at the seventh hole of the Rancho Mirage golf course, California.

Herbert "Zeppo" Marx (1901–1979), youngest of the Marx Brothers comedy team, also an actor, theatrical agent, and inventor. Ashes scattered at sea.

Marilyn Maxwell (1921–1972), actress in B movies. Ashes scattered at sea.

Joel McCrea (1905–1990), movie leading man of the 1930s and 1940s; starred in *Foreign Correspondent, The Palm Beach Story, Union Pacific, Wells Fargo,* and *Sullivan's Travels,* among scores of other films. Ashes scattered at sea.

Steve McQueen (1930–1980), movie star best remembered for leads in *The Great Escape, The Magnificent Seven, The Thomas Crown Affair, Bullitt,* and *Papillon.* Ashes scattered in Santa Paula Valley, California.

Henry Miller (1891–1980), American author who lived in Paris, later in Big Sur, California; his books were banned in the United States for decades because of frank sexual content. Ashes scattered off Big Sur.

Charles Mingus (1922–1979), jazz musician and composer. Ashes thrown into the Ganges River, India.

Jessica Mitford (1917–1996), one of Britain's famous Mitford sisters and author of *The American Way of Death,* an exposé of the funeral home industry. Ashes scattered in Pacific Ocean.

Robert Montgomery (1904–1981), popular movie actor of the 1930s and 1940s; best role probably was in *Night Must Fall,* also in the noir *Lady in the Lake* and *Ride the Pink Horse;* father of Elizabeth Montgomery. Ashes given to family.

Zero Mostel (1915–1977), master comic actor who shone in *The Producers, A Funny Thing Happened on the Way to the Forum,* and in the Broadway production of *Fiddler on the Roof.* Location of ashes unknown.

Anaïs Nin (1903–1977), writer and memoirist. Ashes scattered over Santa Monica Bay, California.

Larry Parks (1914–1975), actor who portrayed Al Jolson brilliantly in *The Jolson Story* and *Jolson Sings Again,* but whose film career was ruined by being blacklisted for Communist ties during the McCarthy era. Ashes buried at his home in Studio City, California.

Anthony Perkins (1932–1992), star of many films in a long career, but best remembered as Norman Bates, the psychopathic killer in Alfred Hitchcock's *Psycho.* Location of ashes unknown.

River Phoenix (1970–1993), promising young actor (*Stand By Me* and *My Own Private Idaho*) who died of drug overdose. Ashes scattered at family ranch in Florida.

Vincent Price (1911–1993), actor who played in *Laura, The Three Musketeers, Edward Scissorhands,* and many other films, but best known for his horror movies. Buried at sea, 3 miles from the Santa Monica shore.

Richard Pryor (1940–2005), actor and revolutionary stand-up comedian whose stunningly original performances influenced many younger comics. Ashes given to family or friend.

Tony Randall (1920–2004), longtime actor of stage and screen, but best remembered for his role as Felix Unger on television's *The Odd Couple,* for which he won an Emmy. Ashes given to family or friend.

Christopher Reeve (1952–2004), actor, best known for his role as Superman in four movies. Ashes given to family.

Lee Remick (1935–1991), beautiful actress who starred in *Days of Wine and Roses, Anatomy of a Murder,* and *The Omen;* died of cancer. Ashes given to family or friend.

Thelma Ritter (1905–1969), character actress who stole many a film, played in *All About Eve, Rear Window,* and scores of other movies. Ashes given to family.

Anne Shirley (1918–1993), born Dawn O'Day, ingenue in *Anne of Green Gables, Stella Dallas,* and other movies. Ashes given to family or friend.

Jay Silverheels (1919–1980), born on the Six Nations Indian Reservation in Ontario, played Tonto to the Lone Ranger from 1949 to 1957. Ashes scattered in Canada.

Dr. Benjamin Spock (1904–1998), noted pediatrician and author of *Baby and Child Care,* the primer on child care for generations of parents. In later life he was an activist protestor of the Vietnam War. Location of ashes unknown.

Barbara Stanwyck (1907–1990), high-profile movie star of almost eighty films, many of them blockbusters, including *Stella Dallas, Double Indemnity, Meet John Doe, Ball of Fire,* and *Sorry, Wrong Number;* later starred in television's *Big Valley* in the 1970s. Ashes scattered in Lone Pine, California.

Inger Stevens (1934–1970), Swedish-born actress who starred in movies (*Hang 'Em High*) and on television; committed suicide. Ashes scattered at sea.

General Joseph W. "Vinegar Joe" Stilwell (1883–1946), commander of the China-Burma-India theater in World War II. Ashes scattered in Pacific Ocean.

Jacqueline Susann (1921–1974), author of *Valley of the Dolls* and other best-selling novels. Ashes given to family.

Hunter S. Thompson (1937–2005), flamboyant self-styled "gonzo journalist" and author of *Fear and Loathing in Las Vegas, Fear and Loathing on the Campaign Trail,* and other books; committed suicide. Ashes shot from a cannon (to the tune of Bob Dylan's "Mr. Tambourine Man") on his Owl Farm estate, Wood Creek, Colorado; costly farewell memorial event paid for by Thompson friend Johnny Depp, with scores of disparate friends in attendance (including senators George McGovern and John Kerry).

Franchot Tone (1905–1968), handsome movie leading man and second lead with a flair for comedy; starred in *Mutiny on the Bounty, The Lives of a Bengal Lancer,* and scores more; was once married to Joan Crawford. Ashes scattered.

Lana Turner (1921–1995), glamorous Hollywood star of the mid-twentieth century who was in more than fifty movies, though more a star than an actress. Ashes given to family or friend.

Thorstein Veblen (1857–1929), sociologist-writer who authored the trendsetting *The Theory of the Leisure Class.* Ashes scattered in Pacific Ocean.

David Wayne (1914–1995), stage, film, and television actor whose best roles were on Broadway, as the leprechaun in *Finian's Rainbow* and as Ensign Pulver in *Mister Roberts.* Ashes given to executor of his estate.

Edward Weston (1886–1958), pioneer photographer who lived in California and was the first person to receive a Guggenheim Fellowship for photography. Ashes scattered over Pacific Ocean at Point Lobos, California.

OVER THERE—BURIALS ABROAD

Josephine Baker (1906–1975), African-American dancer and entertainer who made an international reputation for herself as the star of the Folies-Bergeres and queen of Paris nightlife. Buried in Monaco.

Ingrid Bergman (1915–1982), Swedish-born, internationally famous, stage and Oscar-winning film actress of the 1940s and 1950s; star of *Casablanca, Joan of Arc, Gaslight, Spellbound, Notorious, Intermezzo, Anastasia*, and many other films. Buried in Stockholm, Sweden.

Charlie Chaplin (1889–1977), British-born comic genius of silent movies and early talkies, notably *The Gold Rush, The Great Dictator, Monsieur Verdoux,* and *Limelight.* Buried in Corsier Cemetery, Switzerland.

Claudette Colbert (1903–1996), megastar of the 1930s and 1940s in films from *Cleopatra* and *It Happened One Night* to *The Egg and I* and beyond. Buried in Parish of St. Peter Cemetery, Barbados (where she had a home).

Marlene Dietrich (1901–1992), glamorous movie star featured in *Blue Angel, Judgment at Nuremburg, Destry Rides Again,* and many other films. Buried in Friedhof III, Berlin-Friedenau, Germany.

Alec Guinness (1914–2000), British actor who starred in many stage plays and movies, as believable in comedy (*The Lavender Hill Mob, The Captain's Paradise*) as drama (*The Bridge on the River Kwai, Lawrence of Arabia, Doctor Zhivago*). Buried at St. Lawrence's Church, Petersfield, Hampshire, England.

Princess Grace Kelly of Monaco (1929–1982), movie star whose films included *High Noon, Rear Window, To Catch a Thief,* and *High Society;* later married Prince Rainier of Monaco; tragically killed in a car accident. Buried in Monaco.

Hedy Lamarr (1913–2000), sexy Viennese-born movie star of the 1930s and 1940s, known more for her beauty than her acting talent; surprisingly, she was also an inventor. Ashes scattered in an Austrian forest near Vienna.

Vivien Leigh (1913–1967), British-born movie and stage star, forever Scarlett O'Hara in *Gone With the Wind,* but also Blanche Dubois in *Streetcar Named Desire.* Ashes scattered on a lake at Tickerage Mill in Sussex, England.

Freddie Mercury (1946–1991), lead singer of the British rock band Queen. Ashes scattered on the shores of Lake Geneva, Switzerland.

Jim Morrison (1943–1971), American rock idol and lead singer of the Doors. Buried in Père Lachaise, Paris, France, his grave is one of the most visited in the cemetery, causing such a traffic jam that the cemetery officials would like him evicted, returned to the United States.

David Niven (1910–1983), British-born actor who appeared in *Separate Tables, The Charge of the Light Brigade, Around the World in Eighty Days, Casino Royale,* and *The Pink Panther,* among scores of other Hollywood movies. Buried in Château d'Oex Cemetery, Switzerland.

Laurence Olivier (1907–1989), British-born stage and film actor, considered the best of his generation. Buried in Poets Corner, Westminster Abbey, London, England.

General George S. Patton Jr. (1885–1945), commander of the Third Army in World War II, on whose military exploits the movie *Patton* was based. Buried in Luxembourg American Cemetery, Hamm, Germany.

Dennis Potter (1935–1994), British screen and television writer, creator of TV's *Pennies From Heaven* (which later became a movie) and *The Singing Detective.* Buried in St. Mary's Church, Hereford, England.

John Reed (1887–1920), journalist and subject of the Warren Beatty movie *Reds;* buried in the Kremlin wall, Moscow, Russia.

Arthur Rubinstein (1887–1982), celebrated classical pianist. Ashes in the Jerusalem Forest, Israel.

Robert Ulrich (1946–2002), television actor in series *Vegas* and *Spenser for Hire.* Ashes buried at his family vacation home in southern Ontario, Canada.

Evelyn Waugh (1903–1966), British author of *Handful of Dust, Black Mischief, Brideshead Revisited,* and *The Loved One* (a satire supposedly based on Forest Lawn), among others. Buried in St. Peter and Paul's Churchyard, Combe Florey, Somerset, England.

Orson Welles (1915–1985), brilliant actor, director, and screenwriter best known for *Citizen Kane,* also *The Lady from Shanghai, The Third Man, Touch of Evil,* and *Chimes at Midnight.* Ashes buried in a well in Ronda, Spain.

HABEAS CORPUS

James M. Cain (1892–1977), author of hard-boiled detective fiction, including *The Postman Always Rings Twice* and *Double Indemnity.* Body donated to medical science.

Lon Chaney Jr. (1906–1973), actor in *High Noon, Of Mice and Men,* and other films, but never achieved the fame of his father. Body donated to medical science.

Bobby Darin (1936–1973), popular singer ("Splish Splash") who made "Mack the Knife" a pop hit and whose life was the subject of Kevin Spacey's film *Beyond the Sea.* Body donated for medical research.

Christopher Isherwood (1904–1986), British-born author of *I Am a Camera* and *Berlin Stories,* which later inspired *Cabaret.* Body donated for research to UCLA Medical School, Los Angeles.

Walter Pidgeon (1897–1984), handsome actor of the mid-twentieth century who starred in *Mrs. Miniver, Saratoga,* and *How Green Was My Valley,* among other films. Body donated for research to UCLA Medical School, Los Angeles.

RETURN TO SENDER, WHEREABOUTS UNKNOWN

Ambrose Bierce (1842–1913), author of *The Devil's Dictionary* and *An Occurrence at Owl Creek Bridge.* Disappeared in Mexico; body never found.

Amelia Earhart (1898–1937), famous aviator who set records. Presumed to have crashed in the Pacific Ocean; body never found, but speculation persists to this day.

Leslie Howard (1890–1943), English actor famous as Ashley Wilkes in *Gone With the Wind* and as a foppish nobleman/spy in *The Scarlet Pimpernel.* Killed in a plane crash in World War II; body never recovered.

Jim Thompson (1906–1967), officer in the OSS (Office of Strategic Services) in Thailand during World War II and later a successful silk exporter, considered the postwar savior of the Thai silk industry. Disappeared into the Malaysian jungle in the Cameron Highlands and never seen again; foul play suspected but never proved; his disappearance remains one of the world's most intriguing, long-running mysteries.

INDEX

D

S

About the Authors

Patricia Brooks has written other guidebooks (not all of them funereal), including *Where the Bodies Are* and *Permanently New Yorkers* (both Globe Pequot). When not under-taking graveyard tours, she resides peacefully in Connecticut.

Jonathan Brooks, who spent years at an entertainment-based cable TV station digging up information on many of the people he writes about in this book, is a freelance journalist living uncryptically in Los Angeles, where he never misses a *dead*line.